S

SECOND WIND

Navigating the Passage to a Slower,
Deeper, and More Connected Life

DR. BILL THOMAS

SIMON & SCHUSTER PAPERBACKS

New York   London   Toronto   Sydney   New Delhi

S

305.26
THO

Simon & Schuster Paperbacks
A Division of Simon & Schuster, Inc.
1230 Avenue of the Americas
New York, NY 10020

Copyright © 2014 by Dr. Bill Thomas

First Simon & Schuster trade paperback edition March 2015

For information about special discounts for bulk purchases,
please contact Simon & Schuster Special Sales at 1-866-506-1949
or business@simonandschuster.com.

The Simon & Schuster Speakers Bureau can bring authors to your live event. For more information or to book an event contact the Simon & Schuster Speakers Bureau at 1-866-248-3049 or visit our website at www.simonspeakers.com.

Designed by Ruth Lee-Mui

Manufactured in the United States of America

1   3   5   7   9   10   8   6   4   2

The Library of Congress has cataloged the hardcover edition as follows:

Thomas, William H., 1959–
Second wind : navigating the passage to a slower, deeper, and more connected life /
Dr. Bill Thomas. — First Simon & Schuster hardcover edition.
pages   cm
Includes bibliographical references.
1. Baby boom generation—Social aspects—United States.
2. Older people—United States—Social conditions.   3. Longevity—
United States—Social aspects.   4. Conduct of life.   I. Title.
HN58.T46   2014
305.26—dc23   2013035558

ISBN 978-1-4516-6756-1
ISBN 978-1-4516-6757-8 (pbk)
ISBN 978-1-4516-6758-5 (ebook)

For Kavan

Contents

PART III: THE SECOND CRUCIBLE

PART IV: LIFE BEYOND ADULTHOOD

Preface

I spent the first half of my working life serving as a physician, a geriatrician—a specialist in the care of the old. Close observation and professional training have schooled me in the many and varied difficulties that can accompany entry into old age. My practice also revealed how heavily our society's blatant and unapologetic ageism weighs upon young and old alike. It is customary in our time for people to console themselves with the belief that age is simply a state of mind. When they close their eyes, millions of people can still hear Joni Mitchell singing, "We are stardust. We are golden."

Years spent in the company of very old people offered me a unique perspective from which to view the difficulties that accompany youth. The elders I cared for generously shared their most poignant memories with me, and their lived experience helped me grasp a handful of truths about my life and the world in which I live. The stories elders told me also led me to ask questions about the future of my generation. What stories would we be eager to tell as we looked back at the history through which we lived? How might time and experience change our values and our priorities? What do we still have to learn about the things that matter most?

A half century or more now trails behind those born in the aftermath of the Second World War. Though many still deny the fact, youth slipped from their grasp a long time ago. The mirror, however, remains a teller of truth. The complicated mixture of feelings we experience when we study our own reflections is both very personal and shared by millions of our peers. These emotions are, in fact, connected to some of the most unsettling and dangerous features of contemporary culture. Out of sight, and almost always out of mind, aging is remaking us and our society. With the same gentle power that allows water to carve stone, time is having its way with those who would be forever young.

Those born after World War II are changing in important ways, but the mythology they created about themselves remains suspended in time. As the gap between this generation and its youthful self-image picture of itself grows, so does the feeling that life is, somehow, out of balance. This conflict between mythology and reality would be incidental to current events but for the fact that the postwar generation was endowed, by history and demography, with the power to transform personal troubles into pressing public issues. The struggles of the 1960s and 1970s, which are supposed to have arisen from a generation's fervent embrace of rebellion, were actually the product of a divisive and highly volatile conflict over the structure, function, and meaning of adulthood and maturity.

The story of the postwar generation's first coming of age is exceedingly well worn. For decades people have been accustomed to hearing this story being told from rooftops, televisions, and radios. Accordingly, there is a pervasive sense that nothing new can be wrung from so familiar a tale. During the years I spent caring for elders, I came to understand that the more often a story is repeated, the more likely it is that the teller is using it to conceal rather than to reveal.

My natural disposition and professional experience have caused me to be interested in the reinterpretation of the postwar generation's era. Because I was born in 1959 and was therefore a child during the sixties rather than a child of the sixties, I have always trailed behind the vast bulk of the postwar generation. I've been close to its cultural center of gravity without actually being part of its many dramas. In the conventional telling, this is a mythology that continues to celebrate a long vanished youth. I have done my best to reinterpret and extend this story because I am fascinated by the questions surrounding who these people may yet become.

Some will ask why a physician should be so concerned with history. In fact, the art of medicine is primarily a history-taking profession. The skillful physician takes care to ask probing questions about what preceded the so-called present illness. Details of the patient's medical history are supplemented with an occupational history; a family history; and, when necessary, a travel history. The following pages explore the developmental challenges that lie ahead of the postwar generation and in doing so cannot help but ask "How did we arrive at this moment?" This generation's emergence out of childhood comprises a colorful and eventful period in our shared history. It also carries important clues about the cultural forces that will shape the postwar generation's fitful journey into a new life phase, a life beyond adulthood.

During the course of my career I have listened to hundreds if not thousands of life stories. People have tearfully confessed to me youthful sins and foibles that now lie seventy years past. I did my best to receive these stories with tenderness and compassion. The life story of an elder rightly understood offers us the distilled essence of life as one human being has lived it. All of the great story *listeners* in history have understood that opening one's mind can change a familiar tale into something new, something that can change how we see the world.

While I freely admit to its faults, biases, omissions, and errors, this book is my attempt to retell the foundational generational tale of our time. In writing this book I have done my best to unmask the lazy generational self-justifications that have been allowed to pass as conventional wisdom. I have attempted to retell the postwar generation's now tattered story and complete it with an exciting, though yet to be realized, developmental journey that can lead the postwar generation into the uncharted terrain of life beyond adulthood. We are approaching a second great coming of age that will change how members of the postwar generation see themselves and the world in which they live.

This is where they will form the legacy they will leave for those who follow in their wake.

This is a time of new beginnings. A vast and undiscovered country beckons from what was once but is no longer a distant shore. Those willing to venture there will find an exquisite treasure of meaning and purpose that is now and will always be unavailable to the young.

Dr. Bill Thomas
June 5, 2013
Ithaca, New York

SECOND
WIND

SECOND
WIND

O

SOMETHING'S HAPPENING

The wheels of Continental flight 107 touch down at Newark's Liberty International Airport, on schedule, on August 14, 2011, at 5:35 a.m. eastern daylight time. In seat 2A, fifty-three-year-old Rita Sorrentino startles awake. She groans softly, leans forward in her seat, and rubs the back of her painfully stiff neck. Experience long ago taught her that only a good night's sleep in her own bed could relieve the dull throb in her temples. She's been a member of the Million Mile Club for years but has never developed the knack for sleeping well on airplanes.

She's spent a week in Hong Kong, ten days in Sydney, and an overnight in Tokyo. Now she is almost home. Rita raises the window shade. The terminal looks smooth and sleek in the dawn's soft pink light. She doesn't care. She feels like shit. It has taken nearly two weeks out of her life but she's been able to undo most of the damage the new VP of marketing had caused in a single day. He has a Harvard MBA, a big mouth, and little concern for what anyone else thinks of him. He'll be gone before the year is out.

The plane jerks to a stop. Rita trudges up the Jetway and heads toward baggage claim. There, she stares blankly at the carousel's parade of black roller bags. Hers has a lime-green tag. She majored in accounting in college and joined the firm in her early thirties, a lifetime ago. Except for the year the twins were born, she's been climbing the ladder ever since. Most of the firm's clients had been in the New York area until two—no—three CEOs ago. That one had been big on the "Pacific Rim," and Rita has been on a red-eye at least two or three times a month ever since.

She finds her car and drives home.

The house is empty, as she knew it would be. The girls are grown and out of the house; Bob will be at work until seven, at least. She stands in the shower and lets its hot rain wash the grime of travel from her body. It feels good to close her eyes. She is tired but knows that it would be a mistake to sleep. There is work to do. She wraps her hair in a towel and palms an opening in the misted mirror. Her face leaps into view and surprises her. *Old.* She pushes the word away and remembers the L'Oréal ad she saw on the plane. "Worried about wrinkles? We'll help you fight back." Fight. Yes, she would fight.

What is she fighting?

LIFE OUT OF BALANCE

The world is changing and we are changing with it. We find ourselves eating faster, walking faster, and talking faster than we used to. Without knowing how or why it is so, there is always more to do and less time in which to get it done. We fill and then overfill our days. Every race goes to the swift, every contest to the aggressive, and every prize to the powerful. Without our consent, seemingly immutable concepts like "time," "money," and "meaning" have been stretched, compressed, and distorted as if they are being viewed in a funhouse mirror.

The Hopi language contains a term that English needs but doesn't have. It is an ancient and, to nonnative ears, strange-sounding word.

koyaanisqatsi [koyɑːnisˈkɑtsi]: life out of balance, a way of living that
calls for another way of living

We are living in a way that calls for another way of living. Many
can describe the unease that steals the pleasure from our days and the
sleep from our nights, but few can name its true source. The ceaseless
effort to balance family and work roles that felt so natural and comfortable for so long has gradually and confusingly begun to feel constricting.
It is as if one's favorite pair of well-worn sneakers began to raise blisters
on one's heels. We blame ourselves. We blame our shoes. The fault,
however, lies with the road we are traveling.

America's postwar generation, which consists of the nearly 80 million people born between 1946 and 1964, has, over the past half century, constructed a pervasive and self-serving mythology. This story is
based on a lovingly embroidered version of the ongoing American ro-
mance with dynamism and energy. At every turn and in every particular
this generational narrative celebrates the brilliance, the power, and the
beauty of youth—its youth. Rita's fealty to the virtues associated with
youth and her willingness to allow a millstone of meetings, business
documents, and travel to grind away the years of her life are, in large
part, based on her belief in this story. Her story, and millions more like
it, help us see the flaw that lies at the heart of this mistold tale. Time is
passing and the postwar generation's faith in its own boundless energy is
now pressing up against a set of immutable biological and demographic
facts.

Koyaanisqatsi.

People most often experience the conflict between the postwar
generation's mythology and life's urgent realities as purely personal
problems, but the sense that life is out of balance actually arises from
profound but little understood changes in our culture. The postwar
generation's tremendous size and its position in history have endowed it
with the extraordinary ability to bend, shape, and transform American

culture. Over time, the changes it has inspired have nearly all served to flatter and ennoble the postwar generation's potent and relentlessly youthful self-image. Adulthood, for example, is not what it used to be: it has been amplified. For the past forty years, members of this generation have occupied and reconstructed adulthood. Previously humdrum virtues such as reliability, productivity, and effectiveness have been magnified in the popular imagination and held up as cardinal cultural virtues.

A SOCIOLOGICAL IMAGINATION

Among America's most insightful twentieth-century sociologists, C. Wright Mills was just forty-five when he lost his life to heart disease in 1961. Throughout his brief career he sought to clarify and explain the role that society plays in shaping an individual's life. In other words, he explored how we can best "think ourselves away" from the familiar routines of daily existence and gain access to the forces that are constantly at work. In books such as The Power Elite, White Collar, and especially, The Sociological Imagination, he charted the often hidden complexities that define life in industrial societies. While historians examine large impersonal forces and biographers dig for the telling details that best illuminate the life of an individual, Mills always sought "the vivid awareness of the relationship between experience and the wider society." He named this perspective "the sociological imagination" and never wavered in his belief that "neither the life of an individual nor the history of a society can be understood without understanding both."

According to Mills, the most efficient way to locate the often hidden connections between "personal troubles" and "public issues" is to combine insights gained from three distinct lenses:

History: How does a society come into being and then perpetuate itself? How does it create history and what are the stories that members of a given society tell one another about their shared past?

Biography: How is the life cycle defined? What kinds of lives does this life cycle enable? What kinds of "possible lives" does it forbid?

Social Structure: How do a society's most important and powerful social structures operate and interact? How do they pull the society together? How do they drive members of a society apart?

Unfortunately, Mills died before he could analyze the extraordinary role that the postwar generation would play in reshaping American society. What would he have made of the turbulent years that saw the postwar generation come of age? How did this unprecedented youth boom shape the events of the day, and more importantly, the decades that followed? Examining the postwar generation's story through Mills's carefully aligned lenses of history, biography, and social structure, we can begin to appreciate how intimately the personal and the public are connected.

THE GENERATIONAL CRUCIBLE

In the chemistry lab, a crucible is a vessel in which compounds are heated to and transformed by incandescent temperatures. This book employs the broader and much less technical meaning of the word.

> crucible: a test or severe trial brought about by the confluence of cultural, economic, and political forces within a society

We are well aware of the angst that so often accompanies adolescence; the awkward, ill-defined space between childhood and adulthood can make daily life quite difficult. Life, during these years, almost always seems to be out of balance. Most parents know the sound of a bedroom door slamming followed by a wail of anger and self-pity. One sixteen-year-old might sneak a cigarette behind the barn, but a massive generation of young people can amplify adolescent rebellion in ways that rattle the foundations of a nation.

The postwar generation's size relative to the rest of the population and its position in history allowed it to inject its concerns and its obsessions directly into the heart of American culture. The postwar generation has, from the end of its childhood onward, been both the creator of and a participant in a self-referential narrative. During the years that the bulk of the postwar generation emerged out of childhood (roughly 1961–1971), young people's private lives and personal problems erupted into the public realm. The struggle to enter into adulthood was so intense and chaotic that it led to a society-wide crucible experience.

This was the postwar generation's First Crucible. Few expected or could even believe that a generation born into relative peace and prosperity would come so swiftly into such pointed conflict with the settled norms and expectations of the dominant culture. This "youthquake" is remembered best for its trends, styles, and attitudes, but its true legacy has been broader and much more disruptive than is commonly understood.

During the decades following this First Crucible, the postwar generation fashioned a new adulthood, one that was remade in its image. Like all rising generations, these young people were buoyed by a youthful vigor that led them to be aggressive and achievement-oriented. What made the postwar generation different was its remarkable capacity for altering a life stage as it moved through it. In doing so, it changed the way that people of all ages and backgrounds experience time, money, relationships, and meaning in their daily lives.

A generation long accustomed to the advantages conferred by youth is now rounding a final and decisive corner. Compelled by the iron law of time, members of the postwar generation are now approaching the end of adulthood. The necessity of their entry into life's third age will plunge American society into a Second Crucible. The struggle to outgrow adulthood (unlike entry into adulthood) is poorly understood and offers few culturally sanctioned milestones. Members of the postwar generation have an exceptionally limited understanding of the developmental struggle that lies ahead and little preparation for changes that will likely be even more challenging than those of the First Crucible.

For nearly four decades, we have been reassured that adulthood is

SECOND WIND ～ 7

both the apex of human development and a permanent state of being. Both of these ideas are wrong. The first step down the road toward a useful understanding of life beyond adulthood will require members of the postwar generation to admit a difficult but unalterable fact—not only are they not as young as they used to be, but each morning they wake up one day older. When honestly confronted, this simple truth can generate powerful personal and cultural insights. The retelling of the postwar generation's story that unfolds across the following pages is intended to help readers see beyond the limitations and weaknesses inherent in adulthood and begin an exploration of life beyond adulthood.

Historical context is essential to such an effort, and so this book includes five chapters that offer a kaleidoscopic view of news, art, politics, and culture at key points in the postwar generation's evolution. The events included are all historical facts, but as Caltech's Robert Rosenstone has observed, "History is not a collection of details. It is an argument about what the details mean. The moment you start connecting facts into a meaningful story, you are indulging in certain forms of fiction." Because this book endeavors to "connect facts to a meaningful story," it does rely, at least in part, on fiction. Interwoven throughout this text are episodes, impressions, and incidents drawn from four composite biographies. The descriptions of events in the lives of the composite characters (Tom, Rita, Flo, and Melanie) are based on real life events gathered from interviews with dozens of people.

These characters serve to dramatize the developmental turning points that have been and will be experienced in the course of a lifetime. One generation, many stories. In order to distinguish these composite biographies from historical events, they are presented in italics, and each entry will begin with the character's name in bold type.

Tom Whitmore (born 1946) is the son and grandson of upstate New York dairy farmers. He recalls his youth as a golden age of hard work, high school dances, and homecoming games. At his father's urging Tom volunteered to fight in his generation's war—Vietnam. When he returned home, he married his high school sweetheart and settled into a comfortable life on the farm. The collapse of milk prices and a taste for alcohol reshaped Tom's life in difficult and often painful ways.

Florence ("Flo") Marsh (born 1950) is the daughter of a Baptist minister. Her father (like Tom's father) served in World War II. On returning home from Europe he entered seminary and while still a young man was appointed to the pastorship of the Zion Baptist Church in Charleston, South Carolina. Flo's mother was a loving but stern taskmaster who encouraged the development of her daughter's academic and musical talents. Both of her parents were active participants in the Civil Rights movement.

Rita Sorrentino (born 1956) is the granddaughter of immigrants from Italy. Her mother's mother came to live with them when "Nonno" died. Italian was the language of home, while English was spoken at work and school. She grew up in Vineland, New Jersey, surrounded by a large and fractious extended family. From spelling tests to cheerleading to her job at the public pool's concession stand, Rita always felt the need to outdo her peers.

Melanie Weber (born 1961) is the daughter of a nurse and a luthier, and her roots plunge deep into the hills of Appalachia. Her father thought that there might be a better market for his instruments in the city, and so her parents moved to Nashville, Tennessee, before she was born. For the rest of their lives they spoke of West Virginia as home. Her mother rose from nurse's aide to licensed nurse to registered nurse. Every weekend of her youth, Melanie's home echoed with mountain music made by her parents and their friends.

Something is happening in our society. There is a growing awareness that the lives we are living are, in important ways, out of balance. We are indeed living in a way that calls for another way of living. Though we rarely, if ever, think of it in such terms, we live at the intersection of history, biography, and demography, and we need access to each of these perspectives if we are going to find the true source of koyaanisqatsi. The answers we seek are hidden inside the mistold tale of a generation, the postwar generation. To find our way past the nostalgia, the lazy self-justifications, and deliberate distortions that we have so long accepted, we will need to retell this story.

PART I

THE

FIRST CRUCIBLE

01

WATSON
VERSUS SPOCK

The postwar generation's story begins, appropriately, with a crash. On September 3, 1929, the Dow Jones industrial average hit what was then an all-time high. This good news led economist Irving Fischer to proclaim, "Stock prices have reached what looks like a permanently high plateau." He was spectacularly wrong. The first clouds to darken America's blue-sky optimism arrived on October 24, "Black Thursday," when share prices dropped 9 percent before the closing bell. The market rebounded slightly the next day. But on October 28, "Black Monday," stocks dropped another 12 percent. The Roaring Twenties' deathblow, delivered by a 13 percent plunge on "Black Tuesday," made it clear that the good times were over.

Reflecting on the hardships imposed by this era, historian Piers Brendon showed how "unemployment, hardship, strife, and fear" reinforced each other until what began as a stock market crash became "one great political thunder-cloud." Writing in the *New York Times* in 1957, Henry Steele Commager remembered the Dark Valley:

In the bright sunshine of prosperity we have tended to forget, many of us, how black the desperation was. . . . By 1932 there were 18,000,000 unemployed, but less than one-fourth of these were receiving public aid. In Gastonia, N.C., 14-year-old girls worked sixty-six hours a week for $4.95; lumber workers got 10 cents an hour; Connecticut sweatshops hired girls for $1.10 for a fifty-five hour week. From 1930 to 1933, 9,100 banks closed their doors. The president of the National Association of Manufacturers announced that the unemployed mostly didn't want to work; Samuel Insull, with eighty-five directorships and sixty-five chairmanships, went about with a bodyguard of thirty-six men; the Morgan partners paid no income taxes during these depression years, and President Hoover said to Raymond Clapper, in February of 1931, that "If someone could get off a good joke every ten days I think our troubles would be over."

Unfortunately, jokes (even good ones) proved to be ineffective. The nation's troubles continued to worsen.

Profound economic dislocation inevitably gave life to radical political movements in the United States and around the world. The growth of revolutionary ideologies on the right and the left provoked crackdowns by those in authority. Even before the world war erupted, nativism, racism, xenophobia, and the violence they inspired delivered the most terrible blows imaginable to millions of ordinary people.

In April of 1945 war correspondent Ernie Pyle was killed by machine-gun fire on the island of Ie Shima. His last column was found in his pocket.

Those who are gone do not wish to be a millstone of gloom around our necks. But there are many of the living who have had burned into our brains forever the unnatural sight of cold dead men scattered over the hillsides and in the ditches along the high rows of hedge throughout the world. Dead men by mass production—in one country after another—month after month and year after year. Dead men in winter and dead men in summer. Dead men in such familiar promiscuity that they become monotonous. Dead men in such monstrous infinity that you almost come to hate them.

Less than a month after the nuclear attacks on Hiroshima and Nagasaki, General MacArthur presided over the signing of the Japanese surrender documents on the deck of the battleship USS *Missouri*. On that very day, a little more than two thousand miles away, Ho Chi Minh issued the "Declaration of Independence of the Democratic Republic of Vietnam." The document's first sentence reads, "All men are created equal; they are endowed by their Creator with certain inalienable rights; among these are Life, Liberty and the pursuit of Happiness." One war was over and another had begun.

America's passage through the Dark Valley had required the mass mobilization of society and compelled individuals to consistently subordinate their desires to the needs of the group. Living under the pall of dire necessity had, over the years, led people to value the habit of conformity, and society came to reward the willingness to elevate duty over self. Through it all, hardship nourished the dream that happy days would, someday, return. The postwar period's frenzy of construction and consumerism made Americans proud, but there was another, vastly more important rebuilding effort under way. The Dark Valley's many trials instilled in millions of young postwar parents a fervent wish that their children have a better childhood than the one they had known. This desire became part of a pivotal but little-remembered struggle between two radically different visions of child rearing put forth by two very different men.

A finance columnist publishing under the pen name Sylvia performed the first recorded mating of the terms *baby* and *boom*. In 1951 she wrote, "Take the 3,548,000 babies born in 1950. Bundle them into a batch, bounce them all over the bountiful land that is America. What do you get? Boom. The biggest, boomiest boom ever known in history." The "babies" were to become, oddly enough, the first generation to be defined primarily by their parents' fertility. The generation's eventual 80 million babies were living proof that, at long last, America had emerged from a dark valley.

The flush of postwar affluence led young parents to seek out new sources of guidance. Where child-rearing advice was once offered face-to-face, with grandparents in a position of preeminence, the increased physical mobility of families and the rise of credentialed "experts" often led postwar parents to distrust their own instincts and seek professional advice from popular books on the subject. Members of the white middle class were especially eager to seek the advice of professional authorities and then conduct their parenting in accordance with that counsel.

These circumstances led to an interesting and unexpected natural experiment that pitted two distinctively different sets of child-rearing practices against each other. Both of these practices were based on unstated, but highly idealized, cultural agendas. One approach elevated the virtues of science, authority, control, and obedience. The other relied upon and set about to strengthen the natural good judgment of loving parents.

DR. WATSON

The postwar era's champion of top-down autocratic child-rearing protocols was born the son of an alcoholic, womanizing, hard-luck farmer and his long-suffering, deeply religious wife. In 1878, the year of John Watson's birth near Greenville, South Carolina, few would have guessed that this child would, one day, launch the field of behavioral psychology, transform America's approach to parenting children, and invent the practice of "branding" products.

After earning his doctorate at the University of Chicago, Watson joined the department of psychology at Johns Hopkins in 1908. His ambition and intelligence fueled a career that made him chairman of the department when he was still in his thirties. Credited with being the first to build and use mazes for the study of learning and behavior, his invention set off a rat maze craze that led one rival to grump that "psychology is becoming the psychology of white rats."

This work also led Watson to ask why, if the behavior of rats could be understood without employing the concepts of consciousness or free will, the same might not also be true of human beings. He soon shifted his focus from rats to babies and began conducting "behaviorist" experiments on very young children. The most famous (or infamous) of these studies was conducted on a healthy nine-month-old boy who later became known as "Little Albert."

Watson began his work with Albert by demonstrating that the boy "had no negative response when presented with a white rat but cried and withdrew his legs when researchers clanged a metal bar with a hammer just behind his head." Watson then paired the loud noise with the appearance of the white rat. Not surprisingly, Little Albert soon began to cry when the rat appeared even when there was no loud noise. Watson discovered that the child's fearfulness quickly "generalized" to other white furry objects, including a Santa mask and (no surprise here) Watson's own white hair. Mercifully, the boy's mother removed him from the study before Watson could carry the experiment any further.

Soon after he published the results of the Little Albert experiments, Watson was caught up in a scandal involving one of his female students. The university formally, and quite euphemistically, accused him of conducting "unauthorized research on the human sexual response." The student in question became Watson's second wife soon after the professor's dismissal, and the newlyweds left Baltimore for New York. There Dr. Watson took a job as vice president of the J. Walter Thompson advertising agency.

Determined to bring modern scientific methods to the business of marketing, he persuaded the agency to conduct blindfolded "taste tests" with smokers and found that only one in ten could actually taste the difference between brands. People, Watson concluded, were prone to creating irrational associations between the products they purchased and certain very specific emotions. The advertiser's job, he argued, was to identify and deepen these associations. Watson's radical concept of "brand loyalty" transformed American business. He went on to guide advertising campaigns on behalf of Camel cigarettes, Johnson's Baby Powder, and Pond's Extract.

During Watson's years as an advertising executive he also wrote a handbook on child rearing. Titled *Psychological Care of Infant and Child*, it was published in 1928 and quickly became a best seller. As late as the 1950s and 1960s it was still common to hear those who had been the parents of young children during the 1930s and 1940s dispensing Watsonian advice. Watson offered stern warnings against "spoiling" children with excessive displays of affection. He believed that parents should let wailing babies "cry it out." Rereading his book, one has little doubt that if today's parents diligently followed his commandments, they would soon find the people from Child Protective Services on their doorstep.

It is a serious question in my mind whether there should be individual homes for children—or even whether children should know their own parents. There are undoubtedly much more scientific ways of bringing up children, which will probably mean finer and happier children.

Here is the schedule for a typical day in a Wastonian home.

Children should be awakened at 6:30 A.M. for orange juice and a pee. Play 'til 7:30. Breakfast should be at 7:30 sharp; at 8:00 they should be placed on the toilet for twenty minutes or less 'til bowel movement is complete. Then follow up with a verbal report. The child should then play indoors 'til 10:00 A.M., after 10:00 outside,

a short nap after lunch, then "social play" with others. In the evening a bath, quiet play until bedtime at 8:00 sharp.

Watson also placed severe limits on the expression of affection by
parents toward their children.

> Treat them as though they were young adults. Dress them; bathe
> them with care and circumspection. Let your behavior always be
> objective and kindly firm. Never hug and kiss them, never let
> them sit on your lap. If you must, kiss them once on the forehead
> when they say good night. Shake hands with them in the morning.
> Give them a pat on the head if they have made an extraordinarily
> good job on a difficult task. Try it out. In a week's time you will
> find how easy it is to be perfectly objective with your child and at
> the same time kindly. You will be utterly ashamed of the mawkish,
> sentimental way you have been handling it.

Watson viewed children as complex and little-understood machines
that, with proper management, could be molded into the form their
parents (or society) thought best. He believed, most of all, in the power
of science to guide human interactions. "No one today," he concluded,
"knows enough to raise a child. . . . Radium has had more scientific
study put upon it in the last fifteen years than has been given to the first
three years of infancy since the beginning of time." Despite, or perhaps
because of this cold, imperious bluster, another voice was preparing itself to be heard—one that would reduce the estimable Dr. John Watson
to a dusty historical footnote.

DR. SPOCK

Benjamin McLane Spock was born in New Haven, Connecticut, in
1903, the same year that John Watson earned his PhD. The oldest of
six children, Spock is said to have taken an active role in the care of

his numerous younger siblings. Originally intent upon becoming an architect, he decided to become a pediatrician after spending a summer working at a camp for disabled children. While enrolled at Yale as an undergraduate, the six-foot-four Spock qualified as a member of the rowing crew that won a gold medal at the 1924 Olympics in Paris. Five years later, he graduated from Columbia University's medical school and began his training in pediatrics. Dr. John Watson's book on child-care was highly regarded by the faculty at the hospital where Spock trained.

Spock found that, practically speaking, many of the questions that young parents brought to him had a psychological basis, so he enrolled in a six-year psychoanalytic training program. When he finished, he was the only "baby doctor" in America who had also trained in psychiatry. He established his medical practice in the depth of the Depression and, for many years, found it hard to make ends meet. Daily practice as a pediatrician led Spock to place a premium value on the mother-child bond and he encouraged the mothers who consulted him to cuddle their babies and show them affection because "every baby needs to be smiled at, talked to, played with, fondled—gently and lovingly." Mothers should be "natural and comfortable with and enjoy their babies."

Working during the evenings and with the dedicated assistance of his first wife, the former Jane Cheney, Spock wrote an American classic. *The Common Sense Book of Baby and Child Care* (1946) was composed mostly of insights drawn from his practice of medicine. "I never looked at my records," he said. "It all came out of my head." Written in a friendly, reassuring style, the book was a radical departure from the precise authoritarianism favored by most childcare experts.

Spock's book sold nearly a million copies a year during the 1950s. It went through seven editions (the last was released shortly after his death) and was translated into thirty-nine languages. Today it ranks second only to the Bible in total number of copies sold. Spock's mother, after reading the book for the first time, is said to have remarked, "Why, Benny, it's quite sensible." *Baby and Child Care* became the definitive child-rearing manual for the parents of the postwar generation. Indeed it was Spock's gentle insistence that parents should be flexible and see their children as individuals in their own right that broke Watson's iron grip on parenting advice.

In the early years of his career, Spock's political beliefs remained in line with those of his father, who believed that "Republicans created all the wealth in the United States, and the Democrats, incapable of creating wealth or anything else, used politics to try to cut a slice for themselves." When President Kennedy began sending American troops to Vietnam, however, Spock became an early and insistent critic of the war. During the late 1960s, Spock intensified his opposition to the war, and in 1968, America's pediatrician was put on trial for "illegally conspiring to aid and abet resistance to the draft." Speaking in his own defense, he told the jury that the war was "totally illegal, immoral, un-winnable, and detrimental to the best interests of the United States." This impassioned plea did him little good; he was convicted and would have spent two years in prison if the verdict had not been overturned on a technicality.

Spock's pacifism enraged conservatives, and they actively linked his supposedly permissive approach to parenting to the growing disor-der and violence within the antiwar movement. Vice President Spiro Agnew denounced the "Spock-marked generation" for its individualism and lack of respect for authority. Spock's political activism also hurt sales of *Baby and Child Care*, but its author was not deterred. "People have said, 'You've turned your back on pediatrics,' " Spock said in 1992. "I said, 'No. It took me until I was in my sixties to realize that politics was a part of pediatrics.' " He became the People's Party's candidate for president in 1972 and garnered 75,000 votes. By the time he turned eighty, he had been arrested more than a dozen times for acts of civil disobedience. He never tired of reminding audiences that "war is not healthy for babies or other living things."

Like all giants, Spock walked on feet made, at least in part, of clay. Feminists objected when early editions of his book uniformly referred to the caregiver as "she" and the child as "he." The text was littered with thoughtlessly sexist clunkers such as, "My prime concern is that, back at the childhood stage, parents and schools not encourage girls to be competitive with males if that is going to make them dissatisfied with raising children, their most creative job in adulthood." These failings were eventually corrected, but it took time and steady criticism from the emerging feminist movement to compel the change.

Though his political allies praised him in life and after his death, the members of his immediate family held a somewhat less charitable view of Benjamin Spock. Thomas Maier larded his *Dr. Spock: An American Life* with unflattering quotes given by his subject's children. One son called his father "a scary person." Despite the counsel he gave to millions of American families, the doctor was, much like his own father, an emotionally distant parent. Jane (Cheney) Spock struggled for decades with alcoholism, prescription drug abuse, and nervous breakdowns. The divorce, after forty-eight years of marriage, and his prompt remarriage to a woman thirty years his junior, undid his image as the ideal family man.

Whatever his personal faults and shortcomings, Spock successfully challenged and then overthrew the then-contemporary belief that experts alone possessed the scientific knowledge needed to guide children from birth to adulthood. He restored America's faith in common sense where it matters most of all, within the home and family. His rebuttal to the "condescending, scolding [and] intimidating" child-rearing advice of his time changed our world.

It was the Ivy League baby doctor's daring reassurance, "Trust yourself, you know more than you think you do," that defined parenthood in the postwar era. The chapter titles in Spock's book, "Parents Are Human," "Planning Your Homecoming," "Enjoy Your Baby," and "Diapers" seem mundane to us now, but they electrified the parents of the 1940s and 1950s. Spock's views also supported a subversive reordering of cultural priorities. His belief that regular people could solve life's most vexing problems sprang from his confident endorsement of both individualism and the value of thoughtful cooperation. Postwar parents responded warmly to Spock's offer of a happier, gentler family life. They chose Spock.

A TENSION UNRESOLVED

Although Dr. John Watson slipped into obscurity, Spock's victory over Watsonian ideology was never complete. The idea that children should submit to being molded by responsible adults was and remained especially attractive to the leaders of America's most powerful institutions and corporations. Millions of people whose experiences in the Dark Valley led them to share Watson's reflexive fear of disorder and his insistence on conformity found comfort in his strict prescriptions. In the postwar era, however, Watson's threadbare vision of childhood was easily overpowered by Spock's gentle wisdom. The clash between these ideologies can be seen, in retrospect, as a proxy for the tensions that were being encoded into the postwar generation's formative experiences.

The conflicts that erupted as members of the postwar generation began the difficult trek out of childhood and into adulthood dealt primarily with the irresolvable tensions between individualism and conformity, freedom and control. These struggles would soon develop into a fierce, sustained, and highly public struggle over the meaning, worth, and value of adulthood in the postwar era. As we will see, those who embraced Watson's views on power and conformity would return to play another, larger, and vastly more influential role on the American stage.

O2
1961

January

5 Miles Davis in *Ebony* magazine: "Sometimes a broad will walk up and ask for an autograph and get mad because I don't carry a pen around with me to sign one. I sign an autograph every time I make a record, that's my signature." **9 Tom Whitmore** *turns fifteen. As always, his mother bakes a chocolate birthday cake for him. After supper, his grandmother, parents, and younger sister gather round and sing for him. Outside, starlight makes the snow sparkle; icicles hang from broad, sheltering eaves.* **13** Future *Seinfeld* star Julia Louis-Dreyfus is born. **17** In his final speech to Congress, President Dwight Eisenhower warns America of an "immense military establishment and arms industry [that] is new in the American experience. The total influence—economic, political, even spiritual—is felt in every city, every statehouse, every office in the federal government. We must never let the weight of this combination endanger our liberties or democratic processes." **20** John F. Kennedy gives his inaugural address: "The torch has been passed to a new generation of Americans—born in this century, tempered by war, disciplined

by a hard and bitter peace." **23 Flo Marsh** *The* Charleston Chronicle *reports, "Florence Marsh's performance of Claude Debussy's "Nocturne" was the highlight of Mrs. Jordan's Winter Piano recital. Although she is only 11 years old, Miss Marsh is already making an impression on all those who enjoy classical music. Her parents, Pastor Fred Marsh, of the First Zion Baptist Church, and his wife, the former Augusta Catlett, have every reason to be proud of this remarkable young lady."* **24** A judge in Mexico grants playwright Arthur Miller and actress Marilyn Monroe a divorce on the grounds of incompatibility.

February

2 Stanley Ann Dunham, an eighteen-year-old student at the University of Hawaii, marries Barack Hussein Obama, a twenty-five-year-old graduate student from Kenya. **9** The Beatles perform for the first time at the Cavern Club. **11** Robert C. Weaver becomes administrator of the Housing and Home Finance Agency. He is the first African American to lead a major US government agency.

March

1 President Kennedy officially launches the Peace Corps. His brother-in-law, Sargent Shriver, becomes the program's first director.

April

1 North Central Bible College dropouts Jim Bakker and Tamara Faye LaValley get married. **4** President Kennedy polls a dozen advisers on whether to go ahead with the Bay of Pigs invasion. All vote in favor of proceeding. **6** New York governor Nelson Rockefeller signs a bill authorizing the construction of the World Trade Center. **12** The Soviet Union launches Yuri Gagarin into outer space. On reentry he ejects from the capsule and parachutes safely to earth. A farmer and her daughter come upon him dressed in a bright orange suit with a large white helmet. Gagarin later recalled, "When they saw me in my space suit and the parachute dragging alongside as I walked, they started to back away in fear. I told them, 'Don't be afraid, I am a Soviet citizen like you, who has descended from space and I must find a telephone to call Moscow!' " 13 James Stewart accepts an honorary Oscar on behalf of his friend Gary Cooper, who is unable to attend the ceremony. Stewart's emotional speech hints that Cooper is seriously ill. 15 Del Shannon's hit "Runaway" holds steady at number one in the US and the UK. 17 An underwater demolition team of five American frogmen enters the Bay of Pigs on the southern coast of Cuba. 19 Radio Havana reports that Cuban antiaircraft batteries brought down a US military plane piloted by a US airman. Papers found on the American pilot's body identify him as Leo Francis Bell. 20 NASA rocket scientist Werner von Braun tells Vice President Johnson: "We have an excellent chance of beating the Soviets to the first landing of a crew on the moon. . . . With an all-out crash program, I think we could accomplish this objective in 1967 or '68." 21 President Kennedy accepts responsibility for the Bay of Pigs invasion: "There's an old saying that victory has a hundred fathers and defeat is an orphan. What matters," he says, is only one fact: "I am the responsible officer of the government." 25 Tom *stumbles upon a moldy January 1955 edition of* Playboy *while cleaning out the storage shed behind the barn. Bettie Page is on the cover. He sneaks it into his bedroom and hides it under the mattress.*

May

1 Singer Tony Orlando breaks into the top forty for the first time with "Halfway to Paradise." The song peaks at number thirty-nine. 9 FCC chair Newton Minow calls the majority of television a "vast wasteland." 11 US Army Special Forces arrive in South Vietnam's Central Highlands to train Montagnard tribesmen in counterinsurgency tactics. 13 Gary Cooper, renowned for his quiet, understated acting style and

star of over one hundred films, dies. He is sixty years old. **14** A Freedom Riders' bus is firebombed near Anniston, Alabama, and the civil rights protestors are beaten by an angry mob. **15 Flo** *is sent upstairs when a dozen people from the church arrive unexpectedly at the front door of the parsonage. The talk goes late into the night. Flo falls asleep to murmured voices of men and women talking about the Freedom Riders.* **25** President Kennedy declares that the nation will commit itself to achieving the goal, before the decade is out, of landing a man on the Moon and returning him back safely to the earth. **26** Dr. Jack Kevorkian's transfusion of blood from cadavers into live patients stirs controversy when *Time* magazine reports on "Blood from the Dead." Kevorkian acknowledges that the practice has an "undercurrent of repugnance which makes it difficult to view objectively." **28** Peter Benenson writes, "The technique of publicising the personal stories of a number of prisoners of contrasting politics is a new one. It has been adopted to avoid the fate of previous amnesty campaigns, which so often have become more concerned with publicising the political views of the imprisoned than with humanitarian purposes." His essay, "The Forgotten Prisoners," becomes the founding document of Amnesty International. **31** In trouble for riding in stolen cars, Jimi Hendrix enlists in the army and is assigned to the 101st Airborne Division. His commanding officers ultimately consider him to be a subpar soldier and he is discharged after just one year in the service.

June

14 Country music star Patsy Cline and her brother Sam are involved in a head-on car collision on Old Hickory Boulevard in Nashville. The impact throws Cline into the windshield, nearly killing her. **15** American cigarette consumption peaks at 3,986 cigarettes per person per year. **19** Iraqi president Abdul Karim Qasim announces that he considers Kuwait a part of Iraq and lays claim to its territory. A British diplomat cables London, "We are dealing with an unbalanced man whose actions are unpredictable. We conclude that the threat to Kuwait's independence is as grave and imminent as it could be."

July

2 Ernest Hemingway is found dead of a self-inflicted shotgun wound in the head. His wife, Mary, claims that he had killed himself accidentally while cleaning the weapon. **5** *Melanie Weber is born in Vanderbilt Hospital, where her mother works nights as a nurse. Her father paces the waiting room floor until the doctor emerges to give him the news. He has a beautiful, healthy baby daughter. Ten fingers. Ten toes.* **9** *Melanie comes home to the little house on Maple Street for the first time. Her mother nurses her as she sits in a rocking chair. Her father plays "Hobo's Lullaby" for his little girl on the first mandolin he ever made.* **11** The *Steubenville Herald Star* carries an advertisement for a new hair coloring product for men. The copy warns readers to "Beware of imitations and insist on the original 'Grecian Formula 16.'"

August

1 The Six Flags over Texas theme park officially opens to the public, offering the world's first log-flume ride, first free-fall ride, and first mine-train-style roller coaster. **4** Barack Obama is born at Kapi'olani Maternity and Gynecological Hospital in Honolulu, Hawaii. **13** Troops in East Germany build a wall between East and West Berlin, shutting off the escape route for thousands of refugees from the East. **14** *Tom nervously grooms his prize heifer Amazing, out of Glasson by Shottle. She is a sleek registered Holstein. This is his third year showing at the Madison County Fair. Even though she is a town girl, Brenda Cobb comes to see the Youth Livestock show. She has known Tom since they were both five years old.*

September

3 The minimum wage in the United States rises from $1.00 an hour to $1.15 an hour. 4 Richard Nixon makes a hole in one at the Bel Air Country Club's golf course. He tells a reporter, "It's the greatest thrill of my life. Even better than being elected." 5 *Rita Sorrentino's grandmother stands on the sidewalk and watches as her daughter and granddaughter pass through the front door of Vineland, New Jersey's D'Ippolito Elementary School. It is Rita's first day of kindergarten. At the end of every school day for the next seven years, the grandmother will wait on the sidewalk for Rita and then walk her home.* 6 Afghanistan breaks off diplomatic relations with Pakistan. 8 *Flo walks straight home after school and, under her mother's watchful eye, starts her homework. She then practices piano for two hours. After supper, Flo joins her parents at church for the Wednesday night service. Neither parent nor child makes any allowance for half measures or for putting forth less than one's best effort.* 11 *The Rejected*, a documentary on homosexuality, is broadcast on KQED TV in San Francisco. 17 The Minnesota Vikings beat the Chicago Bears in their first regular season NFL game. Bears' coach George Halas later describes the loss as "the most embarrassing defeat of my life." 18 The word *ain't* is formally accepted into the English language.

October

1 Pat Robertson launches his career as a televangelist on WTFC Channel 27, in Portsmouth, Virginia. 3 The Motion Picture Association of America's production code is modified to allow "homosexuality and other sexual aberrations" to be suggested but not actually spelled out. 3 *The Dick Van Dyke Show* premieres on CBS. 8 *Melanie bats at the toys her father holds in front of her.* 13 President Kennedy issues a top secret order to his defense secretary to "introduce the Air Force 'Jungle Jim' Squadron into Vietnam for the initial purpose of training Vietnamese forces." 18 *Tom, a sophomore sensation for the Madison Tigers, scores*

the winning touchdown in the closing minutes of the Madison County high school football championship game. With the winning score under his belt and 167 yards of rushing, Whitmore is named the game's Most Valuable Player. **29** The USSR detonates a fifty-megaton hydrogen bomb in the largest man-made explosion in history; it has ten times the combined power of all the explosives used in World War II.

November

8 Rita *tells her mother that she wants a Chatty Cathy Doll, more than anything in the world. Her mother tells her not to get her hopes up because it's very expensive.* **9** Test pilot Neil Armstrong sets a world record reaching a speed of 3,989 miles per hour in an X-15 rocket plane that he helped to design. **10** Estelle Griswold is arrested in Connecticut and charged with providing contraception to married couples. Eager to use her trial to challenge the law, Griswold volunteers to help find former patients who would testify against her in court. **11** *Catch-22*, which was originally titled *Catch-18*, is published. Joseph Heller's novel tells the convoluted story of Captain John Yossarian, a member of a US bomber crew stationed on the Mediterranean island of Pianosa during World War II. **13 Rita's** *grandmother, without telling anyone, puts a Chatty Cathy doll on layaway at the department store. She returns to the store every week to make payments on the doll.* **15** The Mattachine Society of Washington is organized to "secure for homosexuals the right to life, liberty, and the pursuit of happiness; to equalize the status and position of the homosexual with the heterosexual; to secure for the homosexual the right to develop and achieve his full potential; to inform and enlighten the public about the homosexual; and to assist, protect and counsel the homosexual in need." **19** Lucille Ball marries Gary Morton.

December

11 The first American helicopters arrive in Saigon along with four hundred US military personnel. "Please Mr. Postman" becomes the first number one pop hit for the Marvelettes and Motown. **15 Flo** *wants The Shirelles' Tonight's the Night LP record for Christmas, but neither her mother nor her father approves of that sort of music.* **22 Melanie** *sits in her mother's lap and babbles happily as her parents sing together.* **25 Rita** *squeals with delight even before she opens the package. She knows from the size and shape of the box what it contains. Her entire body trembles as she tears off the wrapping paper. Her grandmother watches, her eyes smiling.* **30** Conservative talk show host Sean Hannity is born. **31** The Beach Boys play their first paying gig, at the Ritchie Valens Memorial Dance in Long Beach, in a show headlined by Ike & Tina Turner. Brian Wilson later recalls that they were "five clean-cut, unworldly white boys from a conservative white suburb, in an auditorium full of black kids" and realizes that "success [is] all about R&B, rock and roll, and money."

03

YOUTHQUAKE

In the early 1960s, perceptive observers of art, music, and fashion sensed that the zeitgeist was changing. Among the first to embrace this new energy was *Vogue*'s editor in chief, Diana Vreeland. She coined the term *youthquake* to describe what was happening around her. The name was well chosen because these changes really were, in cultural terms, seismic. For the first time, established designers began attending to the preferences expressed by young people, people who were, in many ways, not yet adults.

So-called youthquakers such as Jean Shrimpton, Twiggy, Penelope Tree, and Edie Sedgwick graced the cover of Vreeland's magazine month after month. This abrupt disruption of the status quo annoyed many of the leading figures in fashion. While skirt length could be seen (and measured), the new direction fashion was taking presaged a far more substantial challenge to the status quo. The "tailored little dresses with bold geometric shapes" that were splashed across the cover of *Vogue* reflected the emerging tastes of a rising generation. Suddenly, the styles favored by mature adults were no longer what mattered most.

The 1960s and 1970s marked the first time that young people became the driving force behind changes in popular fashion, music, and art. This youthquake was so powerful and so distinctive in its outlook that the style of those years remains instantly recognizable half a century later, even to people who were not alive at the time. Diana Vreeland once boasted, "The bikini is the most important thing since the atom bomb." It may have seemed that way (especially to the editor of a fashion magazine), but her perspective failed to distinguish the rising choice-making power of this generation from the choices being made. It was actually the ability to choose the bikini, rather than the bikini itself, that was "the most important thing since the atom bomb."

PIGS, PYTHONS, DOGS, AND TAILS

Demographers have long used the analogy of the "pig in the python" to illustrate the impact the enormous postwar generation has had on American society. In this metaphor, the python represents the traditional distribution of age groups in society. Members of the postwar generation are said to be the pig inside that python. A python who's swallowed a pig develops a distinct bulge that slowly travels the length of the snake until it reaches the inevitable outcome. The metaphor makes for a vivid image but, unfortunately, also implies, wrongly, that the postwar generation is a passive entity.

While it is true that, during its years in the Dark Valley, American society *acted* on the parents of the postwar generation (the rigors of the Depression and the war gave them very little choice in many important matters), the postwar years have been shaped to a remarkable degree by their children's rapidly growing capacity to *act on* society. The postwar generation's tremendous size and unprecedented density—combined with a new power of choice—endowed it with the ability to reshape American culture more to its liking. A much more apt metaphor for the youthquakers' relationship with American society would be that of a tail that discovered how to wag the dog.

SQUARES, ACTIVISTS, AND HIPPIES

The postwar generation's passage out of childhood and into adulthood was defined by and is, even now, remembered in terms of the subcultures that dominated the era. While the dominant culture of a nation or people seems as transparent as air—and nearly as ubiquitous—subcultures stand out. People find subcultures hard to ignore because they are so obviously made up of people who "should be" loyal to the dominant culture but who have chosen instead to willfully and publicly violate the dominant culture's accepted beliefs and behaviors. The existence of a subculture is evidence that the dominant culture has failed to solve some urgent problem. In this case the problem was "How can we find our way out of childhood and into adulthood?"

Subcultures are, by definition, informal entities and can often be fully defined only after they cease to exist. They do not hold meetings. They do not issue membership cards. Some people affiliate openly with a subculture, while others who are clearly aligned with its beliefs deny any connection. Furthermore, people's allegiances change over time. They go through phases, some of which they enlarge and embroider in their memory; others they diminish or forget entirely. Despite these limitations, the exploration of a subculture can provide useful insights into the world in which we live.

How subcultures are remembered is heavily influenced by nostalgia, prejudice, and self-deception. Subcultures exist because of a perceived failure on the part of a dominant culture, and not surprisingly, this dominant culture is rarely generous when it comes to writing the history of a subculture. In fact, conventional wisdom often emphasizes the most superficial and ephemeral aspects of a subculture while dismissing or distorting the beliefs and practices that actually lay at its core. Clothing styles, hair lengths, slang terms, and hemlines have been attributes of many different subcultures, but such things rarely tell us much about why people chose to embrace a particular subculture.

The size and density of the postwar generation and its position in the wake of the Dark Valley compelled its members to improvise the transition into adulthood rapidly and on a massive, continent-wide scale. This necessity fractured the Spockian consensus around childhood. While it might seem that these millions of people would discover, explore, and traverse a myriad of paths into adulthood, the truth is that the number of options available to them were actually quite limited. In a more traditional society, the young would have been carefully prepared for the rituals that would deliver them directly from childhood to adulthood. Instead members of the world's largest generation living in a mass society with the benefits of peace and prosperity were left to improvise their own rites of passage.

Young people of the era were ultimately led to choose among three basic developmental strategies for emerging out of childhood. They could (1) accept adulthood as it was lived by one's parents, (2) embrace the power of adulthood as an instrument of social change, or (3) reject the adulthood on offer and explore new, nonadult ways of living beyond childhood.

These three orientations toward adulthood went on to form the foundation for the postwar generation's three dominant adolescent and early adult subcultures: Squares, Activists, and Hippies. These were the primary colors that defined the postwar generation's passage out of childhood. Combined and recombined, these three basic perspectives on adulthood gave rise to millions of distinct variations. Members of the postwar generation who read the following chapters will likely insist that they were never really fully part of any one of these subcultures. This is true. Human beings are complicated creatures. We have many dimensions, and a simple scheme that posits three major generational subtypes cannot possibly capture life as it was lived by individuals during these years. In fact, we are all the product of multiple influences and we all change affiliations over time. And we are all revisionists when it comes to how we choose to remember and tell our own story.

Squares

In the 1940s, jazz musicians started referring to people who didn't or couldn't appreciate their music as "squares." It is said that the term was derived from the square shape that a conductor's hand gestures traced when leading a band in a regular four-beat rhythm. Squares were dull, conventional people who congregated around or lived in Squaresville. The Beatniks took up this idea and used it to divide the world into the hip and the square; they left no doubt which they preferred.

The use of *square* as a negative term gradually seeped out of these subcultures and entered into more mainstream use. With the rise of the counterculture in the 1960s, young Squares increasingly stood out among their less conventional peers. What others saw as repressive, stereotyped, and one-dimensional thinking, they saw as honorable, forthright, and responsible. While others tested the outer limits of art, music, and fashion, Squares were content to stay well inside established norms. The negative and dismissive use of *square* became so widespread that, in 1971, the Cub Scouts of America felt compelled to delete the phrase "to be square" from the Cub Scout promise; they replaced it with the words "to help other people."

We rarely recall the Squares because they left so little impression on the culture and history of the First Crucible era. Art created by young people who find coming of age to be a relatively straightforward endeavor is rarely memorable. The Squares could see and were eager to make use of the same well-worn developmental passages that had launched their parents into adulthood. No matter what geographic region or social class they sprang from, Squares were pleased to imagine themselves living out an adulthood very much like that of their parents and grandparents. Squares, like well-behaved women, rarely made history.

Squares understood that the dawning of the Age of Aquarius would not change the fact that their lives would be much like the lives of their parents. There would be happiness and grief, hardship and triumph, and each would come in their own time. Squares believed that when one is a child, one speaks as a child; but when one comes of age, one puts away childish things. These were the people who knew how to make the world work. Clarity of purpose and responsibility were more than just ideals. These young men and women did their jobs, they went to war, they went to school, all largely without complaint.

Merle Haggard was singing for them when he crooned his pride in being an Okie from Muskogee where "even squares can have a ball." People knew that, when the time came, Squares could be counted on to do what they believed was right, and that is exactly what happened.

Activists

Members of the Activist subculture were suspended between fervent idealism and a genuine grown-up taste for opportunity and success. The dominant culture may have respected their energy and drive, but it also strongly disapproved of the Activists' goals and their methods. The myth of the "bra-burning" feminist, to cite just one example, remains in circulation four decades after its invention. The Activist's commitment to social justice was sometimes less than it appeared to be. Activist Abbie Hoffman addressed the tendency to value form over function in his underground classic *Steal This Book*. Beginning with his observation, "It's perhaps fitting that I write this introduction in jail," Hoffman went on to offer the following admonition:

> The duty of a revolutionary is to make love and that means staying alive and free. That doesn't allow for cop-outs. Smoking dope and hanging up Che's picture is no more a commitment than drinking milk and collecting postage stamps. A revolution in consciousness is an empty high without a revolution in the distribution of power.

The members of the Activist subculture were, it must be said, blessed with an abundance of ambition. (Hoffman started his own publishing company and sold more than 250,000 of his books in less than a year.) They were eager to take power and willing to set aside conventional approaches to organizing in favor of inflammatory rhetoric and dramatic action. Like America's financial and political elites, Activists were concerned with power and its uses. Unlike those elites, they had little experience with or knowledge of the instruments of social change and control. Although they were endowed with a desire for change, they often lacked the skill and experience needed to create and sustain it effectively. Civil rights, environmentalism, feminism, and social justice—all these things were (and remain) radical aspirations, and we can now see that decisive and enduring victories in these areas can rarely be won by people so very young.

It was in their embrace of adulthood that Activists most resembled Squares. Both groups found it easy to endorse the inevitability and desirability of coming of age, and both groups viewed the passage out of adolescence in primarily practical terms. They differed greatly, however, in *why* they valued adulthood. Squares saw, and looked forward to, an adulthood bounded by work, responsibility, family, and community. Activists, in contrast, wanted to use that power of adulthood to create and then enforce a social order that relied upon new approaches to wealth, power, and social justice. Activists for the most part rejected the purity of pacifism and saw simple appeals to "peace" and "love" and "understanding" as being ineffective if not explicitly counterproductive.

Hippies

Timothy Leary was one of the first to articulate the *counter*cultural perspective embodied in the Hippie subculture. Born in 1920, he served honorably as a sergeant in the Medical Corps during the Second World War and, like so many other veterans, got married in 1945. He earned a master's degree in psychology in 1946, and the couple's first child, a daughter named Susan, was born in 1947. Leary later recalled the 1950s as a time when he lived as an "anonymous institutional employee who drove to work each morning in a long line of commuter cars and drove home each night and drank martinis . . . like several million middle-class, liberal, intellectual robots."

He was teaching at Harvard University when he began conducting psychology experiments using drugs such as psilocybin and LSD, which were legal at the time. As part of that work he oversaw the so-called Marsh Chapel experiment in which theology students were given psilocybin and then questioned about their perspective on religion. The university began to receive complaints from parents that Leary was distributing hallucinogenic drugs to their children. The CIA began to monitor his research.

In 1963, Leary, along with his associate Richard Alpert, were fired from their faculty positions. No longer bound to the university, both men greatly expanded their explorations of transcendental consciousness. This led, inevitably, to problems with the law. During the 1960s and 1970s, Leary may well have set a world record by being held in a total of twenty-nine different prisons throughout the world. President Richard Nixon described Leary as "the most dangerous man in America."

Leary attempted to define the Hippie subculture:

Hippy is an establishment label for a profound, invisible, underground, evolutionary process. For every visible hippy, barefoot, beflowered, beaded, there are a thousand invisible members of the turned-on underground. Persons whose lives are tuned in to their inner vision, who are dropping out of the TV comedy of American Life.

It was not the bellbottoms, the beads, the hirsutism, or the slang that generated friction between Hippies and mainstream American culture: millions of Squares and Activists dabbled with such things. It was the Hippies' rejection of the belief that growing up was inevitable that shocked and outraged the dominant culture. The requirements of a responsible, capable adulthood, which seemed immutable to everyone else, were being questioned—and changed.

Despite what American culture was telling them, Hippies understood that entry into adulthood was *not* mandatory. As a group, they explored the uncharted realms of not-adulthood and chose to live outside both childhood and adulthood. Although their cultural leap is dismissed today as blatant immaturity, it is actually fantastically difficult to go beyond and then actively question the foundational belief of one's own culture. Comparable leaps of imagination were taken by the artists who first painted the cave walls in Lascaux, the Renaissance astronomers who first questioned the Earth-centric model of the cosmos, and the amateur political philosophers who brought forth a democratic republic in North America.

The Hippies' cultural heresy fostered the growth of a vibrant and, most of all, creative subculture. Their commitment to beauty, peace, and love, which seemed so fragile to so many, actually served as a solid foundation on which they were able to develop and implement a wide range of social and cultural innovations. Because they were largely excluded from employment in traditional businesses, Hippies often became entrepreneurial. They started businesses, organized cooperatives, and made innovative use of technology.

In the past, mystics, prophets, and sages who were willing to turn their back on society and explore realms of altered consciousness had nearly always been solitary figures. The Hippie subculture embraced "enlightenment" on a mass scale. The source of this vast cultural disturbance was, however, remarkably small. Even at its height in 1968, the number of people self-identifying as Hippies was estimated to be less than 0.02 percent of the US population. Still, their insights into the harsh reality that lay behind the American dream formed the most important cultural innovation of the First Crucible era. Millions of Squares and Activists who could not or would not "tune in, turn on, drop out" embraced elements of the Hippie sensibility, especially its fashion, music, and art.

Unlike any other cultural subgroup, Hippies had the audacity to criticize the form and function of adulthood as a life phase. They understood that while physical maturity was a biological necessity, entry into adulthood was a cultural practice. They chose to explore a new and radically unfamiliar world that lay *outside both childhood and adulthood*. The dominant response to this choice was to interpret the Hippie way of life as either an overextended childhood or an underdeveloped adulthood.

It was the Hippies' radical iconoclasm that ignited the First Crucible's most heated conflicts. As the 1960s wore on, negative reactions from Squares and Activists, buttressed by what was then referred to as the "Establishment," gave life to a sustained campaign of ridicule, vilification, and fear. These attacks battered and then destroyed the Hippie movement, and with its collapse, American culture lost its only effective critique of adulthood. Though it was celebrated at the time as a triumph of order and common sense, this collapse also opened the way for adults and adulthood to make an unprecedented assertion of power.

1971

January

1 A compromise with broadcasters moves the start of a ban on television advertising for cigarettes back one day, thus allowing these commercials to run (for the last time) during telecasts of college football bowl games on New Year's Day. **2 Melanie,** *eleven, goes to her first sleepover at her best friend's house. While the other girls cluster in the bedroom, play 45s, and giggle about the boys at school, she curls up on the couch and watches* The Art of Love *with Dick Van Dyke and Angie Dickinson.* **8** A pod of twenty-nine pilot whales beach themselves on San Clemente Island. **9 Tom** *celebrates his twenty-fifth birthday, at home with his family. He cuts a big corner piece out of his chocolate birthday cake. Brenda is due any day with their first child.* **12** All in the Family, starring Carroll O'Connor as Archie Bunker, debuts on CBS. **12** Satchel Paige, who famously asked, "How old would you be if you didn't know how old you are?" becomes the first player from the Negro Leagues to be elected to the Baseball Hall of Fame. 23 **Flo**, *twenty-one, is in the first year of a doctoral sociology program at the University of Michigan.* 25 Charles Manson and three female Family members are found guilty of the 1969 Tate-LaBianca murders. 30 **Tom**'s *son Wayne Dillard Whitmore is born after a normal pregnancy and delivery. Tom holds him gingerly as he squalls. "Good lungs!" he crows. Wayne weighs eight pounds, six ounces.* 31 The number one song in America is "Knock Three Times" by Tony Orlando and Dawn. It goes on to sell 9 million copies.

February

1 The soundtrack album from the movie *Love Story*, starring Ryan O'Neal and Ali MacGraw, is certified as a gold record. 2 In opposition to apartheid, the General Assembly of the Episcopal Church petitions GM to end production in South Africa. 3 Davy Jones announces he is leaving the Monkees. 9 An earthquake measuring 6.5 on the Richter scale hits San Fernando, California, killing sixty-two people. 13 Backed by American air and artillery support, South Vietnamese troops invade Laos. 17 **Rita**, *sixteen, at her first practice with the varsity cheerleading squad, already knows every cheer by heart. She has been preparing for this moment for an entire year. One of the varsity girls, a junior, has twisted her knee and will be out for the rest of the season. Rita knows that if she performs well, that varsity spot is hers. She does well.* 25 A nineteen-year-old US army recruit named Chapin J. Paterson hijacks a Seattle-bound Western Airlines plane by pretending to have a bomb in a brown paper sack. He orders the pilot to go to Cuba. When the crew explains that the 737 does not have enough fuel for such a long journey, Paterson replies, "All right then, take me to Vancouver." Patterson, a self-described conscientious objector, surrenders to police on arrival in Vancouver. 27 **Melanie** *and her sister spend the evening singing harmonies in their family's living room as a group of her parents' friends play "old timey" music."*

March

1 A bomb explodes in a men's room in the United States Capitol. The Weather Underground issues a communiqué claiming the bombing was "in protest of the U.S. invasion of Laos." 2 *Tom and Brenda go out to the Hofbräu for the first time since Wayne was born. They have the fish fry in a booth in the back corner of the restaurant. Brenda pulls out a battered manila envelope that contains the love letters they wrote to each other when Tom was in Vietnam. They take turns reading them out loud to each other. The Charlie Pride hit "I'd Rather Love You" plays on the jukebox.* 3 Levi Strauss & Co., the San Francisco–based jeans maker, goes public. 7 *Flo joins the Black Women's Organization against War and Racism.* 8 In the "Fight of the Century," boxer Joe Frazier defeats Muhammad Ali at Madison Square Garden. 8 President Nixon is recorded, in the Oval Office, expressing bigotry toward women, blacks, Mexicans, and Italians. 8 Hanoi broadcasts Jimi Hendrix's "Star-Spangled Banner." 18 Soft contact lenses are approved by the FDA. 20 In what is billed as "An Evening with the Grateful Dead," the band plays to a sellout crowd at the University of Iowa in Iowa City. They close the second set with an extended version of "Turn Your Lovelight On." 22 After ten years of employment, Carole A. Gerdom is fired from her job as a flight attendant with Continental. She had been suspended without pay eight times for exceeding her maximum weight. Continental based her termination on the fact that she had exceeded her maximum weight for ninety days. Gerdom, who is five feet five and a half inches tall, weighed 146.5 pounds, thirteen pounds above her maximum weight. 28 *The Ed Sullivan Show* airs its final episode. 29 Lt. William Calley is found guilty in the murder of twenty-two people in the My Lai Massacre. 30 George Harrison's ode to Hare Krishna, "My Sweet Lord," hits number one on the UK charts.

April

9 Charles Manson is sentenced to death. (In 1972, the sentence for all California death row inmates will be commuted to life imprisonment.) **12** Pregnant and in jail on charges of conspiracy, Black Panther Party member Afeni Shakur defends herself in court and wins acquittal. **23** In testimony to the Senate Foreign Relations Committee, army veteran John Kerry asks, "How do you ask a man to be the last man to die in Vietnam? How do you ask a man to be the last man to die for a mistake?"

May

1–3 Over 12,000 anti-war protesters are arrested in Washington, DC, during a massive demonstration against the war in Vietnam. **3** A Harris Poll reveals that 60 percent of Americans are against the Vietnam War. **12** The Civil Service Commission bans gender-specific job descriptions. **17** The musical *Godspell*, by Stephen Schwartz and John-Michael Tebelak, opens off-Broadway. **18** *Rita is hired to work the "Snack Shack" at the local community pool for the summer.* **19** The Mars probe *Mars 2* is launched by the Soviet Union. **23** *Rita, with her parents and Nonna watching proudly, strides across the stage of the auditorium and is inducted into the National Honor Society's Vineland High School chapter.* **28** President Nixon orders John Haldeman to conduct wiretapping and political espionage against the Democrats. The orders are recorded on tape. **30** The Mars probe *Mariner 9* is launched toward Mars by the United States. **31** A proposal is made to the North Vietnamese that includes a cease-fire in place, US withdrawal, and the return of prisoners.

June

10 President Nixon lifts a twenty-one-year-old embargo against trade with China, permitting exports to and imports from China to proceed on the same basis as trade with other Communist countries. 13 The *New York Times* begins to publish previously secret documents known as the Pentagon Papers. They detail America's involvement in the Vietnam War. 17 In a press conference Nixon names drug abuse as "public enemy number one in the United States" and coins the term "War on Drugs." 18 Southwest Airlines opens for business with flights between Dallas, Houston, and San Antonio. 20 *Flo is back home in Charleston. She is going to be the maid of honor in her best friend's wedding. Her mother asks her if "there is anyone special." Flo shakes her head. "There's so much to do, I'm too busy for that." Her mother nods but says nothing.* 27 Concert promoter Bill Graham closes the Fillmore East in New York City with a final concert featuring the the Allman Brothers Band, the Beach Boys, and Mountain.

July

3 Jim Morrison, lead singer of the Doors, is found dead in his bathtub in Paris. 4 The Fillmore West is closed in San Francisco with a final show featuring Santana, Creedence Clearwater Revival, and the Grateful Dead. 5 The Twenty-Sixth Amendment to the United States Constitution, formally certified by President Richard Nixon, lowers the voting age from twenty-one to eighteen. 10 In her "Address to the Women of America" speech, Gloria Steinem declares, "Sex and race, because they are easy, visible differences, have been the primary ways of organizing human beings into superior and inferior groups, and into the cheap labor on which this system still depends. We are talking about a society in which there will be no roles other than those chosen, or those earned."

August

1 Neil Armstrong leaves NASA to become a professor of engineering at the University of Cincinnati. 3 *Tom hears his wife's screaming over*

the dull thrum of the tractor. He races to the house and finds her cradling Wayne. He is not breathing. With fumbling fingers Tom calls the fire department. They send an ambulance but it is too late. His father stays behind to do evening chores while they make the long drive into town. **5** *Wayne Dillard Whitmore's obituary runs in the* Courier Dispatch. **9** India and Russia sign a friendship treaty.

September

1 Tom *receives the coroner's report on Wayne in the mail. The cause of death is listed as sudden infant death syndrome.* **5 Tom**'s *sister Vicky leaves home to go to beautician school. She is the first in her family to continue her education after high school.* **17 Melanie**'s *father refuses to buy a television, so Melanie and her family go around the corner to the Bakers' house to watch* Hee-Haw. *Buck Owens will be playing a guitar her father made and everyone is excited to see it on TV.* **29** The Florida Highway Patrol issues a statement indicating that as many as 300,000 people might try to be among the first to get into Walt Disney World.

October

10 James Michener's novel *The Drifters* hits number seven on the *New York Times* Best Sellers list for fiction. **16** John Lennon and Yoko Ono move to New York City.

November

3 The UNIX *Programmer's Manual* is published. **5 Tom**, *his wife, and his parents all vote a straight Republican ticket. Every morning they play the radio while doing barn chores, and news of antiwar protests never fails to anger Tom. He complains to his father that they both served their country and that "these damn Hippies are lazy cowards." He knows that life is hard. He knows that the only way to survive is to work hard and take care of your*

48 ~ DR. BILL THOMAS

own. **12** President Richard M. Nixon sets February 1, 1972, as the dead-line for the removal of another 45,000 American troops from Vietnam. **25** *Melanie's grandparents, on her father's side, come to visit from West Virginia. Their car is loaded with luggage and food. The house echoes with her grandfather's laughter.*

December

3 War breaks out between India and Pakistan. **4** Montreux Casino burns down during a concert by Frank Zappa. The fire was started by a fan. **8** *Ms.* magazine is launched, beginning life as an insert in *New York* magazine. **12** **Tom** *and Brenda go to the VFW for Saturday night with Tom's parents. Like his father, Tom has had little to say about his combat experiences. After a couple of beers, his parents surprise the young couple with a deed to a parcel of land from the farm.* **14** Senator Robert Taft Jr. introduces a bill that would grant amnesty to draft evaders who return to the United States and agree to perform public service. The measure fails by a wide margin. **19** **Melanie** *brings her report card home. She has A's in every subject.* **23** **Tom** *is shopping for Christmas presents. His sister Vicky is the easiest to buy for: she wants the Partridge Family Christmas album.*

PART II

THE
RISE TO POWER

PART II

THE
RISE TO POWER

O5

THE CULT OF ADULTHOOD

The chaos associated with the most intense First Crucible years generated a powerful and unintended *counter*-counterculture. In place of "flower power" and "the struggle," America was offered what Rick Perlstein in *Nixonland* calls an "Orthogonian" worldview. In its pure form, this ideal embraced the virtues of a productive, humble, and obedient adulthood. The Squares' furious rejection of the First Crucible's social and cultural dislocations led them to push their counterreformation forward with relentless energy and dedication.

The postwar generation's Squares may have been young, but they had much more in common with their parents than with the Activists and Hippies. Like their parents, they found the upheaval generated by the First Crucible to be very disturbing. Richard Nixon had read them right. The postwar generation's Squares eagerly placed themselves within his "Silent Majority." By 1970, the Squares had had enough. They went on the offensive and quickly proved themselves to be especially skillful culture warriors.

THE END OF ACTIVISM

Our culture continues to mislead us with a false narrative surrounding these tumultuous years. The Squares' counter-counterculture detested the protests, the marches, the hairstyles, and the drugs that captured America's collective attention. No matter how one feels about such things today, all of these things were, in fact, ephemera. The real story, the genuine *revolution*, was conceived by, led by, and won by the postwar generation's Squares. Our culture's chaotic passage out of the First Crucible presaged the rise to power of a Square ideology that inspired the hypertrophied adulthood which would dominate American culture for the next four decades. Compared to the plodding and uncertain nature of most social change movements, the Square revolution unfolded with dizzying speed and power. Even today it remains hard to believe that the very people who had seemed so peripheral to the First Crucible's swirling energy and creativity went on to carry out an enduring program of cultural transformation vastly more radical than even the wildest dreams of Hippies with flowers in their hair.

How did Squares manage to become the new lords of adulthood? To begin with, they had a huge numerical advantage. Even though their influence *during* the First Crucible was muted, Squares were always far more numerous than Activists and Hippies combined. They were also blessed with powerful allies. Leaders in the government curried their favor by instigating violent crackdowns on unrest. Right-of-center politicians increasingly took pleasure in deriding Activists regardless of the merits of the questions they posed. The Rolling Stones sang, "I went down to the demonstration, to get my fair share of abuse," but as the close of the decade drew near, the level of that abuse escalated sharply and the willingness of people in charge to accommodate Activist demands nearly vanished. The cost of "demonstrating" soon came to exceed the benefits.

Everybody loves a winner, and Squares soon found that it was surprisingly easy to add "former" Activists to their ranks. Among the most prominent of these converts was Yippie party cofounder and former

Chicago Seven defendant Jerry Rubin. In the post–First Crucible years, Rubin embraced the role of "businessman" and proclaimed "wealth creation" to be the "real American revolution." By emphasizing the power of Square adulthood (along with its material advantages), Square ideology effectively diminished and diverted energy that had been channeled into dissent. In the end, the Activists saw which way the wind was blowing, and most surrendered to the inevitable.

THE DEMOLITION OF
THE COUNTERCULTURE

In the post–First Crucible years, Squares and their growing legions of allies went to work dismantling and stigmatizing the Activist and Hippie subcultures. They insisted, at every turn, that the only valid perspective on adulthood would be theirs. There are few examples in American history of one faction so completely and totally dominating and destroying its cultural adversaries. Even during Reconstruction the remnants of the Confederacy, impoverished by war and shattered by military defeat, remained a lethal force.

The mythology that now surrounds this era makes all of this seem inevitable. The Hippie movement was *obviously* doomed by sex, drugs, and a terrible lack of seriousness. The reality, however, is much more complicated. Far from being the crude caricature created by its most vicious and dedicated opponents, the Hippie movement was actually vibrant, effective, loving, kind, and human. It consistently gave rise to innovative businesses, art, music, poetry, and literature, some of which endures (in altered guises) to this day.

The Hippie subculture was attacked and destroyed not in spite of these successes but rather because of them. So-called freaks dared to imagine and then act upon a radical reinterpretation of the human life cycle. Instead of marching straight into adulthood, as their parents had done, they sought a life based on peace, love, and understanding. Because the Hippies had demonstrated an ability to support this vision with specific and often very effective innovations, the leaders of the

Square Revolution saw them as a serious threat to an emerging consensus that was developing around the meaning and structure of an explicitly adult-centered life.

While the political supporters of Nixon, Agnew, and Reagan were happy to ascribe the relative calm that prevailed in the aftermath of the First Crucible to the crackdowns and get-tough policies initiated by their heroes, a more important factor was the passage of time. The ascendance of the Squares and the movement of the postwar generation's center of gravity out of adolescence and into adulthood weakened the Activist and Hippie subcultures. The Squares absorbed ex-Activists and, with much more difficulty, ex-Hippies and then merged fully with the dominant national culture. Yippies became Yuppies.

This confluence created the illusion that all three of these subcultures vanished after the end of the First Crucible. Tellingly, in the Squares' version of events, the capacity of the postwar generation to distort the surrounding culture is explicitly confined to the crucible years of adolescence. This terrible power, which had created such unrest during the "turbulent sixties," is supposed to have somehow disappeared with the close of the First Crucible. In fact, the power that the postwar generation was able to exercise over American life increased dramatically in the post–First Crucible decades.

America's emerging post–First Crucible adulthood aligned perfectly with the historic American preoccupations with wealth, status, and power. The postwar generation's vast capacity for culture making and an established ethos of "rugged individualism" combined to create something new, something that transcended conventional limits. The postwar generation's magnified adulthood began to function less like a cultural trait—and more like a cult.

The idea that adulthood, or more precisely, an unthinking devotion to a hypertrophied adulthood, could *function* in the manner of a cult seems, at first blush, to be ridiculous. After all, the cults of our popular imagination always feature bearded heretics energetically leading their followers into the maw of disaster and death. Charismatic cults operate outside of and in opposition to the dominant culture and are, therefore, easily identified and stigmatized. The Charles Manson/Jim Jones variety of cult is the one we know best but is not the only or even the most dangerous form a cult can take.

A culture's most cherished symbols and rituals can act as camouflage for the most insidious and dangerous cults. In these cases, the weirdness, the obvious and alarming strangeness that we associate with charismatic cults melts away. These society-wide cults operate in plain sight and propagate their beliefs with the active assistance of a society's most revered figures. One important sign that such a cult has come to power: the society applies simplistic, ideological solutions to a diverse set of complicated problems.

Cults of this type have repeatedly altered the course of human history. During the twentieth century, for example, the works of an obscure expatriate nineteenth-century German philosopher and his ideas about the "ownership of the means of production" became the basis of a cult that went on to hold dominion (at its height) over a quarter of the earth's population.

The Square Revolution was founded upon a deeply felt certainty that young people had a duty to enter peaceably into adulthood. It was intended to restore the early post–First Crucible era's comparative social tranquility and allow people to get on with the ordinary business of living ordinary lives. Unfortunately, it did not stop there. Instead of a simple (and nostalgic) return to the gray flannel virtues of hard work and reliability, this revolution began to enlarge upon and then distort the ideals associated with adulthood. Starting in the early post–First Crucible years, a virulent new form of adulthood began to emerge.

The postwar generation brought forth a cult of adulthood and installed it at the center of American culture. This cult of adulthood proclaimed an ideology that magnified the postwar generation's swiftly growing ambition. They were young; they could set the world on fire and burn brighter even than the sun. Youth lay at the core of their strength, and so they set out to celebrate the virtues associated with being young adults. In this way, youth became the most important interpretive lens of the postwar generation.

Virtues like success, efficiency, productivity, and individualism, which had long been tempered by the competing values of shared sacrifice, trust, and cooperation, were released from almost all constraints. Those who objected to the installation of this hyperactive, hyperacquisitive, hypercaffeinated adulthood at the heart of the American cultural experience were branded as deviants and heretics. They were dirty Hippies. The postwar generation's refashioning of adulthood magnified and amplified its authority within our culture. The resulting cult of adulthood has been both extremely potent and largely invisible.

The most important difference between Mansonesque personality cults and society-wide cults is that while the former depends upon the skillful manipulation of interpersonal relationships, the latter colonizes and then employs existing social structures in order to enforce its orthodoxy. The contemporary cult of adulthood is no less jealous, no less reactionary, and no less suffocating than the nineteenth and twentieth centuries' cult of female domesticity that worked to exclude women from the public realm. In twenty-first-century America we are immersed in a culture that worships the secular virtues of reliability, achievement, and effectiveness.

Becoming fully conscious of the cult of adulthood and the power it holds over us is much more difficult than one might expect. Adulthood's increasingly malignant authority blends seamlessly with some of our culture's most beloved and least questioned assumptions about success, independence, and autonomy. The best way to see what is now hidden from us is to embrace the "consciousness raising" methods of feminist writers such as Betty Friedan and Simone de Beauvoir. During the twentieth century, their writings excavated and then exposed the rotted pillars on which the cult of domesticity rested.

In the case of the contemporary cult of adulthood, the best way to reveal how it has shaped our lives is to examine how this overweening adulthood has redefined seemingly immutable understandings of time, money, and relationships. Because they surround us so closely, the changes these concepts have undergone remain deeply felt but poorly understood. In purely cultural terms, adulthood has used time, money, and our yearning for belonging to forge the bars, the locks, and the walls that hold us all captive.

06

EFFICIENCY PORN

America's "efficiency" revolution began, somewhat inauspiciously, with pig iron, a strong back, and a man with a stopwatch. The man with the stopwatch was Frederick Taylor, who in his 1911 treatise *The Principles of Scientific Management* described his early efforts to increase worker efficiency. Real improvements, he believed, could only come through the "enforced standardization of methods, and enforced cooperation on the part of the worker. The duty of enforcing a rigorous adherence to a set of standards rests wholly with the management, alone." In support of his theory, Taylor often told the story of a man he called Schmidt who worked ten hours a day, six days a week loading 92-pound pig-iron ingots onto waiting railroad cars.

When Taylor met "Schmidt," the man was loading 12.5 tons per day and earning less than a dollar for his effort. Believing that there was "one right way" to do everything, Taylor demanded that Schmidt alter his routine and begin performing the task of loading ingots precisely as he was told. In Taylor's telling, Schmidt's production nearly quadrupled from 12.5 tons of pig iron loaded per day to 47 tons a day. The workman's pay rose as well, climbing from seventy cents to a dollar eighty-five a day.

When the novelist Upton Sinclair read about Taylor's experience with Schmidt, he observed that the wage increase was far less than the 362 percent increase in work. There were other problems with the proofs Taylor offered for his theory. He gave varying accounts of the Schmidt episode over the years, often altering details in ways that flattered the beliefs of the audience he was addressing. It also turned out that his "experiment" wasn't at all scientific. An independent account of Taylor's activities at the Bethlehem Steel Works tells of a group of "Hungarians" who were asked to be part of the experiment but refused to participate. At Taylor's request, the men were fired. A second call for volunteers went out and five laborers responded. The "Pig-Iron Experiment" actually lasted just five days, and four of the five men quit before it was over. Schmidt was the only man to complete Taylor's assignment. It was later revealed that Schmidt was in fact a man named Henry Noll. Taylor often described Noll as being both stubborn and tightfisted. He also, grudgingly, acknowledged that a large part of Noll's motivation came from the fact that he was "building a house and needed money."

This strange and not very persuasive tale (along with many others like it) became the seeds from which an entire American efficiency industry grew. Since Taylor's time, management consultants and "efficiency experts" have remained a constant feature of the American economy. The belief that there could be only "one right way" to do any job and that it was management's duty to *enforce* that method upon its workers became an article of the businessman's faith. Although Taylor sometimes protested that his methods were supposed to be used to find the "rate of work that was both the fastest and the most equitable," factory owners were much more interested in the former than they were concerned with the latter.

Early twentieth-century time and motion gurus demanded that workers surrender control over the smallest details of their work. The financial benefits that flowed from this surrender to authority, however, went mainly into the factory owners' pockets. Unions and trade associations fought Taylorism aggressively and won some battles. The efficiency experts, however, won the war. With their triumph came an almost religious faith among the nation's business and political leaders in the value of efficiency. Not only was efficiency rigorously pursued in the practical sense (more tons of pig iron loaded per day), it was also elevated into a moral virtue. In the post–First Crucible years, this faith in efficiency would be used as the basis for a major expansion of control over American workers, one that would take Taylor's principle of "enforced cooperation" to a terrifying new level.

THE COVEY EMPIRE

As the postwar generation poured out of the First Crucible and into the Squares' responsible, productive adulthood, a new generation of management gurus and efficiency experts were waiting for them. Business books exploded in popularity during the 1980s and 1990s. Authors like Tom Peters, Peter Drucker, Ken Blanchard, Peter Senge, and Jim Collins sold millions of books. Like Benjamin Spock, they caught hold of the postwar generation's zeitgeist and did not let go. One of the least prolific but most successful of this generation of experts was a religious educator turned management guru, a man named Stephen Covey. The biography his publisher posted on its website (in 2013) practically glitters onscreen:

> Recognized as one of *Time* magazine's 25 most influential Americans, Stephen R. Covey has dedicated his life to demonstrating how every person can truly control their destiny with profound, yet straightforward guidance. As an internationally respected leadership authority, family expert, teacher, organizational consultant, and author, his advice has given insight to millions. He has sold over 20 million books (in 38 languages), and *The 7 Habits of Highly Effective People* was named the #1 Most Influential Business Book of the Twentieth Century. His most recent major book,

The 8th Habit, has sold nearly 400,000 copies. He holds an MBA from Harvard, and doctorate degree from Brigham Young University. He is the co-founder and vice chairman of FranklinCovey, the leading global professional services firm with offices in 123 countries. He lives with his wife and family in Utah.

Covey was also the most dangerous and authoritarian of the crop of business experts that flourished during these years. Covey succeeded in polishing his image until it consisted of a single gleaming surface. Even after his death in 2012, his public reputation remained that of a selfless and fervent proponent of "effectiveness." Behind this public relations triumph, however, lies a disturbing shadow that the members of the postwar generation were unwilling or unable to see, until now.

Stephen Covey built his empire atop seven carefully crafted mantras: "Be proactive. Begin with an end in mind. Put first things first. Think win-win. Seek first to understand, then to be understood. Synergize. Sharpen the saw." He used these ideas to radically and successfully redefine the sources of success away from the ideals of shared sacrifice and cooperation and toward a new and terribly impoverished concept of individual effectiveness. In this, he went farther than Frederick Taylor ever dared. In a highly cultish fashion he demanded that his followers submit not just their actions but their very selves to his ministrations. Covey wanted his acolytes to become loyal agents of Frederick Taylor's "enforced cooperation." His "seven habits" were designed to put the man with the stopwatch *inside* every worker.

First published in 1989, *The Seven Habits of Highly Effective People* lays out a puerile vision of conformity that, he claimed, was derived from "200 years of success literature." An early edition of the book was endorsed by the then president of the Saturn Corporation, Skip Le-Fauve, who touted "the major role" the book played in the development of "Saturn's operating system and philosophy." During the 1990s, Covey reported having signed on three-quarters of the Fortune 500 as clients. In a typical, gushing report, *Acumen* magazine reported that at the close of 1994, half of Conoco's 19,000 employees had been trained in Covey's program. The company's director of personnel development estimated that Covey's business principles had saved the company $12 million. No specifics, however, were offered in support of this remarkable claim.

COVEY'S IDEOLOGY

Stephen Covey sought to provide his readers with a "singularly effective tool for establishing an outcome-oriented, efficiency-based, and performance-centric worldview." Fortunately for Covey, his "worldview" arrived on bookstore shelves just as the middle of the postwar generation was moving into the twenty-five-to-forty-three-year-old age bracket. Although it was published, shelved, and sold as a "business/management" book, the *Seven Habits* actually offered readers something much more akin to a fairy tale, a sugary confection designed to delight a generation intent on exploring the outer reaches of adult power and ambition.

Given its careful use of "enduring values" as intellectual camouflage, it remains difficult to see this book for what it was. The *Seven Habits* was an especially dangerous and damaging species of "efficiency porn." Erotic pornography titillates the human capacity for longing and desire while at the same time demeaning and objectifying its subjects. It stimulates sexual desire by presenting idealized and unrealistic images of the human form but fails to satisfy the resulting desire. Covey's writing had nothing to do with carnality and everything to do with a lust for pure and unbridled "effectiveness."

Frederick Taylor's stopwatch and pseudoscientific approach to management was designed to seize control of the motions a worker used to accomplish his assigned duties. Covey aspired to something much more invasive and dehumanizing. He sought to penetrate the minds of his readers. Having done so, he hoped that the "habits" he instilled there would continue to grow. True "effectiveness" required a complete surrender to and acceptance of his carefully developed formulas for success.

In the opening section of his book, Covey criticizes the falsity of what he calls the "personality ethic." He complains that mere attitudes and behaviors cannot yield true, lasting success. Just as Taylor condemned "soldiering" (the practice of pretending to do useful work while actually goofing off), Covey attacked the idea that a worker could reserve or protect *any interior space*. One's thoughts, one's habits, one's most cherished ideals all had to be brought into the service of "effectiveness." He argued that the presence of any reservations would doom the entire enterprise. The nightmare scenario of standing naked in the public square was nothing compared to what Covey was demanding. He intended to strip the individual bare, from the inside. This was, truly, efficiency pornography.

In its prime, the *Seven Habits* spent 250 weeks on the *New York Times* Best Sellers list. How did a flaccid collection of anecdotes and truisms, which even its author admitted contained "no new ideas," achieve such success? The answer lies in Covey's unique ability to communicate a vision of the meaning and purpose of adulthood that the postwar generation was eager to rally around. As his success with the Fortune 500 demonstrates, he simultaneously sold corporate America on a new and better system for maintaining control over its workforce. His book managed the extraordinary feat of simultaneously flattering the egos of a great mass of young adults living near the peak of their adult vitality while at the same time delivering those acolytes ever more completely into the control of their employers.

Covey's mercenary and dehumanizing methods were largely cloaked by his book's folksy embrace of what he called "universal and enduring values." He elevated banal truisms to the status of ancient and unquestionable truths. He asked for, indeed he demanded, extraordinary forms of exposure, vulnerability, and change from his readers while offering virtually nothing in the form of proof for his assertions. Given the extraordinary claims Covey made on behalf of his "habits," he should have been held to an extraordinary standard of proof. Instead, we find a book that is heavily and lazily larded with the sort of aphorisms favored by coaches, valedictorians, and eulogists.

This hoary chestnut appears early on:

What lies behind us and what lies before us are tiny matters compared to what lies within us.

Covey attributes this quote to Oliver Wendell Holmes. It isn't clear if he means Oliver Wendell Holmes Senior or Oliver Wendell Holmes Junior. Such details matter little to him. What *matters* is his larger goal of making the struggle for worth and meaning an entirely personal concern. Given that Covey explicitly ties his insights to America's success literature, and because he reassures the reader that he studied this literature while earning his doctorate, the reader is simply expected to embrace all his conclusions—based solely on his authority as an expert.

In fact, it seems likely that Covey stumbled on this quote while thumbing through some collection of notable sayings. He likely scribbled it down on a three-by-five card and never investigated its origins. If he had done so, he would have soon discovered that neither Oliver Wendell Holmes, father or son, had anything to do with it. The quote actually first appeared in a book published in 1940 titled *Meditations in Wall Street*. The book consisted entirely of the reflections of longtime Wall Street operator Henry S. Haskins. Among many other shortcomings, Haskins had been "effectively expelled" from the Stock Exchange for "reckless and unbusinesslike dealing."

Covey, like Frederick Taylor, was much more interested in reaching predetermined conclusions than in contending with irksome trivialities such as science and scholarship. It is useful, in fact, to ask what Covey would have done if he had become aware of his error. What if he had known these were actually the words of a disgraced Wall Street trader? Would the quote have been useful to him if he had found it alongside Haskins's other bon mots?

It is the brain which does the thinking, not the thought; it is the soul which moves us forward, not ourself.

Glory lies in the estimation of lookers-on. When lookers-on perish as countless generations have done, glory perishes, as countless glories have done.

With some whose nerves have a deep covering of fat, happiness is less of a problem than it is an accident of anatomy.

Covey also fills many of his pages with suspiciously convenient anecdotes. This anecdotal evidence is presumed to be adequate to the task at hand because, as Covey reminds the reader, his is a work based on "enduring principles." Here lies a stunning, and almost entirely unremarked upon incongruity. A writer with an audience of millions asks his readers to change what they believe, what they value, and how they act while scores of major corporations invest hundreds of millions of dollars in his books and its associated trainings all without the benefit of any significant science, philosophy, or logic.

The postwar generation surrendered itself into the hands of an exceptionally skillful proselytizer who, as we shall see, stated overtly and in writing that his most important insights involved concealing religious concepts within his advice on career success. The *Seven Habits* is in fact that most frightening and dangerous species of writing, a hermetically sealed system of thought whose ultimate authority depends solely on the author's personal beliefs, faith, and feelings, while at the same time posing as an impartial moral arbiter for society as a whole.

Despite this, the *Seven Habits* book flourished for much the same reason that Baba Ram Dass's *Be Here Now* succeeded during the First Crucible. The *Seven Habits* validated an emerging cultural consensus that was vastly larger than and independent of the author and his book. After the First Crucible, the postwar generation's ferocious enlargement of a hardworking, successful, and productive adulthood needed a secular but still sacred text that could validate this ascension. Covey's *Seven Habits* became that text. It defined the span of acceptable adult behavior within a tight range bounded on every side by the virtues of speed, independence, and effectiveness.

Not coincidentally, this sleight of hand also served the changing needs of the American corporation. During the 1990s there was a growing desire on the part of corporations to be free from the encumbrance of loyalty. Businesses wanted to be able to "right-size," "off-shore," and "outsource" without having to include worker loyalty in their calculations. Hence the appeal of the Haskins quote, "What lies behind us and what lies before us are tiny matters compared to what lies within us." Covey was more than just a generational voice (like Dylan or Ram Dass); he was also handmaiden to an emerging loyalty-free corporate culture and, as we will see, the energetic servant of another, undisclosed ideology.

A SECOND LOOK AT THE SEVEN HABITS

Covey's "Habits" served first and foremost as a love letter to the postwar generation. Its members, newly in thrall to adulthood, delighted in the power, strength, and vitality that coursed through their veins. They simply knew that Covey was right: success was almost exclusively a matter of diligence, persistence, and conformity. Covey's "habits" served as amulets; they were magic totems that could not fail—they could only be failed. Let's briefly consider each of these habits in order.

Habit 1: Be proactive.

Covey asserts that it is between the "stimulus" of an experience and a person's "response" to that experience that we find the freedom to choose. For this reason, people are "response-able" for their actions. The choice, he insists, is always between acting and being "acted upon." The reader is urged to discount the value of his or her initial response to a situation. In place of this authenticity the reader should insert a new, Covey-approved response. The obvious but unstated consequence

SECOND WIND ~ 67

of this position is that Covey seeks to "act upon" his readers. He wants to fill the space between stimulus and response with his values and his beliefs because his values and beliefs are time-tested.

Habit 2: Begin with the end in mind.

This aphorism went on to become so well known to so many people that it long ago descended into parody. When and if it is used today, the speaker is almost certainly employing it ironically. This is what people say in a meeting when no one knows what else to say. As usual, Covey is content to take a perfectly ordinary idea (people ought to think ahead) and pass it off as a deep insight. What Covey fails to ask or answer is how do we know what matters most? Who gets to decide which ends are the most appropriate in a given situation? This "habit" is actually so vacuous that it could easily be commandeered and used as a tag line for the national convention of any organization. Covey, seeming to appreciate this failing, takes care to suggest that there is actually only one set of approved ends, all of which also happen to bolster his vision of an "effective" adulthood.

Habit 3: Put first things first.

A spectacular (and terrible) sense of entitlement and privilege hangs over this "habit." Covey begins with the unquestioned assumption that all people can always choose their own priorities in any situation. Covey spent his adult life at the head of a large (and I am sure quite loving) family and as the CEO of a business he started. Such a man might be forgiven his natural biases if he didn't also actively dismiss the reality of the sexism, racism, ageism, and flagrant economic injustice that pervade American society. It is only in Covey's rich fantasy life that people, and their preferences, can float free and unencumbered inside a fantastical cultural vacuum chamber.

Habit 4: Think win-win.

This "habit" is even more revealing than the first three. It presents us with Covey's vision of a fully corporatized human life. His admonition to "seek mutual benefit in all interactions" is, of course, trite, but his real audience are the managers of large corporations. Frederick Taylor, after all, might well have been thinking "win-win" as he was ordering Henry Noll around the Bethlehem Steel rail yard. After all, Noll got a pay raise, Bethlehem Steel got more pig iron loaded, and Taylor got an international reputation as an "efficiency expert." It was really a case of win-win-win!

Bitter experience has taught most people, however, that Upton Sinclair was onto something when he observed that one side seemed to be doing most of the winning and it wasn't Henry Noll. Covey completely discounts the tremendous power disparity that exists between a corporation and its employees. The "win-win" conceit actually serves to anesthetize the sensation of unfairness. Habit 4 actually validates this disparity and normalizes its inevitable consequences for employees.

Habit 5: Seek first to understand, then to be understood.

Covey's endorsement of listening is both useful and commonplace. Good listening skills are valuable in every part of our lives. There is, it should be noted, precious little between the covers of his book that suggests Covey is, on a personal level, a good listener. In fact, the book's consistently patronizing tone savagely undercuts its rhetoric of empowerment.

Habit 6: Synergize.

Few, if any, people outside the world of corporate consulting have ever thought of, spoken of, or espoused "synergy." Once the idea is removed from its native corporate environment, it immediately turns to mush. The call for respecting and integrating differences rings hollow when the bulk of the book is dedicated to the author's insistence on conformity. Perhaps sensing weakness, Covey makes the case for parenthood as a metaphor for the proper relationship between the corporation and its employees. The most accurate label for this point of view is *paternalism*.

Habit 7: Sharpen the saw.

Covey's summons to physical, mental, and spiritual fitness seems, at first, to be perfectly at home within the conventions of traditional "success" literature and even common sense. But there is much more afoot here. The *Seven Habits* program is at its core a secularized shadow of Mormon dogma, repackaged and sold as management training. Covey openly supposes that all moral behavior is based on obedience to universal natural laws that are absolute and immutable. These include, for example, fairness, integrity, honesty, human dignity, service, quality, and excellence, and they are the foundation of what he calls "principle-centered leadership."

In a personal note appended to the end of the book, he writes, "I believe that correct principles are natural laws, and that God, the Creator and Father of us all, is the source of them, and also the source of our conscience." He continues, "I believe that to the degree people live by this inspired conscience, they will grow to fulfill their natures; to the degree that they do not, they will not rise above the animal plane." This is theology drawn directly from the Mormon pulpit.

Joseph Smith announced in 1844, "God himself was once as we are now, and is an exalted man . . . you have got to be Gods yourselves, and to be kings and priests to God, the same as all Gods have done before you, namely by going from one small degree to another, and from a small capacity to a great one." As we will see, this doctrine is the true source of Covey's seventh habit.

Stephen Covey began his career as a religious educator and, in many ways, never wavered from that ambition. Indeed, none of his writings reveal any interest in or understanding of how modern corporations actually operate. His concern with business seems, in retrospect, to be incidental to his true purpose. His most urgent concern lies with the souls of his readers. Frederick Taylor was content with taking control of a worker's actions and employed what might be called an outside-in approach to efficiency. Stephen Covey insisted on working from the inside out, demanding belief without offering proof, obedience without consent.

THE DIVINE CENTER

Few people realize that the *Seven Habits* is essentially the third revision of Covey's first book. The earlier versions were much more forthright about the religious dimensions of his message. The first of these precursors, *Spiritual Roots of Human Relations* (published in 1971), presented the familiar seven habits but connected them overtly to the author's Mormon faith. The first chapter of this book is titled "Our Purpose Here: Obedience." The first paragraph reads:

> By obedience to the principles and the ordinances of the eternal
> gospel of Jesus Christ, man will gradually become a partaker of the
> divine nature and will feel comfort and confidence in the presence
> of his Eternal Father and his Elder Brother, the Lord Jesus Christ.
> This is the purpose of my life.

Covey's real commitment was to "success" as defined by Mormon doctrine. He believed wholeheartedly in the Mormon idea of "growth toward Godhood" as preached by Joseph Smith, and he skillfully repackaged that theology for consumption by unsuspecting corporate audiences.

This earlier book is also the source of many of the anecdotes that would later populate the *Seven Habits*. A story about his daughter's birthday party tantrum, for example, was originally included in this book. Covey also poses a question that is familiar to readers of the *Seven Habits*: "How can we break bad habits and form healthy new ones?" The answer he offers in this first book begins, "The Savior gives us insight into the process in the following magnificent parable."

Over the next ten years Covey reworked and revised this material. The result was his second book, *The Divine Center*, released in 1982. This book is still in wide circulation among Mormons, including an ebook version complete with spiritual self-improvement worksheets. It is in *The Divine Center* where he first reveals that "I have found in speaking to various non-LDS groups in different cultures that we can teach and testify of many gospel principles if we are careful in selecting words which carry our meaning but come from their experience and frame of mind." Among the most important of these "gospel principles" was the concept of "the upward spiral." In the *Seven Habits* he frames the principle in these terms: "Renewal is the principle—and the process—that empowers us to move on an upward spiral of growth and change, of continuous improvement." Reading *The Divine Center*, one quickly realizes that this is actually a skillful reworking of the Mormon doctrine of "eternal progression."

The true aim of this "saw sharpening" is not mere "success" but rather a "constantly expanding upward-spiraling movement in the development of the human soul which constitutes the road to perfection." Cultivating the correct habits, namely those endorsed by the Church of Jesus Christ of Latter-day Saints, "liberates man" and "releases his divine potentialities." Covey's extravagant faith in the idea that all people are always in possession of unlimited potential is derived directly from the Mormon doctrine that "since we truly are sons and daughters of God the Eternal Father, we possess in embryo his nature and potential."

Stephen Covey succeeded in converting a religious tract into a celebration of "effectiveness." He then brought it to a mass audience. The reason this was not immediately apparent was that the book also, flawlessly, plucked the chords of the postwar generation's frenetic adulthood. The book's thin sourcing, its trite anecdotes and vapid moralizing mattered much less than its highly effective endorsement of success as a purely individual enterprise.

Throughout his life, Stephen Covey maintained a fervent desire to advance the theological principles of the Church of Jesus Christ of Latter-day Saints. Despite his immense publishing success, there is little evidence that his "secular" books ever materially advanced the interests of the Mormon church. What is clear is that Covey's work did validate and strengthen the postwar generation's overweening adulthood. In doing so, it also undermined the faith in family, love, loyalty, and community that he clearly revered. Rarely has the real-world impact of a book diverged so profoundly from the professed intentions of its author.

07

GREED AND GOD

Before Harry Potter, there was Ragged Dick. Though his first novel was published in 1868, everyone still knows the name of Ragged Dick's creator. Horatio Alger was a prolific author who published nearly a hundred "coming of age" novels, including six about Ragged Dick, in the years following the Civil War. He specialized in "bouncy little books for boys" that espoused "the merits of honesty, hard work, and cheerfulness in adversity." Although Alger's name became synonymous with triumphant tales of "rags to riches," his work actually celebrated a much more restrained (and pious) Protestant ethic of "rags to respectability."

Alger's stories lauded scrappy bootstrap pullers who sought a "hand up, not a hand out" and white-washed the greed, poverty, and corruption of America's Gilded Age. He never varied from this simple formula and it served him very well. Although he is little read today, Alger was one of the nineteenth century's best-selling authors. Viewed from the perspective of the voracious, no-holds-barred materialism that, increasingly, defined the post–First Crucible years, Horatio Alger's saccharine novels seem terribly quaint.

The important moral distinctions that separate the cult of adult-hood and the Gilded Age become obvious when comparing the following quotes. The first is taken directly from Alger's first novel:

"In here, young gentlemen," said a black-whiskered individual, who appeared suddenly on the scene. "Walk in."

"It's a swindlin' shop," said Dick, in a low voice. "I've been there. That man's a regular cheat. He's seen me before, but he don't know me coz of my clothes."

"Step in and see the articles," said the man, persuasively. "You needn't buy, you know."

"Are all the articles worth more'n a dollar?" asked Dick.

"Yes," said the other, "and some worth a great deal more."

"Such as what?"

"Well, there's a silver pitcher worth twenty dollars."

"And you sell it for a dollar. That's very kind of you," said Dick, innocently.

"Walk in, and you'll understand it."

"How does he manage, Dick?" asked Frank, as they went on.

"All his articles are numbered, and he makes you pay a dollar, and then shakes some dice, and whatever the figgers come to, is the number of the article you draw. Most of 'em ain't worth sixpence."

The second quote comes from the movie *Wall Street*. The film was released in 1987, just as the American religion of money was seeping into the bones of the postwar generation. This is Gordon Gekko's famous address to the stockholders of Teldar Paper:

The point is, ladies and gentleman, that greed—for lack of a better word—is good. Greed is right. Greed works. Greed clarifies, cuts through, and captures the essence of the evolutionary spirit. Greed, in all of its forms—greed for life, for money, for love, knowledge—has marked the upward surge of mankind. And greed—you mark my words—will not only save Teldar Paper, but that other malfunctioning corporation called the USA. Thank you very much.

While Alger was always careful to keep Ragged Dick's ambition well inside existing social and moral constraints, Wall Street's Gekko gleefully elevates the pursuit of money above virtues such as love, knowledge, friendship, and loyalty. While the "greed is good" speech may have been intended as satire, it was received as bracing honesty. In his book The Growth Illusion, Richard Douthwaite argues that American society is wearing "a pair of spectacles which give short-term economic issues such prominence that they obscure our vision of the future." The "spectacles" to which Douthwaite refers are part of a generational mythology designed, refined, and implemented with the specific goal of ennobling the fantasies of the postwar generation.

The post–First Crucible years saw a restoration of domestic tranquility but also a decisive shift away from what had been a widespread engagement with art, music, and all kinds of creativity as intrinsically worthy activities. For example, sales of acoustic guitars collapsed in the mid-1970s and did not recover their previous peak for nearly fifteen years. The growing fixation on adult values like success, effectiveness, and prestige ensured that many millions of Fenders, Martins, and Gibsons went into the closet or under the bed and stayed there. The abundance of personal artistic expression that characterized the 1960s gave way to a new emphasis on activities judged to be productive. The postwar generation traded in their notebooks with poems, lyrics, political theories, and introspective essays for day planners and personal strategic planning documents.

MONEY AS RELIGION

Philip Goodchild, author of The Theology of Money, argues that Americans, always eager to make a buck, have severed the bonds that had long restrained our ambition. Money has been elevated to the position of a supreme value against which all other values are to be compared. He perceptively notes that "debt has replaced God as the guarantee for human cooperation." Money, and the pursuit of money, now function in many ways like a civil religion. The unlikely theologian of this new fiduciary faith was a woman named Ayn Rand.

In a collection of essays titled *The Objectivist Ethics*, Rand argued that markets and the selfishness that animated them provided the best, most rational guidance for human behavior. "When I say 'capitalism,' " she wrote, "I mean a full, pure, uncontrolled, unregulated laissez-faire capitalism—with a separation of state and economics, in the same way and for the same reasons as the separation of state and church." Stephen Covey, the devout Mormon, and the atheist Rand might have seemed an odd couple, but when it came to the *logic* of success, they were intellectual soul mates.

When we examine Covey's *Seven Habits* and Rand's *Objectivist Ethics* from a generational perspective, it becomes obvious that these books were much more important as cultural totems than as intellectual arguments. They validated the cultural consensus that was developing around the power and "rightness" of the postwar generation's surging adulthood. More than anything else, what we find in these books is an unabashed celebration of individuality and a contemptuous dismissal of the moral and practical value of collective action in pursuit of a common good.

Sociologist Christopher Lasch coined the term "the culture of narcissism" to describe this massive generational rejection of the communalist ideals that had animated American society as it passed through the Dark Valley. The values of cooperation, consensus, and community were increasingly subordinated to a debt-fueled consumerism and the careerism that was necessary to support this lifestyle. Gordon Gekko's naked faith in greed aligned perfectly with the aggressive materialism that was remaking American society. If this had been a passing phase or if it had been a sentiment that was confined to the real Wall Street, the movie *Wall Street* would have been forgotten as quickly as Michael Douglas's follow-up movie, *Black Rain*.

Covey's "habits," Rand's objectivism, and Gekko's greed speech became powerful cultural totems that validated the postwar generation's new hypertrophic, hyperacquisitive adulthood. During the 1980s and 1990s, the middle class began to stagger under the burdens created by a "winner take all" economy, and a large chunk of the nation's wealth would be redistributed into the pockets of the most fortunate. Job security, along with our faith in the social structures that enable collective action, began to crumble.

The growing concentration of wealth, in particular, ceased to be proof of a failure to protect the common good and instead became evidence that the "market" was working its ordained magic. Rising levels of income inequality, which in earlier times were understood to represent a threat to democratic self-government, were reinterpreted as evidence of the triumph of the "fittest." At the same time, those who continued to advocate for communal action in pursuit of the common good were derided as weaklings whose real agenda involved taking from others a slice of the success that they could not achieve *on their own*.

When we compare the impact of the postwar generation's flirtation with youthful rebellion to its embrace of the cult of adulthood, it becomes clear that, even though the former looms large in our cultural history, the latter has remade every dimension of American society. All along the way, the era's most powerful people and institutions eagerly endorsed this unprecedented expansion of adult power. The postwar generation and its members working in the media were free to elevate the "business of business" into a new and unfettered civil religion. But there was more to come. American culture had, in the past, largely avoided the obvious mixing of money and faith, but that taboo would be broken as well. The cult of adulthood brought forth a new and unseemly effort to hybridize money and faith.

RELIGION AS MONEY

As the power of the postwar generation grew, some religious leaders began to espouse a direct link between wealth and worth. This new theology dismissed Protestantism's historic emphasis on modesty, moderation, hard work, savings, and charity. Among the leading proponents of the "prosperity gospel" was Robert Tilton. According to Pastor Tilton, "it is the will of God for all to prosper. . . . I do not put my eyes on men, but on God who gives me the power to get wealth." Pastor Kenneth Copeland offers a somewhat more specific claim: "Since God's Covenant has been established and prosperity is a provision of this covenant, you need to realize that prosperity belongs to you now!" Although these names may be unfamiliar to some readers, they are superstars in the world of Evangelical Christianity.

Prosperity gospel rests on an especially slender scriptural reed. According to Matthew 7:9–11, "Or what man is there of you, whom if his son ask bread, will he give him a stone? Or if he ask a fish, will he give him a serpent? If ye then, being evil, know how to give good gifts unto your children, how much more shall your Father which is in heaven give good things to them that ask him?" In other words, all the faithful need to do in order to be blessed with material abundance is ask for it in prayer. This belief has been derided by more mainstream figures as a "blab and grab it" or "name and claim it" theology.

In its most basic form, the prosperity gospel rests on five controversial assumptions:

1. Material wealth is a good thing because it signifies God's love and approval.
2. The failure to accumulate material wealth should be understood, primarily, as the consequence of a lack of faith in God.
3. Good health is given to those who ask for it in prayer, and illness is evidence that the individual is not being faithful to God.

4. The faithful must continue praying until the desired amount of money is acquired. Giving up on prayer guarantees failure.
5. Contrary to popular belief, Jesus lived his earthly life as a rich man and he wants his followers to be rich as well.

This is the Bible recast as a contract between God and man with faith and prayer providing the means for people to collect on God's contractual obligations. This inversion of conventional religious doctrine emphasizes God's *obligation* to keep his promises. This ambition has made Deuteronomy 28:11–12 and its divine pledge that "the Lord shall make thee plenteous for good, in the fruit of thy body, and in the fruit of thy cattle, and in the fruit of thy ground" especially popular in prosperity gospel circles.

The influence exercised by prosperity churches has been more cultural than organizational: they rarely affiliate with long-established Protestant denominations. Instead, the usual arrangement features a single, charismatic pastor who is often assisted by members of his family. Joel Osteen is a popular "prosperity preacher" whose career offers a good example of this tendency. He grew up in and ultimately assumed control of a church that was started by his father—and now has a net worth estimated at $40 million. Services in these churches typically reserve large blocks of time for teachings about the blessing of wealth and the need to give abundantly as an act of faith.

Not surprisingly, the combination of religious zeal, nepotism, and greed has resulted in a long line of scandals. Among the most lurid was the rivalry between Jimmy Swaggart and televangelists Marvin Gorman and Jim Bakker in the late 1980s. Using their nationally televised ministries to trade accusations from the pulpit, all three eventually stepped down in disgrace over sex scandals. Swaggart helped bring down Gorman and Bakker over accusations of extramarital affairs. Soon after, private detectives captured pictures of Swaggart with a prostitute. In 2007, after media exposés detailed the lavish lifestyles of prominent prosperity gospel televangelists, as well as their fleets of Rolls-Royces, private jets, and multimillion-dollar homes, Iowa senator Chuck Grassley launched a congressional inquiry into the finances of six ministries.

Kenneth Copeland, head of one of them, sounded a defiant note with respect to responding to a subpoena for his records: "It's not yours; it's God's. And you're not going to get it, and that's something I'll go to prison over. . . . And if there's a death penalty that applies, well, just go for it!"

The affinity between the prosperity gospel and the cult of adulthood comes into sharp focus when we contrast its wealth-based theology with the most prominent religious innovation of the First Crucible. At their best, the Jesus freaks blended a communitarian, antimaterialist lifestyle with a love-centric and often transcendental interpretation of the Gospels. The result was a vibrant and diverse subculture. The popular musicals *Godspell* and *Jesus Christ Superstar* represented the Jesus freaks' beliefs fairly accurately, and both were hits with the public. The genial communalism of the Hippie subculture, backed by the cultural power of the postwar generation, gave rise to the Jesus freaks in much the same way that the cult of adulthood popularized the prosperity gospel.

The postwar generation employed religious ideals and imagery to validate a wholly secular and highly destructive exaltation of ambition, materialism, and individualism. There were plenty of "prophets of profit" in the worlds of business and religion, and they often rallied support for one another. This cooperation was readily apparent in the media of the era. Captains of industry and religious leaders were brought out of their relative obscurity and made into celebrities. Federal Reserve chairman Alan Greenspan and televangelist Jim Bakker were two sides of the same coin. Money was the coin of this realm and it could go only to the best, the fastest, and the most faithful.

"NOBODY EXPECTS
THE SPANISH INQUISITION"

During the First Crucible and especially at its chaotic peak, the Squares and their allies in the Establishment advocated for a return to the settled values and virtues that they identified with the Eisenhower years. The Square Revolution led directly to a new cultural consensus, one that seemed to guarantee the order and stability the majority of Americans desired. But Squares' triumph produced unintended consequences. The postwar generation's colonization of adulthood distorted the values associated with Square adulthood in ways that would be much more easily felt than described.

Instead of a comfortable, small c conservative social order, Americans of all ages increasingly confronted a massively enlarged, self-justifying, and ravenous adulthood. The result was the painful irony that is on full display in the life and work of Stephen Covey. In his private life, the man gave every indication of valuing his family, his neighbors, and his community. The emphasis his work placed on the individual as the true source of success, however, undermined and subverted traditional Square values. As the postwar generation entered fully into adulthood, it created a massive cultural disruption that was orders of magnitude larger than anything the First Crucible Activist and Hippie subcultures had thought possible.

Established business and religious leaders of the time had little to say about the pain and dislocation caused by this radical cultural shift. When data on income, income inequality, and work life satisfaction stagnated and then turned negative, these changes were validated as "the new normal." Even as a cultural revolution degraded and destroyed the sources of communal support and protection on which people had long depended, no action was taken to change our trajectory. So-called helicopter parents now hover over their children because they understand that adulthood is a terribly serious business. Accordingly, they endeavor to provide their children with every possible advantage in the struggle for success. Such efforts often push kids into prematurely "adultified" roles. Paradoxically, this highly involved form of parenting can also lead to infantilization and a prolonged period of dependence.

The reason these cultural shifts have been so poorly understood is that they emerged during a time when 75 million people were living at the apex of adult power. This was a generation that could change American culture to *its* liking. Most of those who did see that society was changing believed that the movement was proceeding in the right direction. Rationalizing this cultural transformation was easy because the zeitgeist flattered the postwar generation's growing sense of mastery and it seemed natural that society should acknowledge and celebrate the postwar generation's rise to power.

The destruction of the First Crucible's counterculture vastly diminished the influence of the writers, intellectuals, and artists who were capable of effectively criticizing the status quo. We have long inhabited a society wherein the most prominent voices all belonged to those who assisted, endorsed, and profited from the cult of adulthood. Religious leaders who, in times past, might have rallied support for the poor and disenfranchised were frequently supportive of this muscular new adulthood and its conservative ethos, and many were richly rewarded for their faith. The Squares' commonsense way of life and most sacred values were set aside in favor of a more dangerous obsession with wealth, faith, and fame.

The cult of adulthood's manic distortions of existing institutions, traditions, families, and communities proved to be far more damaging to the structure of our society than anything the First Crucible had to offer. It is the postwar generation's adulthood (not its adolescence) that has inspired a vast reordering of American culture. The Squares conducted a revolution that has remained hidden in plain sight: it is everywhere, it is all around us, and it is, and remains, exceptionally hard to see.

08

THE TIME MACHINE

The classic American silent film *Modern Times* comically exposed how the machine age warped and accelerated time and distressed the lives of ordinary people. The movie's first shot of sheep being driven to slaughter cuts to one of men pouring out of a subway station on their way to work. The symbolism is not subtle. Charlie Chaplin plays a factory worker who tries but fails to keep up with the escalating pace of the assembly line. When he begins to tire, he falls into the machine and becomes entangled in the gears that drive the factory. The experience of being inside the machine drives Chaplin's factory worker mad, and a slapstick disruption of the factory and its assembly line ensues. Chaplin's character is subdued and taken to the hospital. Man, it seems, was not meant to live inside the machine.

For most of human history, humanity's understanding of time was derived from and regulated by nature's circadian and seasonal rhythms. Chaplin's audience saw the movie from this perspective and could use it to critically evaluate the absurdities of man-made mechanical time. The factory with its pitiless gears and sprockets, along with Frederick

Taylor's merciless stopwatch, represented a new form of time, but as is often the case, newer was not necessarily better.

In 1936 moviegoers found Chaplin's exaggerations comical; viewing them now it is easy to feel that they carry the weight of tragedy. After all, we know what those audiences did not. Nature's time would lose its struggle against machine time and the latter would go on to conquer American society. During the long decades of the postwar generation's adulthood, we disassembled the factory that Chaplin so skillfully lampooned and rebuilt it—inside ourselves. No longer is it necessary for the man to be swallowed by the machine; now the machine thrums inside the man. The late twentieth century gave rise to a temporal revolution that refocused nearly all of America's waking hours on "time thought."

The world might still spin on its axis as it used to do, there might still be, strictly speaking, 23 hours, 56 minutes, and 4.090 seconds in a day, but the way in which those hours, minutes, and seconds were perceived was changing. People could increasingly "feel" that time was moving faster. The belief that we all have less time than we used to has become so ingrained in American culture it's hard to convince people that it's not true.

The Bureau of Labor Statistics American Time Use Survey has long carried out a variety of measurements of how Americans use their time. These studies include self-reported time diaries, payroll statistics, and household surveys. Although nearly everyone agrees that we work more and have less time than we used to, these studies show that the average work week has remained very consistent over the past forty years and may even have declined slightly. It is also surprisingly true that the amount of leisure time available to Americans stands at an all-time high of thirty-five hours per week. No matter what the evidence shows, millions of people would agree that it *feels* as if this could not be true. How can we reconcile the objective fact that weekly hours of work have remained fairly consistent over time with the feeling that we almost never have enough time?

Unraveling this paradox requires a quick tour through some interesting avenues of psychology, economics, and demography. How Americans perceive the passage of time is shaped by a complex interaction among seemingly unrelated variables of age, information, and money.

TIME AND AGE

The certainty that time must be moving faster than it used to is not a new phenomenon. William James examined the subjective experience of time's passage in his 1892 book *Psychology: Briefer Course*. Perhaps writing from personal experience, the fifty-year-old professor observed that "the same space of time seems shorter as we grow older." Among the first researchers to rigorously investigate how people of different ages experience that passage of time were Ludwig-Maximilian University's Marc Wittmann and Sandra Lehnhoff. In 2005 they published results that showed few age-related differences in how people evaluate the passage of time in the last week, the last month, or the last year. Older people did, however, experience "time compression" when it came to judging how fast the previous ten years had passed.

There are several theories why older people experience "long-term" time compression so much more acutely than young people. It has been observed, for example, that for a twenty-year-old, ten years is half a lifetime, but for a fifty-year-old, the same span represents just 20 percent of one's life. As we age, a decade becomes an ever-smaller proportion of our life experience. Others have emphasized the fact that, in a ten-year span, younger people encounter more "turning points" than older people. In just ten years, a younger person is likely to graduate from college, woo and win a mate, start a family, and buy a house. Older people, in contrast, can easily pass a decade doing the same job and living in the same house with the same spouse. The absence of frequent life-changing events may partly explain why older people feel that the later decades seem to pass so quickly.

What the research does show is that regardless of one's age, our days, hours, and minutes become "compressed" when we are engaged in a goal-directed activity. This compression is even more pronounced when the outcome is in doubt. It turns out that our perception of time—how much we have and how fast it is passing us by—is shaped, in large part, by the rate at which our minds are processing information.

TIME AND INFORMATION

Joseph Heller illustrated the connection between time and information in his novel *Catch-22*. The book's main character is Captain John Yossarian, a twenty-eight-year-old B-25 bombardier stationed off the coast of Italy during World War II. One of his few friends is Dunbar. The two of them share one important trait—they don't want to die. Dunbar accepts the fact that everyone must eventually die, but he also commits himself to an unorthodox approach to life extension: the pursuit of boredom. "Dunbar loved shooting skeet because he hated every minute of it." Dunbar also liked spending time with Clevinger because "Clevinger annoyed him and made the time go slow."

Heller makes clever and darkly comic use of the psychological truth that time devoted to "boring," low-information pursuits seems to pass very slowly. "Dunbar was lying motionless on his back again, his eyes staring up at the ceiling like a doll's. He was working hard at increasing his life span. . . . Dunbar was working so hard at increasing his life span that Yossarian thought he was dead." Heller understood that our perception of time is highly elastic and that being exceptionally bored makes it seem that time is passing exceptionally slowly.

This trait also reveals itself in those long childhood rides in the back of the car that inevitably led us to the question, "Are we there yet?" In a darkened back seat with nothing to read or do, minutes passed like hours. When we make the same trip as an adult driving the car, chatting on the phone, jumping between radio stations, and taking note of the For Sale signs in front of houses, the journey seems to pass much faster—even though the miles and hours required are the same. As the rate at which our brains process information accelerates, so does the "speed" of time.

In the 1960s psychologist Robert Orenstein investigated the impact of information processing on the perception of time. Some of his most interesting studies tested the accuracy of people's "inner clocks." Orenstein had volunteers listen to audiotapes that were all the same length but had varying levels of interest. The low-information tapes featured a sparse assortment of clicking sounds, while high-information tapes included many more and more varied types of sounds. Orenstein then asked participants to guess how long they believed they had been listening to each tape.

He found that when people listened to the high-information tapes, they believed that the tape was longer than it really was. When they guessed how long the low-information tapes were, they consistently estimated the tape to be shorter than it really was. In other words, the act of processing more information created the sense that the seconds had passed faster and that more time had gone by than was actually true. As Heller and Orenstein would be quick to remind us, when one lives in an "information age" and has access to an unending stream of news, opinions, facts, and statistics, time does seem to pass much more quickly than it did when our access to such things was much more limited.

TIME AND MONEY

Our changing views on money also play an important role in how we perceive the passage of time. A clever study conducted by economist Daniel Hamermesh and provocatively titled "Stressed Out on Four Continents: Time Crunch or Yuppie Kvetch?" took a close look at the connections between time and money. After surveying time budgeting and household income data from around the world, Hamermesh found that "holding market and [home] work hours constant, individuals with higher household earnings are more likely to respond that they are always stressed for time." While common sense suggests that affluence should reduce time scarcity, it actually increases the sensation of "not having enough time." This holds true even when we adjust for number of hours people work and the ability of the wealthy to hire others to do house cleaning, meal preparation, and childcare.

People who make much more money than average also perceive their time as being much more valuable than that of the average person. Affluence has the side effect of making people feel that something valuable is constantly slipping through one's fingers. Robert Levine's pivotal studies on the "geography of time" have confirmed the relationship between time and money. Levine evaluated the "pace of life" in cities around the world and found that, with few exceptions, the world's most affluent cities were also home to its speediest pedestrians. People tend to walk faster when they feel that their time is more valuable. They also commonly associate value with rarity.

Imagine stepping up to the counter at a numismatist's shop and watching as the dealer lays five coins in front of you. She points to one and tells you that it is the rarest of the five. Most people would assume that the rare coin was also the most valuable of the five. Another five coins are laid on the counter and the dealer shows you which is the most valuable of the five. Most people would, quite reasonably, assume that this coin is also the most rare. The same dynamic operates when applied to time. People whose time is extremely valuable are likely to *feel* that their time is also very scarce. As strange as this may seem, it is the perception that one's time is valuable that creates the sensation of scarcity.

Further research has confirmed that the three strongest predictors of "time compression" are a country's gross domestic product, the purchasing power of its citizens, and the level of individualism that prevails in that society. On a generational level, this psychology helps explain how the perception of time changed as America exited the First Crucible and entered into the cult of adulthood. During the postwar generation's adolescence and early adulthood, billions of hours were spent rearranging record collections, writing bad poetry, lying on rooftops, and attending keg parties. All these activities were accomplished with precisely the same number of minutes in a day that the same people have now. Because their time had little monetary value during those years, there was little sense of its scarcity and little concern about the gap between productive and nonproductive uses of that time.

As the postwar generation entered adulthood the value of its time increased for two important reasons. First, the passage out of adolescence and into adulthood also meant that lazy weekends dedicated to friends and part-time jobs were surrendered to more profitable activities. The second factor was technological. The rising productivity of the 1990s was largely fueled by a digital revolution that allowed workers to process vastly more information in the course of a workday. These new technologies increased the value *of* our time faster than they increased compensation *for* our time. Combined with the era's dramatic shift away from communalism and toward individualism, we find a trifecta of time scarcity—a massive generation leaving adolescence and entering adulthood, an information-driven revolution in productivity, and a rising (generational) level of affluence.

PRIMING

If plutocratic angst were all there was to the "time revolution," it might not have mattered. Unfortunately, the feeling that time is passing faster than ever, that we have less time than ever before, is not limited to harried billionaires. Nor is the experience of time poverty limited to members of the postwar generation: this plague affects everyone. It turns out that the *feeling* of affluence can easily be substituted for actual affluence when it comes to how people perceive time. The mechanism by which this happens is known as "priming."

Jeffrey Pfeffer and Sanford E. DeVoe have investigated this phenomenon among college students. They designed a study that asked students to report the total amount of money they had in the bank. Each student was given a paper with an 11-point scale. Half of the participants received a scale that was divided into $50 increments, ranging from zero to $500. The other half was given a scale that was divided into much larger increments, with a maximum of $400,000. Even though all the participants had about the same amount of money, those with the first scale were able to circle a number near the top, whereas those in the second group marked a point much lower on the scale.

Although the impact of these scales on how students felt about their level of affluence might seem trivial, it was enough to lead participants who had marked their bank balance near the top of the scale to report feeling more pressed for time than members of the other group. In other words, simply *feeling* more affluent leads students to experience the same sense of time pressure so often reported by the truly affluent. In American society, people of all ages and income levels are bombarded with messages that reinforce our society's mantra: "We are the most prosperous nation on earth." These messages represent a culture-wide priming, worsening the sense of time poverty even among the less well-to-do.

The most common response to the stress of living on "fast time" involves rigorous efforts to reach ever-higher levels of efficiency and productivity. Unfortunately, such efforts lead to a paradoxical worsening of time stress. The result is a positive feedback loop that drives Americans farther into the embrace of the "efficiency" industry. Sadly, the decades of productivity improvements, the revolution in information technology, and the increased capacity for effective collaboration could have fueled a boom in leisure time. But that is not what happened. Instead, rising levels of productivity have led to an epidemic of stress and time poverty, as well as rising, and unevenly distributed, affluence.

Behind this foundational shift in the meaning, the use of, and the experience of time lay the postwar generation and its relentless drive to magnify its own life stage. As adults, members of this generation were comfortable with and reassured by the influence that they were having over American society. The probing uncertainty, the willingness to explore new ways of living, and the desire to question authority all receded before a new and extremely confining cultural consensus.

SECOND WIND ~ 91

The First Crucible years had fractured and then dismantled America's Spockian consensus about the meaning of childhood. The Square Revolution and the resulting rise to power of a cult of adulthood created a new and distinctly Watsonian vision of what adulthood should be and how adults should act.

The advice Dr. Watson gave in *Psychological Care of Infant and Child* eerily presages the lives that America's *adults* would find themselves living:

> Children should be awakened at 6:30 A.M. for orange juice and a pee. Play 'til 7:30. Breakfast should be at 7:30 sharp; at 8:00 they should be placed on the toilet for twenty minutes or less 'til bowel movement is complete. Then follow up with a verbal report. The child should then play indoors 'til 10:00 A.M., after 10:00 outside, a short nap after lunch, then "social play" with others.

With only minor alterations (such as replacing "be placed on the toilet" with "review proposed budget"), Watson's chronology would feel perfectly at home nestled between the covers of a FranklinCovey day planner. Spock may have won the struggle to define the childhood of the postwar generation, but Watson's ideas about authority, duty, and control resurfaced and then came to dominate the cult of adulthood.

Although the First Crucible continues to loom large in the public imagination, it lasted only about ten years (roughly 1961 to 1971) before it was swept aside. The cult of adulthood, in contrast, has been defining the contours of American life for nearly four decades. Its long tenure as the axis around which our culture turns has primed us with the belief that its tenets are both inevitable and infallible. Adult understandings of success and "effectiveness," the proper role of individualism, and the ennobling nature of wealth are no longer subject to debate or ridicule: they have become articles of faith. Even time, which would seem to be far beyond the reach of a mere generation, has been warped, compressed, and transformed by our era's magnified adulthood. Unfortunately, the consequences of these changes, which felt so normal and appropriate to members of the postwar generation, were not limited to them. People of all ages have become entangled in our era's punishing devotion to "fast time."

09

1991

January

9 Tom *After birthday cake at home, Tom takes Brenda out to the VFW. In the car on the way into town they fight over how much time Brenda has been spending in town.* **10** The number one song in America is "Justify My Love" by Madonna. **12 Flo's** *literary agent calls and tells her that Simon & Schuster has offered her a book contract. She hangs up the phone and sits quietly in her office. She is an eager, if somewhat lonely, junior faculty member climbing the ladder to tenure. She wishes that her parents had lived to share this moment with her.* **13** Soviet military troops attack Lithuanian independence supporters in Vilnius. **14 Flo** *photocopies the job notice announcing an opening for a research assistant for the new book. She wanders through sociology building tacking copies of the notice on various bulletin boards as she goes.* **15** The United Nations deadline for the withdrawal of Iraqi forces from occupied Kuwait expires, preparing the way for the start of Operation Desert Storm. **15** Yoko Ono releases a new recording of John Lennon's "Give Peace a Chance." Its all-star vocal ensemble is quickly dubbed "the Peace Choir." **16** President George H. W.

Bush addresses the nation from the Oval Office. He begins, "Just two hours ago, allied air forces began an attack on military targets in Iraq and Kuwait. These attacks continue as I speak. Ground forces are not engaged." 17 In Baghdad, Saddam Hussein declares that the "Mother of all Battles has begun." He urges the Iraqi people to "stand up to evil." 18 Eastern Air Lines goes out of business after sixty-two years, citing financial problems. 19 *Flo returns to her office after class and finds Alice Perry waiting for her. Alice is holding a slip of paper torn from the job notice Flo posted. She is bright, vivacious, and eager to work on Flo's new book. Alice is ten years younger than Flo.* 21 CBS News correspondent Bob Simon is captured by Iraqis in the Persian Gulf. 27 Whitney Houston sings "The Star-Spangled Banner" at the Super Bowl. The recording is released as a single and immediately becomes a hit. 30 John Bardeen, winner of two Nobel Prizes (the first for the transistor, the second for superconductivity), dies. An exceptionally unassuming man, his biographer notes that because he "differed radically from the popular stereotype of genius and was uninterested in appearing other than ordinary, the public and the media often overlooked him."

February

1 **Rita** *After graduating summa cum laude from Rutgers in 1978, Rita was offered a job with Arthur Andersen. Having risen slowly though the ranks, today she moves into her new, vice president's office. The simple act of unpacking her boxes and arranging the items on her desk gives her exquisite pleasure.* 5 A Michigan court bars Dr. Jack Kevorkian from assisting in suicides. 12 Continental unveils its new blue and gray livery and the "globe" logo. 18 A federal appeals court overturns televangelist Jim Bakker's sentence. Tammy Faye Bakker announces, "I talked to Jim this morning. He is filling out papers right now for his release." 25 Part of an Iraqi Scud missile hits an American military barracks in Dhahran, Saudi Arabia, killing twenty-nine and injuring ninety-nine US soldiers. 25 An amateur video captures the beating of motorist Rodney King by

Los Angeles police officers. **27 Melanie** *attends her 138th Grateful Dead show.*

March

7 Tom *Money is tight, so Brenda takes a job as a clerk in a paint store in town. Their daughter, born two years after baby Wayne's death, will finish high school in June. She wants to go to college. Everything they have goes into keeping the farm running.* **10** In Operation Phase Echo, 540,000 American troops begin to leave the Persian Gulf. **13** The United States Department of Justice announces that Exxon has agreed to pay a billion dollars toward the cleanup of the *Exxon Valdez* oil spill in Alaska. **14** The emir of Kuwait returns to Kuwait City. **14** Tony Orlando releases an album titled *With Every Yellow Ribbon.* **18** Apple computer head Steve Jobs weds Laurene Powell. **20** The Supreme Court rules unanimously that employers can't exclude women from jobs where exposure to toxic chemicals could potentially damage a fetus. **27** New Kids on the Block star Donnie Wahlberg is arrested in Louisville, Kentucky, for a fire in his hotel hallway.

April

1 The Supreme Court rules jurors can't be barred from serving because of race. The minimum wage rises from $3.80 to $4.25 per hour. **4** Senator John Heinz of Pennsylvania and six other people are killed when a helicopter collides with their plane over Merion, Pennsylvania. **5** The United States begins airdrops on Kurdish refugees in northern Iraq. **8** Actor Michael Landon announces he has inoperable cancer of the pancreas. **17** The Dow Jones Industrial Average closes above 3,000 for the first time. **18 Melanie** *is outside the Sam Boyd Silver Bowl in Las Vegas getting ready for her 155th Grateful Dead show since she dropped out of the premed program at Emory to follow the band. After the show, she calls her parents collect from a pay phone. They ask her if she wants to come home.*

She says yes and they arrange for her to pick up airline tickets at a travel agent's office. **21 Melanie** *On board Continental flight 3767 to Nashville, Melanie strikes up a conversation with flight attendant Kevin Ramos. He makes her laugh. As she is getting off the plane, she slips him her parents' home phone number and says that "she'll be there for a while."* **22** Johnny Carson announces that this will be his last year as host of the *Tonight Show*. **22** Boxer Mike Tyson is arrested and charged with the rape of Miss Black America contestant Desiree Washington three days earlier in Indianapolis, Indiana. **31** The Warsaw Treaty Organization officially dissolves in accordance with a protocol calling for a "transition to all-European structures."

May

3 Melanie *Kevin arrives in town and comes to see her. Her parents like him. Her father gives them backstage passes to the Opry and tells them who made most of the instruments that will be played that night. More than one of them will be his.* **6** Journalist Richard Behar publishes an exposé titled "The Thriving Cult of Greed and Power" in *Time* magazine. He writes, "The Church of Scientology, started by science-fiction writer L. Ron Hubbard to 'clear' people of unhappiness, portrays itself as a religion. In reality the church is a hugely profitable global racket that survives by intimidating members and critics in a Mafia-like manner." **7 Flo** *sees Alice at a party at the house of a mutual friend. They fall into an intense conversation. Before Flo leaves, Alice invites her over to her apartment for dinner.* **7** A judge in Macon, Georgia, dismisses a wrongful death lawsuit against Ozzy Osbourne. The suit was filed by a local couple who believed that Osbourne's music had inspired their son to commit suicide. **8** The *New York Times* runs an obituary for Dennis Crosby, son of Bing. The paper notes that "a 12-gauge shotgun was found near a sofa, where Mr. Crosby's body lay." He was fifty-four. **10** Oakland A's slugger José Canseco is seen leaving Madonna's apartment. He says they are "just friends." **13** Apple releases Macintosh System 7.0. **13** Yankee Stadium fans sing "Like a Virgin" to José Canseco. **23 Rita** *Today is her third wedding anniversary. Rita remembers meeting Bob for the first time. He had just become a partner and was leading the division meeting. He couldn't keep his eyes off her. They kept the relationship secret until the wedding date was set. Arthur Andersen disapproves of office romances.*

June

5 Elizabeth Carl is ordained as a priest in the Episcopal Church. She is the church's first openly lesbian priest. **6** NBC announces Jay Leno will replace Johnny Carson as host of the *Tonight Show*. **11** Microsoft releases MS DOS 5.0. **16** It is the twentieth birthday of Tupac Shakur, named after Tupac Amaru, an eighteenth-century Peruvian indigenous activist who led an uprising against Spanish conquistadors. **17** Apartheid laws are repealed in South Africa. **30** Zenith closes the last remaining American television manufacturing plant and moves the operation to Mexico. **18 Rita** *Bob drops by Rita's office and asks if she'd like to discuss the Sheffield account, over lunch. She smiles and says sure. It's their code for "let's get away from the office."*

July

2 Donald Trump proposes to Marla Maples and gives her a 7½ carat diamond ring. **13 Flo** *Alice introduces Flo to her wide circle of friends.* **19** Cal Ripken plays in his 1,500th consecutive game. **29** Yankee Stadium fans throw cups of beer and blow-up dolls at José Canseco.

August

1 Tom *Brenda admits to Tom that she has been having an affair with the Sherburne bank branch manager. They fight and she leaves. The next morning, while Tom is doing chores, she comes back for her clothes. She never returns to the farm.* **6** Tim Berners-Lee announces the inception of the

World Wide Web project and software on the alt.hypertext newsgroup. **14 Rita** *and Bob have their fifth appointment with the fertility specialist. The news is not good. Rita remains determined to get pregnant, deliver naturally, and stay on the fast track at work. In the evening she sets aside the reports she should be reading and pores over books about infertility.* **16** Boston Globe columnist Ellen Goodman writes, "Sooner or later, most Americans become card-carrying members of the counterculture. This is not an underground holdout of hippies. No beads are required. All you need to join is a child. At some point between Lamaze and PTA, it becomes clear that one of your main jobs as a parent is to counter the culture. What the media delivers to children by the masses, you are expected to rebut one at a time." **19** Soviet president Mikhail Gorbachev is put under house arrest while vacationing in the Crimea. The attempted coup, led by Vice President Gennady Yanayev and seven hard-liners, collapses in less than seventy-two hours. **30** Country music star Dottie West's car stalls on the way to a scheduled performance at the Grand Ole Opry. Her eighty-one-year-old neighbor, George Thackston, offers to drive her to the Opry. Frantic about being late, she urges him to speed. Thackston's car careens off an exit ramp and slams into an abutment. West, believing she is not injured as badly as her neighbor, insists that he be treated first. In fact, she has suffered severe internal injuries; her ruptured spleen is removed that night.

September

2 Tom's *daughter, Marsha, starts her first day of classes at the community college. It is a thirty-mile drive to and from school.* **4** During her third operation after the car crash, Dottie West dies on the operating table. She was fifty-eight. **5** Nelson Mandela is elected president of South Africa. **7 Tom** *Brenda takes a job as a clerk in a paint store in Norwich. She is living with her lover and even though the city has only 5,000 people, she feels like she has "arrived."* **11–13** During his confirmation hearings, Anita Hill testifies that Clarence Thomas spoke to her "about . . . such matters as women having sex with animals and films showing group sex or rape scenes." Thomas's testimony includes a vehement and complete denial and the assertion that he is being subjected to a "high-tech lynching for uppity blacks." Hill agrees to take a polygraph test, which finds her statements true; Thomas declines the test. The US Senate confirms Clarence Thomas to the Supreme Court by a vote of 52–48, the narrowest margin since the nineteenth century. **20 Tom** *A property tax bill arrives in the mail. Tom leaves it unopened on the kitchen table. He does not have the money to pay it.* **21 Flo** *invites Alice to move into her apartment; they start house hunting.* **22** Robert Tilton's global televangelism empire is shaken by an ABC-TV *PrimeTime Live* exposé on his extravagant lifestyle and his fund-raising practices. The show reports that Tilton's ministry threw thousands of unread prayer requests into the trash. Tilton responds by claiming that the prayer requests shown in the trash had been stolen and that he prayed over every request he received to the point that he "laid on top of those prayer requests so much that the chemicals actually got into my bloodstream, and . . . I had two small strokes in my brain." **23** Jack Kevorkian attends the deaths of Marjorie Wantz, a fifty-eight-year-old Sodus, Michigan, woman with pelvic pain, and Sherry Miller, a forty-three-year-old Roseville, Michigan, woman with multiple sclerosis. **28** "Shiny Happy People" by REM peaks at number ten on the charts.

October

4 Tom *learns that his daughter Marsha has decided to move in with her mother, who is living in Norwich. He howls with rage as she drives away. She will be closer to her classes and is glad to be free of her father's towering anger, and his drinking.* **7 Melanie** *tells her parents that she is moving to Houston with Kevin. They aren't sure about marriage but want to live together and "see what happens." Her mother smiles and says, "I just want you to be happy."* **11** The California Highway Patrol in Indio, California, pulls over a car for driving on the wrong side of the road. Jimmy

Swaggart is in the car with a woman not his wife. When the patrolman asks her why she was with Swaggart, she replies, "He asked me for sex. I mean, that's why he stopped me. That's what I do. I'm a prostitute." 12 **Rita** *gets a call from the doctor's office. Her pregnancy test is positive and she needs to come in for a prenatal appointment as soon as possible.* 13 The *New York Times* reports that milk prices paid to farmers fell 30 percent in the first nine months of the year. 25 Legendary concert promoter Bill Graham dies in a helicopter crash. He was sixty years old.

November

3 A free tribute concert is held at Golden Gate Park in memory of Bill Graham. Santana, the Grateful Dead, Journey, and Crosby, Stills, Nash & Young perform. 6 The KGB officially ceases operations. 12 Tupac Shakur releases his first album, titled *2Pacolypse Now*. 14 Michael Jackson's music video "Black or White" stirs controversy. It features Jackson smashing windows, vandalizing a car, and causing a building to explode. He also suggestively grabs his crotch while dancing. 22 **Flo** *and Alice host Thanksgiving for their friends. Alice is a natural at creating warmth and joy. Flo feels the pull of companionship and friendship and is willing, for the first time, to let down her guard, to relax with friends, and to set aside her work-related worries.* 24 Queen lead singer Freddie Mercury dies of pneumonia related to AIDs. The day before he died, Mercury issued a statement saying, "I wish to confirm that I have been tested HIV positive and have AIDs. I felt it correct to keep this information private in order to protect the privacy of those around me. However, the time has now come for my friends and fans around the world to know the truth, and I hope everyone will join with me, my doctors, and all those worldwide in the fight against this terrible disease."

December

1 Melanie *starts the flight attendant training program. When she gets home, she throws her arms around Kevin. "I love it! I love you. It's perfect! You're perfect." Over a TV dinner and a bottle of wine they decide to get married.* **4** Pan Am Airlines enters bankruptcy. **8 Rita**'s *first ultrasound shows that she's pregnant with triplets. She and Bob hold each other and cry, their emotions a swirl of joy and fear.* **10** Architect I. M. Pei receives $5 million to design the Rock and Roll Hall of Fame. **20** Oliver Stone releases *JFK.* The movie tells the story of a News Orleans district attorney who becomes suspicious of the official story being told about the assassination of the president. **20** A Missouri court sentences the Palestinian militant Zein Isa and his wife, Maria, to death for the honor killing of their daughter Palestina. **21 Rita** *wakes up knowing that she is bleeding. A panicked call to the doctor leads to a follow-up ultrasound that shows one of the triplets is gone. Now carrying twins, she is placed on bed rest.* **25 Tom** *does the chores, then comes inside to celebrate Christmas with Vicky and his mother. Without Brenda and Marsha there, the house feels empty. He doesn't bother putting up a tree.* **26** The Cold War ends when the Supreme Soviet meets and formally dissolves the Soviet Union.

PART III

THE
SECOND
CRUCIBLE

10

KOYAANISQATSI

America would be a very different place today if the cult of adulthood had confined its influence to the affairs of adults. Instead, we live in an age when the virtues and strengths associated with youthful maturity have become cardinal cultural virtues. The vast expansion of adulthood has ensured that its standards would become the measure of success for people of all ages. Among the casualties of this change was the understanding of the meaning and purpose of childhood that was current in the middle of the last century.

Because American society, as a whole, does not make use of ceremonies or rituals to demarcate and protect childhood, children have been exposed to a relentless and highly aggressive campaign to adultify childhood. Large cultural forces have whipsawed children between two conflicting cultural requirements. They are simultaneously criticized for "growing up too fast" and for failing to be hardworking and "effective" enough to meet adult expectations. Many teachers will be familiar with parents whose urgent desire to see their children succeed has led them to post anonymous comments, like the following, in response to a proposed class trip:

We should be taking educational field trips—it's a school, not a camp or a baby-sitting service. This school seems to spend an inordinate amount of time pursuing "fun" trips and activities away from the classroom—skating trips, water parks, fairs, etc. I don't get it. We did that stuff when I was a kid too, but on weekends, and over vacations—NOT during the 180-day school year. If we are going to use a legally mandated school day, it needs to be an educational experience, not a trip to a water park. I am sure the kids would want to do other "fun" stuff. That is why there are parents and teachers and principals to set guidelines for how the school days are to be used.

A person without knowledge of the recent history of American society might well have expected that when the "Spock-marked" generation became parents they would embrace the approach to child rearing that dominated America during their youth, but that isn't what happened. Current attitudes toward children and childhood now lean decisively toward Watson's highly structured point of view. Parents, teachers, and coaches all feel pressure to schedule, instruct, monitor, and test children as if they were already adults. Childhood has become a job. Stephen Covey's son Sean recognized this social trend and responded with a best seller titled *The Seven Habits of Highly Effective Teens* and its successor, *The Seven Habits of Happy Kids*. FranklinCovey also produced a line of day planners designed specifically to help children become more effective.

Life in American society *is* out of balance and it *does* call for another way of living. Fortunately, help is on the way. The postwar generation, so long accustomed to the advantages conferred by youth, is now rounding a final and decisive corner. Every single morning every single member of this generation wakes up one day older. One day older and one day farther removed from the epicenter of adult vitality, striving, and aggression. The postwar generation may have been able to change how we all perceive time, but it failed to alter the *passage* of time. As strange as it may seem, it is time that now rides to our rescue; it is time that will soon ease the mania of productivity and relieve the epidemic of "hurry sickness." Time will change everything.

Given the well-founded skepticism about "futurology," it is useful to ask, "When can we speak confidently about what lies ahead?" While technology gurus are famous for missing or overstating important trends, there is an important but underappreciated branch of mathematics that actually does a good job of illuminating our shared future. Demographers hold a significant advantage over political and technology prognosticators when it comes to predicting the future. While the lives of individuals or even families are directed by chance and circumstance, the populations of nations are surprisingly compliant with the principles of demography. In particular, *time* changes national populations in highly predictable ways. Demographers have made and continue to make extremely accurate estimations of how old the American public was and will be at different points in time.

As late as 1930, people over sixty-five made up just 5.4 percent of America's population.

In 2010, the oldest members of the postwar generation started turning sixty-five.

By 2012, America's fifty and older population will reach 100 million.

By 2020, for the first time in American history, people over sixty-five will outnumber children under the age of five.

By 2025, members of the postwar generation will be between the ages of sixty-one and seventy-nine.

Barring a catastrophe, all of these predictions will be fulfilled—most of them to the nearest percent. Time and age proceed with clocklike precision. The arrow of time always points in the same direction and not even the power of the postwar generation can change that fact. The center of gravity of the postwar generation now moves, every single day, one day closer to the end of adulthood. This is what makes speculation about the future of the postwar generation so reliable. This force now propels us toward a Second Crucible.

THE IRON LAW

A well-known riddle asks, "What happens when an irresistible force confronts an immovable object?" During its long journey through the life cycle, the postwar generation has functioned as an immovable cultural object. During the First Crucible, Yippie party founder Jerry Rubin insisted that people over thirty should not be trusted and millions agreed with him. During their adulthood, members of the postwar generation gleefully expanded the authority of people "over thirty." Indeed, the definitions of seemingly settled understandings of time, money, faith, and childhood were bent to this generation's will. In the four decades since the postwar generation entered into adulthood, nothing has been able to move it from its place at the center of our society.

The irresistible force is time. It is time that endows water with the power to carve stone. Like stone, the postwar generation must, ultimately, surrender to the passage of months, years, and decades. Each and every day the postwar generation moves farther from the zenith of its adulthood. This change is as slow, steady, and certain as that of a beam of sunlight tracing an arc across a wall. Time leaves no room for choice, its workings will *force* members of the postwar generation to confront the growing chasm between their idealization of youthful adulthood and the disturbing reality that youth is now but a memory. It is this deeply felt but little understood gap that leads millions to feel that their lives are "out of balance," that makes them feel that they are living in a way that calls for a new way of living.

KOYAANISQATSI

The cult of adulthood, which has for so long punished, derided, and dismissed its critics, is gradually becoming less . . . effective.

During the First Crucible, the *biological* imperative of matura-
tion led to a *cultural* upheaval. The postwar generation's adolescence
fractured America's postwar Spockian consensus about childhood and
the Square, Hippie, and Activist subcultures took root within those
fractures. We now approach a second great generational struggle. The
members of the postwar generation, again compelled by the force of
a biological imperative, are now approaching the end of adulthood.
People increasingly feel a new, and still-unnamed, sense of unease that
derives from a growing tension between the postwar generation's manic
adulthood and the relentless workings of time. The apex of adulthood
is already well behind them, while entry into late adulthood looms before them. Although it is hard to believe, a four-decade-long cultural
hegemony created by the postwar generation's occupation of the adult
life phase is drawing to a close. We are approaching the postwar generation's Second Crucible, and with it a spectacular and unprecedented
struggle to discover and enter into life beyond adulthood.

ADULTHOOD'S END

The first sentence of M. Scott Peck's pop psychology masterpiece, *The
Road Less Traveled*, reads, "Life is difficult." An appreciation of the developmental challenges of moving from one life phase to another could
easily inspire a corollary to Peck's declaration: "Life is difficult, but its
difficulties are not evenly distributed." Indeed, we have all encountered
some hardships that were good for us. Many others prove to be not so
good. We take pictures at graduations, weddings, and birthdays because
it's in these moments we can feel our lives changing. Other, less happy
events remain unmarked but are even more vividly remembered. "It's
been three years since . . ."

It is the change that comes upon us slowly that can be the hard-
est to see—and understand. A once-happy marriage dissolves into two
people living in the same house. Both spouses know that the marriage
is over, though neither can say when it ended. A job, once challenging
and fulfilling, no longer suits. When did the change come? It is hard

to say. On a more optimistic note, the process of acquiring a new skill (such as learning to play a musical instrument) often proceeds so gradually that one cannot recall a "moment" when mastery arrived.

During the long decades since they reached adulthood, members of the postwar generation have experienced only inklings of the *need* for change. When asked, most will say that they don't feel any different than they used to. They imagine that adulthood will last, must last, forever. But it won't, and they *are* different than they used to be.

Powerful social and economic forces resist this reality but they cannot and will not alter the course of demography. The postwar generation is, increasingly, subject to the same sort of "false" consciousness that the Inquisition thrust upon Galileo. Placed on trial for his life, the astronomer was compelled to testify under oath that the earth was the fixed and eternal center of the universe. After giving his testimony, he muttered, "Still, it moves." In contemporary America, loud, well-compensated, and well-intentioned voices insist that we are all "as young as we feel." We are constantly reassured that we can "fight" unwanted changes and that, contrary to the available evidence, the postwar generation will always inhabit the delicious zenith of adult strength, beauty, and vitality.

"Still it moves."

Other people living in other places and in other times have understood quite clearly that adulthood is just one phase of life. They understood that as the end of human adulthood drew near, a person could begin to explore the passage that leads out of the constrained life of the adult and into a new way of living. They understood that there was a life beyond adulthood. Around the world and through history people have made use of rituals and ceremonies to help young people make the transition out of childhood and into adulthood. Many of these same societies employed rituals that helped people outgrow adulthood.

ONCE MORE INTO THE FIRE

During the First Crucible, the postwar generation divided along lines that were defined, in large part, by one's approach to the challenge of becoming an adult. Now, as the members of this generation near the end of adulthood, they are contending with unsettling sensations associated with another impending "coming of age" experience. This second great transformation will be very different from the first. In youth this need to grow and change is normalized and celebrated with a "coming of age" narrative that explains, to everyone, what is happening. We are encouraged to identify the stirrings of adolescence not as pain or loss or failure but rather as a summons to a new phase of life. For those nearing the end of adulthood, there is no reassuring cultural consensus they can turn to for comfort and guidance. Contemporary society offers no language, no ceremonies or rituals, no heroic tales of discovery on which people living in late adulthood can rely. For the second time in its experience, the postwar generation will be compelled to improvise their transition from one life phase to the next.

As the end of the postwar generation's adulthood draws near, so does its Second Crucible. This crucible will be different from but even more challenging than the first. During the First Crucible, even the most persistent critics of the postwar generation understood that its members would grow up eventually. As we enter into the Second Crucible, we already find that the "summons to growth" and the sensation of "life out of balance" are being misinterpreted. There are, for example, few Americans living today who believe that adulthood is something that one can and should outgrow.

Because the postwar generation has spent decades enlarging upon adulthood, it will be *especially* difficult for members of this generation to see beyond its limitations. The postwar generation's increasingly strained relationship with adulthood will create entirely new cultural fault lines. During the Second Crucible, these fractures will give rise to unique subcultures with divergent answers to the increasingly urgent question, "What comes next?" Members of the postwar generation will

Deny the necessity of change and endeavor to remain fully and
permanently adult.
Accept but work to minimize the impact of change for as long as
possible.
Embrace change and *choose* to explore life beyond adulthood.

These three perspectives along with their inevitable permutations and combinations are already beginning to divide members of the postwar generation. This generation's approach to the end of its adulthood—and the absence of clear cultural guidance about how to manage the growing sense of koyaanisqatsi—will create enormous cultural heat and pressure. The long-standing consensus around the structure and meaning of adulthood will increasingly be challenged by three emerging Second Crucible subcultures: Denialists, Realists and Enthusiasts.

The Denialists are (and will continue to be) the most vociferous of these subcultures. Members of this subculture loudly and proudly reject the changes that come with aging and embrace an alternative narrative that posits a future where one can be forever young. Youth, they contend, can be, should be, and must be a permanent state of being. A much larger and vastly less ideological segment of the postwar generation is already coalescing into a Realist subculture. Those who are aligned with this subculture pride themselves on their willingness to admit that they are, in fact, changing. They see (and dislike) the changes that come with the passage of years and they are committed to actively resisting those changes. The Enthusiasts are and will likely remain the smallest of the Second Crucible subcultures. They are distinguished by a genuinely countercultural embrace of "life beyond adulthood." Enthusiasts openly acknowledge the difficulties that lie ahead but are also eager to explore the new opportunities for growth that the passage of time brings into their lives. Because of our culture's slavish devotion to youth, the Enthusiasts are essentially disconnected from mainstream thinking about age and aging. They remain underground and are, for now, happy to devote themselves to developing their own rituals, their own language, and their own gatherings.

The Second Crucible will bring us all many difficult days. In much the same way that the Squares, Activists, and Hippies shaped the First Crucible and its aftermath, the Denialists, Realists, and Enthusiasts are poised to exert an outsize influence over our shared culture. Taking time to explore the structure and function of each of the Second Crucible subcultures in greater detail will help us better understand the upheaval that will accompany the postwar generation's fitful journey out of adulthood.

11

DENIALISM

In 1519 Venetian scholar Antonio Pigafetta set sail from Seville under the command of Captain Ferdinand Magellan. He returned to Spain three years later, one of only 18 from the initial crew of 240 to survive the first known circumnavigation of the earth. Pigafetta recorded his observations and speculations in a diary, where he noted, for example, the average Brazilian Indian was between 124 and 140 years of age. Reflecting on this remarkable, if questionable, observation, he concluded that Brazilians lived so long because they retained a primitive innocence similar to that of the Patriarchs who, according to the Bible, lived many hundreds of years.

Pigafetta was not the only European making questionable claims about what he had seen. Thirty years earlier, Christopher Columbus had set the standard for this sort of unbridled optimism. One of the explorer's early letters celebrated the seemingly limitless supply of food available in the New World, noting that the land he had discovered was "a veritable Cockaigne."

Columbus and Pigafetta lived in a time when most people were familiar with the legends of Cockaigne. These stories told of a place where good food and good health came effortlessly—to everyone. While reality offered disease, famine, backbreaking labor, and the prospect of early death, Cockaigne was a land of plenty. As news from the early explorers spread across Europe, rich and poor alike dreamed of Cockaigne. In a time when the average life span was under forty years, epidemics swept across the land, and famines were a common occurrence, who would not dream of a land where idleness was the norm and houses were framed with beams of butter and roofed with meat pies? In Cockaigne, a man who was fond of his drink was paid a silver penny for each "fair-sided" mug of ale he consumed.

Fantasies of roast chickens that fly into one's mouth might seem juvenile to those reared in a time of plenty. Indeed, so great is our distance from the extremities of that era that it is possible to imagine we have outgrown our need to console ourselves with imagined utopias. We no longer dream of a place where fish jump out of the water and into the fisherman's creel. We do, however, indulge in vastly more modern but far less plausible fantasies.

We live in an age that equates youthful adulthood with all that is right, good, true, and beautiful, and it is the bloom of youth that we seek and nothing less. Members of the postwar generation increasingly dream of youth, and this alone is proof that they are no longer young. The truly youthful, after all, have no reason to pine for what is already theirs. These dreams belong most especially to those who long to be immune to the passage of time. They belong to those who lie in their beds sometimes awake and sometimes asleep and imagine living a thousand years and being young on the day they die. These are the dreams of our Cockaigne.

THE NEW PETER PAN

In its mildest forms, Denialism provides us with the comforting illusion that we look and act a bit younger than we really are. We are especially pleased when the deception requires only a small effort on our part.

After all, no one wants to appear tired or careworn, and reasonable people agree that minor cosmetic enhancements do no harm. Such desires are not new. The book *Eighteen Books of the Secrets of Art & Nature*, first published in 1661, presented readers with information on how to use vegetable dyes to change the color of human hair. Grecian Formula 16 has been a popular hair-coloring product for men since its introduction in 1961. It is appropriately named, since its main active ingredient is lead acetate, which, research has shown, ancient Greeks also used to turn gray hair black. In the 1950s fewer than 10 percent of American women colored their hair. By the 1970s that figure had risen to 40 percent, and by 2004 it exceeded 75 percent. A 2008 study, conducted by Clairol, found that 88 percent of women feel that coloring their hair has a positive effect on their confidence.

The desire to be seen acting "young" is also important to Denialism. The retiree who insists, "I'm so busy I don't know how I ever had time to work," is making it known that she remains part of the "time-stressed" adult's frenzied world. The story about a cardiac surgeon who refuses to stop operating even though he is well into his nineties says much more about the surgeon's self-image than it does about clinical acumen. It is easy to see that a politician who continues running for reelection—even though it's been decades since she actually influenced legislation—is in denial. Likewise the American veneration of athletes inspires a seemingly endless series of scandals involving professional athletes who use performance-enhancing drugs. Among Denialists, people are defined by how they look and what they can *do*.

Around the world, the general preference in favor of youth is so well established that it could be said to be a cultural universal. To the extent that we share this view, and almost all of us do to some degree, we are all Denialists. What separates the subculture from the sentiment, however, is the development of a persistent and pervasive fear that stigmatizes all age-related aspects of one's appearance and performance. The center of the Second Crucible's growing Denialist subculture is bounded by this gnawing anxiety.

During the late 1980s and early 1990s psychologist Dan Kiley popularized the idea that young people (especially young men) were increasingly afflicted with what he called the "Peter Pan" syndrome. Those who chose to resist "normal" growth and development and opt instead for stasis and stagnation appalled members of the postwar generation. The book became a best seller. Three decades later, Denialism is beginning to function as a neo–Peter Pan syndrome that describes those who wish to remain adults "forever." The most fervent Denialists are the "lost" men and women of late adulthood.

The Denialist subculture is composed primarily of people who are not content to simply look and act a little bit younger than their actual age. They yearn for something that no human being has ever achieved. There are Denialists who believe (contrary to all evidence) that normal human aging can and will be stopped and then reversed. The Denialists believe that soon-to-be-invented technology will eradicate human aging. This buoyant optimism leads Denialists to endorse techniques that help them simulate the behavior and appearance of people substantially younger than themselves. Aging may continue apace but the appearance of aging is arrested.

HOPE IN A BOTTLE

Currently, the most hotly contested Denialist battlefield is the human face. Those who want to look much younger than their years understand how sensitive people are to the age-related facial characteristics. A popular website (www.guessmyage.net) used this sensitivity as the basis for a surprisingly addictive age guessing game. Users upload photos of themselves and "win" when visitors "guess young." This is a game that Denialists play in real life and one they are always eager to win. The desire to always be the winner of this kind of game makes Denialists easy prey for those who profit from selling "hope in a bottle."

America's ubiquitous anti-aging industry can be surprisingly hard to see because it hides in plain sight on store shelves and magazine covers and on our many glowing screens. Testimonials for anti-aging

breakthroughs are never more than one click away on just about any
ad-supported Internet site. The website for the TV show *The Doctors*,
for example, informs visitors that Dr. Ordon's "HydraFacial" procedure
"takes 15 minutes and makes you look 15 years younger!" Publishers
flood the market with books bearing immodest titles like these:

Beyond the 120 Year Diet: How to Double Your Vital Years
The Longevity Bible
The Hardness Factor
Anti-Aging Cures: Life Changing Secrets to Reverse the Effects of
    Aging
The Youth Pill: Scientists at the Brink of an Anti-Aging Revolution

Alone at the top of anti-aging's first tier is Deepak Chopra, MD.
In 1993 Chopra published *Ageless Body, Timeless Mind: The Quantum
Alternative to Growing Old*. The book's message skillfully validated and
then enlarged upon the postwar generation's worshipful approach to
youth; more than 1.5 million copies were sold. In its pages, Chopra
argues that "we are not victims of aging, sickness and death. These
are part of the scenery, not of the seer, who is immune to any form of
change. This seer is the spirit, the expression of eternal being." For reasons that are never made clear, Chopra bases his formula for immortality on the arcane principles of quantum physics. By "defeating entropy,"
he declares, we can create a "land where no one is old" and where "we
create our bodies as we create the experience of our world." This book
anticipated the Denialist movement and remains in print two decades
after its initial publication.

Chopra followed up on this success with a series of books aimed
directly at the Denialist market, including 2009's *Reinventing the Body,
Resurrecting the Soul: How to Create a New You*. This book begins with
an examination of the restless discontent, the feeling of a "life out of
balance" that has been referred to here as koyaanisqatsi. Building on his
earlier work, Chopra locates the source of this difficulty in an "estrange-

ment of body and soul." His solution involves "transforming [your body] from a material object to a dynamic, flowing process." Chopra contends, without any supporting evidence, that "every cell is made up of two invisible ingredients: awareness and energy." How will the reunification of body and spirit be accomplished? He urges his readers to surrender to inner guidance, embrace a journey to higher consciousness, expand awareness through meditation, ask for guidance, and then wait for it to appear.

The success and longevity of a book promising readers an ageless body and timeless mind naturally raises questions about the author. What has happened to *him* over the past twenty years? Did he change his "quantum reality" and defeat aging? Did he transform his body into a "dynamic flowing process"? We can find the answer to these questions by comparing photos taken of the author when *Ageless Body, Timeless Mind* was released and those taken fifteen years later. When we do, we find, unsurprisingly, that time has changed Deepak Chopra in all the ways that we would naturally expect. Like all his readers, the guru appears fifteen years older fifteen years later.

NEVER

Denialism is a kind of cultural cousin to the First Crucible Activism. Denialists share the Activists' respect for the power of adulthood and their desire to apply that power to the problems they deem to be the most important. While the Activists once struggled for peace and social justice, Denialists want to grab hold of every tool or technology that might allow them to "stop and reverse aging." Where the Beach Boys once sang, "Wouldn't it be nice if we were older," the Denialist hums a tune that goes something like "Wouldn't it be nice if we were younger."

The word that best captures the essence of Denialism is *never*. Like the Peter Pans who cannot bear the thought of leaving childhood behind, Denialists refuse to acknowledge the passage of time and its impact on their minds and bodies. This refusal creates a parallel and very intense need to believe that science or mysticism or ayurvedic medicine or vitamins will, somehow, come to their rescue. Predictably, Denialists have worked to develop a close and highly symbiotic relationship with large corporations. This devotion to youth has brought forth an anti-aging industry that works ceaselessly to create and maintain illusions of youth.

HARDBALL

Among the many ironies that populate the Denialist subculture is the fact that the most fervent advocates of youth are almost never young. Born in 1946, Suzanne Somers is a former television sitcom star, more recently the author of *Ageless: The Naked Truth about Bioidentical Hormones* (2007). In that book, Somers endorsed the so-called Wiley protocol and claimed to be taking sixty pills a day, applying hormone creams, and injecting herself intravaginally with estriol. When several leading physicians issued a public letter calling this approach "scientifically unproven and dangerous," Somers went on the *Oprah* show looking for validation, and she found it. The talk show host introduced Somers this way: "Many people write Suzanne off as a quackadoo, but she just might be a pioneer."

In her book *Selling the Fountain of Youth*, Arlene Weintraub asks how the anti-aging industry could, seemingly, come out of nowhere and reach $88 billion in annual sales. New but untested and unproven remedies like T. S. Wiley's bioidentical hormones have led the way, but members of the medical profession have proven themselves to be very willing accomplices. Botox, custom nutritional supplements, and quirky innovations like Dr. Ordon's patented HydraFacial regime have fueled a boom in medical revenue and profits.

The glue that has, so far, held the industry together is the American Academy of Anti-Aging Medicine (better known as A4M). Founded in 1993, it now organizes conferences and trade shows in the United States and around the world. A4M has also demonstrated a willingness to play legal hardball with critics who demand evidence for anti-aging claims. In 2004 epidemiologist S. Jay Olshansky made what he considered to be "a lighthearted attempt to make the public aware of . . . anti-aging quackery." (He created a "Silver Fleece Award" and gave it to A4M.) The association's lawyers were not amused, and they responded by filing a $150 million lawsuit against him. The *Chicago Tribune* called the action an "almost unheard-of attempt to punish academics for comments made in their professional capacity." Olshansky countersued and, according to a report from CNN, both parties eventually dropped their cases.

Large parts of the anti-aging industry do, however, remain exquisitely sensitive to criticism—and for good reason. The emerging Denialist subculture is the cornerstone on which their industry's profitability rests. The doctors, corporations, actors, gurus, and healers who are active in the field are engaged in a constant struggle to reconcile the promise of a youthful longevity with the humbling truth that such a thing remains impossible. Building a business on promises that can't possibly be kept is a risky business in the best of times. Fortunately for the A4M, the Denialist response to the litany of anti-aging's technical failures has been to swiftly transfer hope from a disappointing reality to the field's next great thing.

AGEISM

Few Denialists appreciate or take much interest in the complex interactions between their perspective and social attitudes about aging. Their intense focus on youth also validates and promulgates negative attitudes about age and aging. This phenomenon is something like the sexism advanced by women who reinforce sexist stereotypes and even entertain friends with jokes that cast women in an unflattering light. In his Pulitzer Prize–winning book *Why Survive?*, Dr. Robert Butler examined the social pressure that leads people to deny the reality that appears before them in their mirror every morning. He called it "ageism."

A recent survey of people over sixty found that nearly 80 percent of respondents reported experiencing ageism. Typical examples included episodes in which others had assumed the presence of memory or physical impairments simply because of a person's age. Duke University's Erdman Palmore found that the most frequent type of ageism—reported by 58 percent of respondents—was being told a joke that pokes fun at older people. Thirty-one percent reported being ignored or not taken seriously because of their age. Does this matter? Yes, it does. Negative stereotypes about aging may well shorten the lives of older people. Becca Levy, PhD, assistant professor of public health at Yale University, followed 660 people aged fifty years and older and found that those with positive self-perceptions of aging lived seven and a half years longer than those with negative self-perceptions of aging.

The passage of time demands that, each and every day, the postwar generation move one day farther away from the apex of adult power. This unyielding reality makes the postwar generation's passage out of adulthood inevitable, but the form that passage will take and what its consequences for the rest of our society will be remain unknown. We do know, however, that America's Coveyesque consensus on adulthood is beginning to erode. The astounding growth and success of Denialism and the anti-aging industry is partly a response to that failure.

If the most extreme elements of the Denialist subculture emerge from this struggle with control over the postwar generation's center of gravity, then their insights, priorities, and beliefs will be amplified in the decades to come. The Denialists already have powerful allies in the media and corporate spheres, and if they define the Second Crucible on their terms, the result is likely to be a series of intense intergenerational conflicts. There will be war—an age war—like nothing we have ever seen before.

12

REALISM

Realists take great pride in their common sense. They hold what they see as a perfectly obvious and sensible position that aging is both inevitable and unpleasant. They know that no one has ever grown young and conclude from this that it is very unlikely that anyone ever will do so. They dismiss the Denialists' most fervent desires as juvenile fantasies. Realists can, and do, state their case plainly, and with little emotion: "There isn't much good to be said about aging, but instead of complaining about it, we should do what we can to avoid the worst of it." Knowing that aging cannot be reversed, they choose to resist its effects. In this effort, Realists make heavy use of low-impact aerobic exercise, number puzzles, blended multivitamins, estate planning, well-balanced diets, and volunteerism.

If Realism had a spokescharacter, it would be Winnie the Pooh's Eeyore.

"It's snowing still," said Eeyore gloomily.
"So it is."

"And freezing."

"Is it?"

"Yes," said Eeyore. "However," he said, brightening up a little, "we haven't had an earthquake lately."

This odd blend of hope and fatalism leads people to embrace Realism and do most of what is asked of them by the "experts." Their diligence in these endeavors is all the more remarkable considering they do all this in the sure knowledge that a cold hard rain is going to fall.

THE SCREAM QUEEN GETS REAL

Jamie Lee Curtis (born November 22, 1958) got her start in movies playing beset-upon young women in slasher films like *Halloween*, *The Fog*, *Prom Night*, and *Terror Train*. She went on to enjoy a long and successful career as an actress, author, and pitchwoman. Although she spent most of her career working in Hollywood, Curtis has, in recent years, emerged as one of America's most prominent Realists. In 2002, she did a photo shoot for *More* magazine wearing only a sports bra and spandex briefs. She went without the makeup, hairstyling, and airbrushing that come standard with celebrity photos because "I wanted to say to women, 'Hello? I look like this. Relax, we all look like this.' I'm 44 and I weigh 150.' "

Like many aging entertainers, she used plastic surgery to stave off her body's encroaching middle age. While the procedures did make her look a bit younger, the surgery left her feeling "misshapen" and "unnatural." Growing up as the daughter of two iconic American actors had allowed her to watch "people age and become buffoons. When you crest in your 30s or 40s and then you don't pull out of the public eye, you become a caricature. You have to have grace, dignity, and gratitude, and walk away kind of slowly, like you're walking away from a bear." Toward that end, she gave up pills, alcohol, and plastic surgery. "I want to do my part, as I develop the consciousness for it, to stop perpetuating the myth. I'm going to look the way God intends me to look . . . with a little help from Manolo Blahnik."

Perhaps as a result of her newfound Realism, Dannon began using Curtis in advertisements for Activia yogurt in 2007. Under the headline "Jamie Lee Curtis Can't Take a Dump, Hypes Dannon's Bifidus Regularis," columnist Steve Hall summarized the social significance of the campaign: "So now we have Jamie Lee Curtis, who has seemingly approached an appropriate age to which women who suffer from this malady can relate to, sitting comfortably on a green couch with just the right amount of gray hair and just the right amount of commercial spunk so as to make this piece of work both good and fodder for middle school bathroom humor." "Bifidus Regularis" sounds as if it ought to be quite scientific but is actually a made-up, copyrighted term used solely for the purposes of marketing Dannon's products to consumers.

In 2010 Connecticut attorney general Richard Blumenthal announced a $21 million settlement against the yogurt maker for allegedly "overstating the digestive, immunity and other health benefits related to Activia yogurt and DanActive dairy drinks." An FTC complaint maintained that the ads in which the actress discussed her more vigorous bowel movements were based on unsubstantiated claims. "In truth and in fact, eating one serving of Activia daily is not clinically proven to relieve temporary irregularity and help with slow intestinal transit time," the FTC said.

Jamie Lee Curtis, movie star and scion of American acting legends, developed a powerful and realistic understanding of what aging is and what it does to our bodies. It was this insight that allowed her to challenge the Hollywood orthodoxy and go public with statements like this: "It's a conspiracy, a complete catastrophe, a surgical industrial complex. Somehow we are being fed this belief that to continue on we have to do this. Yet people are being disfigured. It's shocking what people are doing to their faces." At nearly the same time, she began to make public claims for a product that the FTC maintained to be, "in truth and in fact," unsupported by research. If this seems like a contradiction, it shouldn't. Realists are very willing to criticize anti-aging dogma, especially those methods and procedures that they feel violate the standards of common sense. They are also attracted to seemingly humdrum products, like "probiotic" yogurts, when they see them as augmenting or supplementing normal biological processes.

The Realists hold common sense in high esteem: Curtis's criticism of the repeated use of anti-aging surgical procedures is based on the fact that their use makes people feel "misshapen" and "unnatural." When Curtis says, "I want to . . . stop perpetuating the myth. I'm going to look the way God intends me to look," she is valuing authenticity over the possibility of looking even younger than her actual age. It is the inauthenticity created by plastic surgery, rather than its aims, that give Realists pause. Common sense demands a certain decorum and an unblushing willingness to face up to the unpleasantries created by our aging bodies. It seems to matter little to the Realists that Dannon is alleged to have gained tens of millions in annual sales using deliberate shadings of the truth if not outright lies. What matters is that its pitch to women had "just the right amount of gray hair and just the right amount of commercial spunk." Common sense suggests that a yogurt fortified with "Bifidus Regularis" *should* relieve constipation, and that is enough for them.

THE COMMON SENSE GURUS

Gigi Vorgan and Gary Small, MD, are Realism's power couple. She worked in television and movies (including *Rain Man* and *Red Dawn*) before teaming up with husband Dr. Gary Small to cowrite *The Memory Prescription*, *The Longevity Bible*, and *iBrain*. Their first book, *The Memory Bible*, covered all of the Realists' favorite themes. Middle-aged people, the authors warn, all need to realize that they are "one day closer to Alzheimer's disease." Fortunately, however, it turns out that "great memories are not born, they are made." The book's "innovative memory exercises and brain fitness programs" include encouragement to "minimize stress" and "do puzzles and brainteasers," because these things can "immediately improve mental performance." The authors recommend a "brain diet" rich in memory-enhancing foods like prunes and blueberries. This bible also includes a workbook with a weekly and daily calendar.

Vorgan and Small have an abiding faith in the power of vim and "vinegar" to keep us all young. Dr. Small offers this story about his wife's fiesty 103-year-old grandmother as an illustration of Realism done right:

[She] lived in a third floor walk-up apartment in New York City. Every day she walked up and down those stairs several times to go shopping, to the post office, the dry cleaner's and do other little errands. At 103, she was as sharp as a tack. She never forgot a birthday, an anniversary or a single holiday. And God forbid you forgot to send her a card or call her on her birthday—you'd hear about it for ages. The exercise she got on those stairs and errands may not only have protected her heart so she could live past 100, it may also have protected her brain.

After reviewing the results of several studies on the topic, Dr. Small offers readers a carefully hedged conclusion: "Exercise gets the heart pumping more blood to the brain, which *appears* to reverse cellular deterioration associated with aging." [emphasis added] Self-help books make heavy use of so-called anecdata and those aimed at Realists and Denialists are no exception. Small's recollection of his wife's 103-year-old grandmother may not prove a thing, but it does help the reader feel better about what is admittedly a rather frightening topic.

This emphasis on feeling over evidence is vividly displayed in Vorgan and Small's 2011 book, *The Alzheimer's Prevention Program*. The authors note that because there is currently no cure for Alzheimer's disease (and little reason to believe that a cure is on the horizon), all hope for avoiding this dreaded disease currently lies with prevention. As a Realist and scientist (he is the founding director of the UCLA Memory Clinic and director of the UCLA Center on Aging), Small freely admits, "We don't have a definitive long-term study to prove that we can prevent Alzheimer's disease." Dr. Martha Davis of Northwestern University is even more blunt: "We wish we could tell people that taking a pill or doing a puzzle every day would prevent this terrible disease, but current evidence doesn't support this."

In place of such proof, Vorgan and Small offer a detailed reinterpretation of the "fine print" of certain short-term and epidemiological studies. Readers are encouraged to train but not strain their brains, exercise, eat a brain-boosting diet, and, of course, reduce stress. Asked about his personal efforts to "prevent" Alzheimer's disease, Dr. Small reports:

> I do crossword puzzles, Sudoku, and KenKen every morning after reading the newspaper. If I don't have time to swim or walk the dog for some cardiovascular conditioning, I take the stairs at work or pick up the pace when walking between campus appointments. I work in regular breaks from the computer to stretch, meditate or chat with colleagues. I make an effort to eat plenty of fruits and vegetables, omega-3 fats, and whole grains—but I admit that occasionally my sweet tooth gets the best of me. When that happens, I remind myself that moderation is the key—that chocolate does contain brain-healthy antioxidants.

He gives us, in a single elegant paragraph, the distilled essence of common sense in our time. No reasonable person can object to crossword puzzles, walking the dog, or partaking of an occasional chocolate bar. Neither can a fair-minded person say that any of these things are proven to actually prevent the development of Alzheimer's disease. This conflict would seem to pose a substantial difficulty for aspiring authors of a guide to Alzheimer's prevention. Fortunately for Vorgan and Small, Realists are willing to content themselves with the *feeling* that they are "in control" and the *belief* that what they are doing will make a difference. Given this propensity, *The Anxiety about Alzheimer's*

Prevention Program might have been a properly descriptive title for the couple's book. When we strip away the hype and wishful thinking, we find a sober, practical, and devoutly commonsense approach to managing one's *fear* of developing Alzheimer's disease.

THE DIRTIEST FIVE-LETTER WORD

We naturally admire people who have the courage to adopt "realistic" approaches to life's most difficult problems, and millions agree that a commonsense approach to resisting aging is best. Few would argue with the idea that exercise and healthy diets are good for whatever might ail us. Unfortunately, it is also true that doing the hard work required to stay fit *will never be enough* to actually stop or reverse aging. This unacknowledged conflict explains why, for all their "common sense," Realists are creating a remarkably backward-looking subculture. While their pursuit of health and wellness is laudable, Realists are driven to "exercise and eat right" mostly by a dread of losing their status as adults.

One of the most disabling and demeaning five-letter words in the English language derives its power largely from the Realists' fear of age and aging. If there were a contest to come up with an official word for the Realist subculture, *still* would win. In American society, older people are accorded respect and allowed to maintain their standing as an adult only to the degree that they can *still* . . . Everyone understands this game and knows how it's played. Nieces and nephews boast, "My aunt Myrtle, she *still* drives." Sons and daughters brag, "My dad, he's eighty-two, and you better believe it, he *still* works five days a week." Not even great-grandchildren can resist: "Opa turned ninety-four this month. He just got back from climbing Pike's Peak. He's in Florida and he *still* water-skis—barefoot—in the nude!" We live in an age when older people are deemed worthy only to the degree that, in their thoughts and actions, they resemble young people. This ethos is very rigidly applied and we all know what happens to older people who can't *still* do the things that adults are supposed to do.

They disappear.

The word *still* is intended as praise but actually serves to wound and diminish older people. The prominent place it holds in the Realist lexicon reminds us that, when it comes to people living in the latter decades of life, success is defined by the absence of change, interruption, or cessation. It is a peculiar conception of human life that equates success with a lack of change. Our use of the word *still* reveals an ordinarily unstated assumption: in contemporary American society, any deviation from the parameters of vigorous adulthood, by definition, carries the stigma of failure.

The contradictions that bedevil this position become obvious as soon as we apply its tenets to childhood. It is hard to imagine Dr. Spock or even Dr. Watson endorsing an approach to childhood that is based on thwarting the normal processes of growth, change, and development. The idea of health and wellness programs for children designed and intended to *delay* and, if possible, *prevent* the passage of young people out of childhood and into adulthood would violate some of our most basic social norms. Realists may pride themselves on their devotion to common sense, and they do resist aging with an energetic persistence, but they are also dangerously misguided. Healthy, happy people are meant to grow, and there are crucial moments in our lives when that growth compels us to leave one phase of the human life cycle and enter into the next. It is the Realists' inability to see the value of "life beyond adulthood" that traps them in a desperate and ultimately doomed effort to continue living as adults. This is the tyranny of *still*.

NOTHING MORE THAN FEELINGS

Denialists adhere faithfully to an adultish standard of appearance and performance, and they are always eager to look and act younger than they really are. This ambition also leads them to discard and dismiss any innovation that fails to quickly deliver fully on its promises. If Dr. Ordon's HydraFacial fails to make you look fifteen years younger in just fifteen minutes, he and his trademarked treatment will be abandoned. The same holds true for all the other anti-aging pills, potions, and procedures available today. This uncompromising dedication to results, combined with the blatant ineffectiveness of anti-aging nostrums, accounts for Denialism's fickle nature and weakness for fads.

Realists take a different approach. They are concerned primarily with creating and maintaining the *feeling* that aging is being deterred. The lack of proof that something (for example the antioxidants in blueberries) actually works matters little to Realists. As a result they are much more easily and persistently deceived than those of the Denialist persuasion. Sales figures for Activia yogurt suggest that Realists largely dismissed the fact that government agencies were convinced that Dannon was making false claims on behalf of its celebrity-endorsed, "Bifidus Regularis"-enriched yogurt. The $21 million fine the company paid (even as it denied liability) mattered little, because so many people felt that the product *ought* to work as advertised. Realists, for all their rhetoric about "common sense" and their insistence on authenticity, are actually people in search of a feeling. They will diligently continue buying, using, and believing in products science has proven to be ineffective—as long as doing so fosters the *feeling* of effectiveness.

Realists share the Squares' devotion to adulthood and the virtues American society has attached to life as an adult. They lack, however, the Squares' simple, honest approach to getting on with life by embracing whatever comes next without complaint or ambivalence. Realists prefer to place their faith in a diluted common sense that just might be enough to extend their residence in adulthood—if only for one more year. The task of exposing and correcting the Realists' flawed reasoning and challenging the dangerous excesses promoted by the Denialist subculture will fall, oddly enough, to the Second Crucible's smallest, most obscure, and currently least influential perspective—that of the Enthusiasts.

13

ENTHUSIASM

During the postwar generation's long journey through adulthood, the idea that one could outgrow adulthood vanished from American society. Realists and Denialists attempt to fill this void with a decisively negative vision of aging. Adulthood, they insist, could or at least should last forever. Fortunately, there is an alternative to that perspective. There is a nascent Second Crucible subculture that combines a positive view of aging with a free-flowing, joyful sense of *optimism*.

Most Americans would call *positive aging* an oxymoron and place it alongside perennial favorites such as *enormously small*, *genuine fake*, and *military intelligence*. Our society's pervasive and unrelenting bias against aging makes it hard to take terms like *active retirement* and *healthy aging* seriously. Nor do the words *enthusiast* and *aging* seem to belong together. But they do. Although they remain a small group hidden in the shadows of society, those who embrace aging are creating a subculture that has the temerity to celebrate the normal changes associated with life beyond adulthood. These are the Enthusiasts.

Very few people are aware of this peculiar brand of enthusiasm, and even fewer can say that they know an Enthusiast personally. Indeed, the Enthusiast's perspective is so far removed from the conventional Denialist and Realist interpretations of aging that it remains nearly invisible. Enthusiasts aren't just willing, they are eager to explore life beyond adulthood because they believe this life phase contains far more developmental potential than adulthood. They want to take hold of aging and its opportunities with both hands and use them to further their own growth. Even though most people have never heard of them, Enthusiasts have already developed a rich self-descriptive language and a vibrant network of relationships and gatherings.

NEW GROWTH

During the first-ever conference on "The Poetics of Aging," Josiah Polhemus neatly summarized the Enthusiasts' creed: "As I grow older, the outer world of appearance, prestige and perfection, all influences from outside sources, lessen; the inner world of imagination, grati-tude and tolerance strengthen and keep me seeking wisdom and more breath." Enthusiasts gleefully subvert, mock, and violate the doctrine of youth's perfection. Instead of accepting the idea that youth is best, they draw inspiration from people and cultures from around the world and throughout history who have seen virtue in age.

The Book of Genesis reports that Adam lived nine hundred years. The remarkable longevity of biblical patriarchs was said to be a *reward* for their great piety. Leviticus 19:32 leaves no doubt about the *value* of age and requires the faithful to "rise up before the hoary head, and honor the face of the old man." Postwar Japan established a new holi-day known as Respect for the Aged Day: the media lavishes attention on the lives of older people, and the occasion has become one of the busiest travel days of the year. In 1963 President Kennedy highlighted the connection between age and value:

This increase in the life span and in the number of our senior citi-zens presents this Nation with increased opportunities: the opportunity to draw upon their skill and sagacity—and the opportunity to provide the respect and recognition they have earned. It is not enough for a great nation merely to have added new years to life— our objective must also be to add new life to those years.

Enthusiasts endorse Kennedy's vision of reciprocity, seeking good health not just for their own benefit but, more importantly, so that society can draw upon "their skill and sagacity." Perhaps most importantly, they recognize that human development is not, as so many insist, restricted to the young but continues across the life span. Norm Amundson summarizes the Enthusiasts' powerful urge to explore: "Life is a story with many chapters, the most exciting segments usually come toward the end of the book." The desire to outgrow adulthood is honorable, it is ancient, and in contemporary American society, it is also rare. We need to explore the undiscovered country of aging because there is also compelling evidence that we will find happiness there.

THE U-BEND

Stanford University psychology professor Laura Carstensen has been exploring the emotional terrain of aging for most of her adult life. For a dozen years (1993–2005) she ran a first-of-its-kind study designed to untangle the relationship between age and emotion. Her analysis of the data showed that the older people become, the better they are at controlling their emotions. While conventional wisdom holds that old age is a time of sadness, she found that older people are significantly happier than people in their twenties and thirties. Carstensen concludes that "older people manage negative emotions better than younger people. When negative feelings arise, they don't linger on them the way the young tend to." Decades of research have led her to identify a growing awareness of one's own mortality not as a source of sadness and grief (as is popularly supposed) but rather as a spur to happiness. "So when they see or experience moments of wonderful things, that often comes with the realization that life is fragile and will come to an end.

But that's a good thing. It's a signal of strong emotional health and balance."

This theme was taken up in a cover story published in the *Economist* in December 2010. The article looked at four factors that research has shown to be related to happiness. The first three were gender, personality, and external circumstances. Women are, it seems, slightly happier than men. Extroverts are happier than introverts and, not surprisingly, much happier than those with neurotic tendencies. Personal circumstances of course vary widely, but people who are working tend to be happier than the unemployed. Married people are happier than singles, unless they have small children in the house. While these factors are interesting, the big news was related to the fourth factor they examined—age.

In a paper titled "A Snapshot of the Age Distribution of Psychological Well-Being in the United States," Arthur Sloan and his coauthors explored the relationship between age and the experience of positive and negative emotions. The *Economist* summarized their findings: "Enjoyment and happiness dip in middle age, then pick up; stress rises during the early 20s, then falls sharply; worry peaks in middle age, and falls sharply thereafter; anger declines throughout life; sadness rises slightly in middle age, and falls thereafter."

These findings are at odds with what our culture assures us must be true. Indeed, when people of all ages are asked who is happier, the young or the old, all age groups tell the same story—young people must be happier: they are, after all, young. They are wrong. When the same people are asked how happy they feel, older people routinely report being happier than young people. Nor is this a matter of culture alone. Cross-cultural studies have repeatedly confirmed the existence of the U-bend in countries around the world. Viewed from a global perspective, the *Economist* informs us, the unhappiest age is forty-six. When it comes to happiness, age matters.

Denialists and Realists define aging as an individual enterprise with very individual consequences. Their cultural influence causes us

The Happiness U-Bend
Personal well-being on a scale of 1–10

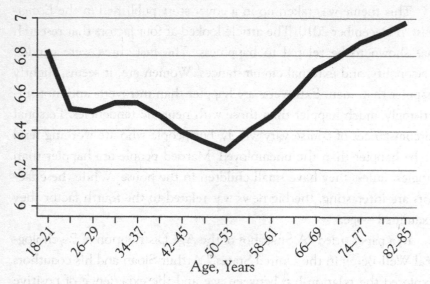

Age, Years

Source: "A Snapshot of the Age Distribution of Psychological Well-Being in the United States" by Arthur Stone

all to be exposed to a steady stream of stories about the "seven steps to a flatter belly" and the "anti-aging miracle that will change your life." Carstensen's research resonates with the Enthusiasts' countercultural view of aging and supports the idea that normal human aging has a virtue that can yield important benefits for people of all ages. The emergence of a new age-positive culture, she writes, could be facilitated by "a large population of emotionally stable, knowledgeable and relatively healthy people." She adds, "The shame is that we're only looking at the problems but we're not looking for opportunities. . . . It's surprising to people when you say something like the number of older people in the world is the only natural resource that's actually growing."

For all their optimism, Enthusiasts are well aware that they live in a world that consistently validates and perpetuates the Denialist and Realist ideologies. Given this stiff cultural headwind, Enthusiasm might seem to have little reason to hope that its perspective will ever become widely shared. Fortunately, the Enthusiast exploration of life beyond adulthood is based on an incisive understanding of human development that has the additional advantage of being supported by the available evidence.

A NEW COUNTERCULTURE

Enthusiasts flatly and uniformly reject contemporary society's slavish devotion to the virtues associated with youth and the young. They are steadily dismantling the conventional wisdom that surrounds adulthood and constructing an alternative language, a vibrant new community, and a set of rituals and ceremonies in its place. The few Realists and Denialists who do become aware of this subculture are quick to criticize what they see as its unwarranted optimism. In fact, Enthusiasts are well aware that aging includes significant decline-related difficulties. They are, however, unwilling to *equate* aging with decline. Members of the Enthusiast subculture are currently experimenting with a broad range of countercultural approaches to life and living that can be described as radical simply because they do not rely on adulthood as the source of worth, dignity, and meaning.

Enthusiasts tend toward a relaxed attitude toward money and material possessions. They value experiences over things and, given the choice, pursue experiences whose rewards come in the form of memories, emotions, and psychological and spiritual insights. Enthusiasts reject the fantasy of human immortality and, in doing so, infuse the decades, years, months, days, and hours that remain to them with depth, richness, and poignancy. They understand that human beings have long relied upon the old to pull hot-blooded youth back from the brink of destruction. If they were to pick a single word to represent their worldview, it would likely be *further*.

This perspective on adulthood recalls elements of the critique developed by and acted upon by members of the Hippie subculture. Although the Second Crucible's Enthusiasts do not look like, act like, or sound like Hippies, they do share the Hippies' rejection of adulthood as the only meaningful framework for organizing one's life and sense of self. The resonance between the two subcultures' foundational beliefs might also explain why the Second Crucible's Enthusiasts have, so far, remained underground. The history of the First Crucible is remarkably clear about what fate lies in store for those who dare to challenge the hegemony of adulthood.

The insights we will need to emerge successfully from the Second Crucible are unlikely to be provided by the Denialists or Realists because their perspectives are founded on the false premise that aging can be stopped, reversed, or even successfully resisted over the long term. Far from the public eye, Enthusiasts are making great progress toward a better understanding of what the end of adulthood means and how outgrowing this life phase can lead individuals toward greater happiness and a greater sense of fulfillment. Even as the media detail every twist and turn in the war on aging, Enthusiasts are fashioning a life beyond adulthood that is based on meaning, worth, and dignity.

BEING AND DOING

In addition to reconsidering the intrinsic merits of age, Enthusiasts are challenging the cult of adulthood's most cherished assumptions about the purposes of human existence. How we experience daily life, our hopes for the future, and our memories of the past are heavily influenced by our understanding of two very simple but vitally important concepts—"doing" and "being."

The conventional understanding of "doing" centers on those actions that allow us to engage with and act upon what is visible and material. Doing things changes the world around us in ways that are measurable and, we hope, to our advantage. Action-oriented adults find time spent doing to be especially important and meaningful. Adulthood's generous supply of energy, ambition, and perseverance lead many adults to center their lives on the power of "doing."

"Being" is a very different thing. We call ourselves human *beings* because we have a unique capacity to see clearly with our eyes closed.

This ability is the taproot of faith, love, poetry, and song. We can *be* in love. We can *be* creative. We can *be* true to ourselves. Complex and mysterious, it is *being* that opens the door to meaning.

Doing and being go together like a wink and a smile, and we experience daily life as an alloy of these two elements. Sometimes doing takes precedence over being: "Sorry, can't go to the party. I've got an exam on Friday." Sometimes being takes precedence over doing. For example, measured solely by the empirical standards of doing, the celebration of a Catholic mass accomplishes almost nothing. Despite its obvious lack of productivity, millions of people find the experience to be intensely moving. The cave paintings at Lascaux feel so wonderfully human because of the skill with which the people who made them blended doing and being. Scientists may analyze the pigments used by the artists, but the beauty lies in the images' exploration of our ancient connection with all that is sacred.

People living in contemporary society are constantly reminded that doing > being. In a survey asking people if they would prefer to (a) have a successful career in shipping, or (b) sit on the dock of a bay and watch the world go by, most would likely prefer the more practical occupation. The Enthusiasts are set apart from the dominant culture in large part by their desire to reverse the cult of adulthood's life equation so that it looks like this: being > doing.

The postwar generation's malignant enlargement of adulthood insists that every race must go to the swift, every contest to the strong, and every victory to the powerful. People have been led to believe that important social issues can be and should be settled exclusively through the exercise of power. The twin dimensions of "what is" and "what ought to be" have collapsed into a tawdry version of the Golden Rule where "he who has the gold, makes the rules." Our well-being and the health of our society are in great need of precisely the being > doing revolution that Enthusiasm is preparing for us all.

THE STRUGGLE AGAINST AGEISM

When the nineteenth-century psychologist William James wrote, "How pleasant is the day when we give up striving to be young—or slender," he was touching on a truth that goes much deeper than perhaps even he realized. Much of the growing sense in late adulthood that life is out of balance is actually derived from an inability to reconcile the divergent demands made by our bodies, our selves, and our culture. James's answer to this riddle was simple: he chose to release his hold on youth and, in doing so, broke free of the hold youth had on him.

Unfortunately, the situation in contemporary society is much less straightforward. Normal changes in our bodies (facial wrinkles, for example) are endowed with seemingly inescapable and highly stigmatizing meanings. The contemporary view of aging alters the perception of self by channeling our minds into a narrow band of experience that is tightly bounded by a morbid fear of disability and dependence. Researchers who ask subjects what it means to "be old" nearly always elicit a litany of negative images and stereotypes.

The nascent Second Crucible subcultures are best understood as distinct strategies for defusing ageism. The Denialists sidestep ageism by refusing to acknowledge the inevitability of aging. They align the self with our ageist culture and, in doing so, become alienated from their own bodies. In the case of the more extreme Denialists, this alienation becomes so intense that it becomes easy to do terrible things to the body, including but not limited to grinding, cutting, peeling, and paralyzing normal, nondiseased tissues.

Realists align the body with the culture. They accept the "fact" that aging is a bad thing and then invest hard work, diligence, and stolid devotion to common sense into the struggle to earn temporary exceptions (I still . . .) to the iron law. In doing so, they inevitably distance the "self" from the body. A Realist will talk freely about the decades he spent working as an engineer at Boeing and will regale listeners with his commonsense approach to "staying active." Rarely, however, will he speak openly of what he might someday become. Realists fear and often openly disdain their future selves. They identify their future self as a traitor, with the only real uncertainty being the date on which the ultimate betrayal will take place.

While the Denialist and Realist perspectives both exacerbate ageism, the Enthusiasts ally the body and the self in opposition to the dominant culture's diminished and demeaning vision of age and aging. Enthusiasts eagerly challenge received attitudes toward aging. For example, some Enthusiasts make a conscious decision to stop coloring their hair and let their "freak flag fly." As we will see later, others are refurbishing and inhabiting historic cultural roles that entitle them to carry on a struggle against the dominant culture and its ageism.

Enthusiasm is a countercultural movement that rejects the narrative of decline and replaces it with a journey of growth and discovery. For now the Enthusiast subculture remains a small, underground movement. If and when it emerges from obscurity, the Second Crucible will take a decisive turn. The cultural history of the past half century suggests that when the bravest among them rise and ask to be recognized, they will be dismissed, mocked, and then attacked. The clash over the meaning and worth of life beyond adulthood will raise the Second Crucible to a white heat, and its outcome will reshape the lives of people of all ages for decades to come.

14

WHAT IF . . . ?

The inevitable movement of a massive and (in demographic terms) extremely dense generation from one life phase to the next cannot help but compel social change. During the First Crucible, the challenge lay in moving nearly one third of the population across what was then a well-marked boundary separating childhood and adulthood. The tempest that accompanied the postwar generation's fitful effort to come of age shook the foundation of our society, and we are still contending with the consequences of that struggle. While the Squares' triumph in the aftermath of the First Crucible seems inevitable to us today, we would be living in a very different world if they had not risen to power.

What if the Activist subculture had emerged as the victor and the postwar generation had applied its culture-distorting power to their priorities, ambitions, quirks, and flaws? Might we all have spent the past forty years immersed within and completely dominated by an earnest campaign for social justice, environmental protection, equality, and peace? Could this effort have made the world a better place? Would the Activists' tendency toward schism have led to the collapse of our political system? Certainly we would all be living different lives, and instead of moldering in obscurity, the *Port Huron Statement* would likely be on display at the National Archives. Its history would be lovingly recalled to hushed schoolchildren and the labor union summer camp where it was written would likely have been named a national historic monument.

This resolutely Activist society is hard to imagine for the same reason that it is hard to "see what's not there." Most people will find even more difficult to imagine what the consequences of a Hippie victory might have been. Post–First Crucible stereotypes of Hippie culture will likely lead some to shudder at the prospect of a patchouli-laced, long-haired dystopia with Abbie Hoffman and Timothy Leary presiding over the Supreme Court. In fact, if the Hippie subculture *had* gone on to define adulthood, it would also have escaped the vituperation and propaganda that Square culture has heaped upon it for decades. Had the Hippies triumphed, their victory would, today, seem just as ordinary and *inevitable* as the Squares' does to us now.

What if the Hippie movement's critical perspective on adulthood had allowed us to avoid the endless striving for effectiveness that has served to define success in contemporary culture? Might we all now be grateful for an adulthood more intrinsically rewarding and vastly less stressful than the one we know today? Love, marriage, work, art, music, and child rearing would all have been remade as the postwar generation enlarged upon both the best and the worst of Hippie culture. In such a world, it is very unlikely that Stephen Covey would have ever become a best-selling author.

We are swiftly approaching a social upheaval that will be far different and, arguably, much more challenging than what we experienced in the 1960s and 1970s. The journey into life beyond adulthood will be especially difficult because our culture offers so few clues to the existence of this frontier or what might lie beyond it. Even so, it must be crossed. Given what lies ahead for all of us, it seems prudent to ask how the still-embryonic Second Crucible subcultures we have just examined might alter our society in the post–Second Crucible years. The unyielding nature of the iron law will, eventually, grant one of these subcultures access to the postwar generation's capacity for culture distortion.

What if the Denialist subculture came to dominate society after the Second Crucible? More precisely, we might ask how a morbidly exaggerated Denialism could remake the lives of people of all ages. A society founded on an abiding hatred for age and aging would raise up its own heroes and celebrities, all of them dedicated to reinforcing a new and much more aggressive regime of ageist beliefs and taboos. As victors in the Second Crucible's *intra*generational struggle, they would be entitled to place their war against aging at the center of American life.

Although our culture's abiding ageism might seem to guarantee a Denialist triumph, such an outcome is not inevitable and, as we will see, may not even be likely. The muted tones and understated ambitions of the Realists might well take precedence in much the same way that the seemingly lackluster Squares emerged as the First Crucible's ultimate victors. What if Realism, and its grudging acceptance of aging, were to reshape our politics, our culture, and our economy? What would its devotion to common sense and its disdain for aging do to our understanding of time, money, meaning, worth, and value?

We must also ask, What if Enthusiasts win the day? How might their open and searching approach to the experience of life beyond adulthood remake the world in which we live? Four decades into a fevered adulthood, the willingness to believe that there might be other ways of living has grown weak. This collapse of possibility will likely lead some to reject the idea of an Enthusiast triumph as untenable. After all, how could something so small, so obscure, and so out of touch with the sterling virtues celebrated by the cult of adulthood have any hope of success? The hopes of the Enthusiasts rest on a single great truth. Adulthood does not and cannot last forever. We stand on the cusp of a new and transformative generational struggle. As always, the postwar generation's trial will be America's as well.

15

AGE WAR

What if the Denialism we know today was subjected to the postwar generation's culture-distorting power? Just as the Square virtues of reliability and hard work were refashioned into a compulsive pursuit of effectiveness, the Denialists' fear of aging would very likely be turned into an obsessive quest for youthful immortality. Instead of "dreaming of Cockaigne," we would find ourselves living in a world obsessed with the fountain of youth.

The straightest path to a Denialist future requires the near-term discovery of a practical, affordable intervention that can actually "stop and reverse aging." Unfortunately, those who claim aging is not inevitable currently rely on exceptionally weak evidence to support their ambition. As richly varied as nature is, a vanishingly small number of its species demonstrate characteristics that could be construed as a conquest of aging. Advocates of anti-aging are, for example, prone to cite *Turritopsis nutricula*'s trick of reverting from its adult, free-swimming form back into its juvenile larval polyp stage as proof that aging can, in fact, be reversed. Replicating this exceptionally rare trait inside a living human being would require a fluency with molecular genetics and cell biology that lies far beyond even the most fevered dreams of biologists working in these fields.

There will be no "anti-aging miracle," at least not in the lifetime of anyone reading this book. Unfortunately, the fact that a concept is unfeasible in technical terms does not release us from the obligation to consider the impact that the *idea* of the thing can have on our culture and society. A Denialist triumph, if it comes, will be contested on cultural rather than scientific grounds.

Because we live in an ageist society, influential voices consistently underestimate the weakness of anti-aging's ideology. Few, for example, are inclined to question the idea that a breakthrough in the technology of anti-aging would have entirely positive consequences for individuals and society as a whole. This presumption of beneficence relies on an especially naive strand of utopian thinking. In fact, history suggests that the discovery of a genuine "fountain of youth" would create a thicket of moral and religious quandaries. Religious belief, in particular, would be sorely tested in a world where a pill allowed people to live a thousand years and be young on the day they die. Would such a miracle be sanctified by religious authorities or condemned as the work of the Devil? We know that a significant number of religious leaders have long opposed the availability of inexpensive and effective birth control; given this history it is hard to imagine them rallying around a technology that would keep their flocks artificially young and healthy—for centuries.

The discovery of a cure for aging, abetted by the law of unintended consequences, would quickly compel scientists to begin work on vastly more effective methods of birth control. After the defeat of aging, the earth would be home to billions of individuals living for hundreds, if not thousands of years in a randy state of youthful fertility. Currently, the US pregnancy rate among women who use oral contraceptives correctly ranges between 2 and 8 percent a year. Without a radical shift toward lifetime abstinence (which is not what the Denialists seem to have in mind), a thousand-year-old woman would likely experience scores of unplanned pregnancies during her lifetime.

If religious leaders did prohibit age control, how could such a ban be enforced? Unlike a prohibition on birth control, it would be easy to identify those who violated the age control ban. In such a world the faithful would grow old and weary while the heretics remain vigorous and young. The promise of an eternity spent in paradise has long served to modify one's conduct in this life. The reality of a never ending youth could easily lead to the extinction of religion as an arbiter of morality in human societies.

When all of the hype and rhetoric are cleared away it becomes clear that Denialism relies on a fanciful approach to science and technology and a savagely self-centered dismissal of the common good. Its current incarnation is sustained entirely by the ability to soothe the tortured psyches of the many millions of people who fear aging more than death.

THE POWER OF BELIEF

Cultural anthropologist Ernest Becker explored the natural and universal desire to escape the limitations imposed by the human body in his Pulitzer Prize–winning book *The Denial of Death*. In its pages he connects our fear of aging and death to our status as "self-conscious" animals. Being aware that, at some indefinite point in the future, our earthly lives will end has always aroused anxiety, and that anxiety has long been a spur to the human exploration of meaning, worth, and altruism.

For millennia people have sought what Becker calls "symbolic immortality" through life projects dedicated to cultural significance. Parenthood, literature, voyages of discovery large and small, and the pursuit of acclaim have all functioned as "immortality projects" through the ages. Indeed, such projects can easily be said to have contributed a large part of what we think of as the best parts of our humanity. We are, all of us, balanced atop a razor-thin wire with the fact of our mortality on one side and the reality-distortion field that is created by our denial of that mortality on the other. Denialism dismisses Becker's symbolic immortality and raises a real, but doomed, physical immortality project in its place.

A heavily fortified post–Second Crucible Denialism would shift the focus of our immortality projects from family and community to ourselves. Its passionate insistence on "never" growing old continues to inflame prejudice against aging and the aged. Although the worship of youth and the pursuit of anti-aging breakthroughs dominate much of the media (and are especially prevalent in publications dedicated to women's interests), a Denialist triumph during the Second Crucible would deliver us into a new era that was *defined*, nearly exclusively, by the fear of growing old.

In the post–First Crucible era, an obscure religious educator with a graduate degree from Brigham Young University became the "voice of a generation." More than anything else, it was Stephen Covey's advocacy on behalf of the Squares' increasingly aggressive ideology that brought him fame in the post–First Crucible years. A Denialist triumph in the Second Crucible would raise up a generation of authorities on anti-aging. They are already out there, preying on fear, most often in pursuit of their own enrichment. A culture founded on the tenets of Denialism would sanctify their exploitation of the fearful. It would venerate them and silence criticism of their work. Like Stephen Covey, they would be elevated to the status of unchallenged, culture-defining gurus.

THE MAKING OF
THE THOUSAND-YEAR-OLD MAN

Deepak Chopra, the man who can be fairly said to have invented modern anti-aging, was born before his time. If his career had coincided with a Denialist triumph, America would have placed him in the firmament of America's greatest thinkers, pioneers, and writers. As it is, he is too old (he turned sixty-seven in 2013) to play the role of anti-aging champion in the Second Crucible era. Although Chopra's work was daring for its time, his belief in transforming the human body "from a material object to a dynamic, flowing process," would be too timid and too conventional to succeed in a truly Denialist culture. This is a case where the students have clearly overtaken their teacher. A Denialist America would need someone far younger and much more audacious than Chopra to lead the way.

Consider the value, in Denialist terms, of a person who is willing to claim that, in the future, "the average age will be in the region of a few thousand years. And remember, none of that time would be lived in frailty and debility and dependence—you would be youthful, both physically and mentally, right up to the day you mis-time the speed of that oncoming lorry." This statement is highly refined, weapons-grade Denialism.

The source of this prediction is an Englishman named Aubrey de Grey. A computer scientist and self-taught biogerontologist, de Grey has developed a research agenda he calls SENS (Strategies for Engineered Negligible Senescence). This research plan will, in his words, "stop people from getting frailer and more prone to life-threatening diseases as they get older, and moreover [will] restore the already frail to youthful vitality."

An article published in the viewpoint section of EMBO (the European Molecular Biology Organization) summarizes de Grey's convoluted proposal:

> To solve the problem of apoptosis in senescent cells, one simply uses "senescence marker-tagged toxins." To cure cancer, one just calls on "total telomerase deletion plus cell therapy." To prop up the failing immune system, one can turn on "IL-7 mediated thymopoiesis." To reverse mitochondrial mutations, one need only use "allotopic [mitochondrial]-coded proteins" of the type favoured by algae. Cell replacement can be accomplished by "stem cell therapy and growth factors," whereas retooling the endocrine system relies on "genetically engineered muscle." Cleavage of

glycosylation crosslinks will involve periodic exposure to phena-
cyldimethylthiazolium chloride, and so on.

This farrago helps sustain de Grey's popular image as the "Cambridge scientist who knows how to help us live forever with telomerase,
allotopic mitochondrial-coded proteins and marker-tagged toxins."
Unfortunately, a rigorous examination by independent scientists who
evaluated SENS found that "each one of the specific proposals that
comprise the SENS agenda is, at our present stage of ignorance, exceptionally optimistic." They concluded that "none of the SENS therapies
has ever been shown to extend the lifespan of any organism, let alone
humans."

The paper reads like a career-ending takedown, but the biologists'
criticism of de Grey's science actually misses the point. The true value
of de Grey to the Denialist-inspired anti-aging movement lies in his
ability to create and sustain a hermetically sealed system of thought. His
is a cultural rather than scientific enterprise. His discussions of "IL-7
mediated thymopoiesis" are intended for people who yearn for a fountain of youth, not professors of cell biology. Indeed, the science, such as
it is, serves as a fig leaf that covers a much more radical intention.

De Grey dismisses his critics for being unfairly biased against anti-
aging. They are, he says, *anti*-anti-aging. "I encounter knee-jerk resistance about the desirability of the ability of postponing aging; and
this arises primarily from the way it is portrayed in the media. In the
media there is a tendency to try to make everyone feel comfortable with
what they are hearing and what they're reading. The whole prospect of
postponing aging doesn't make people feel comfortable because they're
worried that it won't be in time for them." Alone among critics of the
media, he perceives a powerful *pro-aging* bias within contemporary
journalism.

This convoluted and evidence-free line of argument helps to conceal a dangerous fallacy on which a large part of the anti-aging movement depends. People like De Grey routinely conflate an increase in

average human life expectancy with an increase in human longevity or life span. In fact, *life expectancy* refers to the number of years we estimate populations of people will survive. *Longevity* refers to the maximum number of years a human being can live. De Grey is correct when he points out that life expectancy has increased dramatically in the past century. Since 1900, average life expectancy for men increased by more than twenty-five years and for women by more than thirty years. But the largest gains were made before 1950 and were due primarily to decreased mortality among the young, particularly infants.

Extreme Denialists routinely cite this data as reason to hope for similar or even larger increases in life expectancy. What they are reluctant to admit is that during the last hundred years the maximum human life span has not increased by even a single day. True, millions of people have been saved from premature death—but no pill or lotion or therapy has ever stopped, let alone reversed, aging. In fact, Romans who had the good luck to survive infancy and adulthood typically experienced a life span equal to ours today—without the benefit of modern science. Even more ominously, American life *expectancy* actually dropped for the first time in decades in 2010, and children today are the first generation in modern history expected to have a shorter life expectancy than their parents.

Longevity remains a mysterious attribute little understood by modern science, let alone pseudoscientists such as de Grey. We know a mixture of genes, environmental factors, and luck determine our longevity. Of these we can only control environmental factors, and have yet to offer the guarantee of long life. And even if we make stunning breakthroughs in gene therapy or other medical advances, we will not alter the reality that aging is tightly bound to the experience of being *alive*.

While de Grey's faith in a thousand-year life span remains on the fringe of anti-aging ideology, its audacity serves Denialism especially well. His work serves to validate and normalize the less extravagant but still unrealistic claims being made by the cosmetics industry. In a fully Denialist society, the health and beauty industry would move decisively to embrace de Grey's vision and bolster his rhetoric with its own well-tuned media machinery.

Popular women's magazines already brim with anti-aging propaganda. Products with names like Miracle Skin Transformer, Naturopathica Vitamin C Revitalizing Complex, and Intraceuticals Rejuvenate that were big in 2012 would have remained big if they had really worked to "reverse aging." But they didn't and so were overtaken by the next big thing. This unending cycle of hope and disappointment would do much to define the zeitgeist of a Denialist-centered culture. The health and beauty industry would carry much of the load and be joined by powerful allies.

In a Denialist future, doctors would rally to the side of the anti-agers. Despite their professed faith in evidence and the sanctity of unbiased medical research, this would not be the first time that the profession had been seduced by commercial interests and the prevailing prejudices of the time. In the early 1960s, leading physicians and organizations of medical professionals endorsed the use of refined horse urine as a treatment for the normal biological process of menopause. The drug was called Premarin (for "pregnant mares' urine") and the treatment was hormone replacement therapy (HRT). Despite the lack of evidence of safety or effectiveness, Premarin was prescribed routinely to millions of women. The practice was halted when studies belatedly projected that the routine use of HRT led to the premature death of over 100,000 women.

A PLAGUE OF LOCUSTS

Although American society is already home to a powerful bias against age and aging, a Denialist future would use this bigotry to justify a holy war against the old. The ordinary workings of human aging would be redefined as a terrifying malignancy. Wrinkles and "fine lines" would cease to be annoying but harmless folds of skin; they would become fearsome evidence of encroaching decrepitude. The exhibition of common attributes of aging would be cause enough to separate older people from their families and communities. Once committed to institutions designed explicitly to contain them, few if any older people would ever escape.

If the idea of people who show evidence of aging being herded into concentration camps for their own protection seems impossibly dystopian, it shouldn't. America has already constructed an old age archipelago that contains more nursing homes than Starbucks has coffee shops. If aging itself becomes a disease and our culture not only sanctions but propagandizes for and enlists its citizens in a war on aging, no one would be immune. Even young adults would begin to monitor their appearance for signs of incipient aging. The subtlest of these signs would be enough to push young people to submit to ever more dangerous and expensive interventions. Disturbing statistics on the use of plastic surgery already reveal that young people are increasing their use of these procedures faster than any other age group.

In a Denialist future, the faces of older people, their voices, and their stories would vanish completely from our screens and the pages of magazines. As it is, we rarely see, hear, or read about older people, and when we do, they are nearly always presented to us as a fool or as a fortunate soul who happens to look, sound, and act impossibly young. Pro-aging voices and points of view, already rare, would be eliminated.

A society obsessed with the idea that old age is a dreadful and ultimately terrifying disease would be capable of doing terrible things to older people. A subgenre of science fiction/fantasy literature has already envisioned some of the excesses that could become routine in a Denialist future. These authors describe societies in which older people are forced to commit suicide, used as cannon fodder, or reduced to nutrient soup and fed to the young. Kim Stanley Robinson's Mars trilogy explores a future where the invention of abnormal aging catapults the Earth into a disastrous "hypermalthusian" era.

Nonfiction writers who address issues related to aging have had their say as well. The most extreme among them have produced a body of alarmist literature that features titles like *Gray Dawn* and *The Com-*

ing *Generational Storm*. The author of *Gray Dawn* is Peter G. Peterson, the billionaire founder of the Blackstone group. He places the aging of America into this context:

> There's an iceberg dead ahead. It's called global aging, and it threatens to bankrupt the great powers. As the populations of the world's leading economies age and shrink, we will face unprecedented political, economic, and moral challenges. But we are woefully unprepared. Now is the time to ring the alarm bell.

Peterson's focus is budgetary, not cosmetic, and he is "anti-aging" mainly in the sense that he sees the responsibility of caring for frail old people as something that is going to cost too damn much money. Rather than shying away from intergenerational conflict, Peterson embraces its inevitability—if his recommendations are not heeded. "From a society that once felt obliged to endow future generations," he warns, "we have become a society that feels entitled to support from our children. Unless this mindset changes, Americans may one day find that all they really are 'entitled to' is a piece of the national debt." Peterson's agenda has Social Security and Medicare in its crosshairs. Aging, it seems, is a luxury that America can no longer afford.

NASTY, BRUTISH, AND SHORT

The First Crucible's Squares sought a return to a staid and responsible vision of adulthood. Instead, they saw their most cherished beliefs being morphed into a ravenous and ravening adulthood. A Denialist triumph during the Second Crucible could easily transform the natural desire to "look and feel good" and our energetic efforts to create the illusion of youth into something that is dreadful and damaging. Because human beings so often fail to distinguish between the disease and the person living with the disease, the war on aging could very easily disintegrate into a war against the old.

In a Denialist future, the young would be actively encouraged to attack, ostracize, and diminish older people. The very old, in particular, would be stigmatized because their very existence provides irrefutable evidence of the failure of the anti-aging technology. The obsession with youth and the frenzied pursuit of a fountain of youth could inspire culturally sanctioned intergenerational conflict that could easily escalate into a serious and potentially bloody war *between* the ages.

Every human generation has, in its time, yielded (not always happily) to the rising generation following in its wake. The anti-aging movement threatens to break this ancient chain. A manic commitment to an unlimited and unending adulthood and the Denialists' proven capacity to believe in people and ideas that falter under even the most cursory independent inspection disqualify them, or should disqualify them, from leading the way out of the Second Crucible. No matter how willing they are to believe nonsense about living to be a thousand years old and staying young until the day they die, the iron law requires that the Denialists, just like everyone else, wake up each morning one day older.

The passage of time will expose the rapidly diminishing returns that are a property of all anti-aging nostrums. A forty-year-old can trick others into believing he or she is thirty. It is virtually impossible, however, for a sixty-year-old, no matter how much money is spent or how much effort is expended, to pull off the same feat. Despite their current advantaged position in our culture, the most likely outcome for the Denialists consists of a spiraling descent into increasingly ineffective and embarrassing attempts to look and act young. Denialism would condemn the once golden postwar generation to a future in which they become the oblivious objects of mockery and derision.

16

RUST NEVER SLEEPS

While the Denialists' verve and optimism could lead them to victory during the Second Crucible, most people prefer a commonsense approach to solving important problems. During the First Crucible, the Squares offered a stolid, and ultimately very attractive, alternative to the era's discord and discontent. The Realists could well play a similar role in the Second Crucible. Within the postwar generation, Realists are already establishing a reputation for having a no-frills, no-nonsense approach to age and aging. Their earnest commitment to sensible shoes, regular exercise, and plenty of fiber in one's diet won't ever be hailed as "revolutionary," but they are eminently reasonable. Especially when compared to the Denialists' agitated optimism, the Realists' measured approach to forestalling the end of adulthood can be quite comforting. Given these strengths it is reasonable to ask what might happen if the postwar generation magnified the Realist worldview in much the same way that the Squares enlarged upon adulthood in the aftermath of the First Crucible.

Understanding what a Realist future might entail requires an appreciation for the role pessimism plays in their worldview. Research conducted by psychologist Martin Seligman has shown that the most pessimistic people among us are also among the most realistic. The opposite is also true. Denialists are full-blooded optimists who also adhere to the unrealistic belief that a cure for aging is just around the corner. A magnified version of Realism would also, by necessity, amplify the subculture's foundational pessimism. A Realist future would bring with it a searing conflict between a national spirit of optimism and a generational dismissal of life beyond adulthood.

The Realists' unflinching pessimism causes them to suffer much more aging-related anxiety than Denialists, who find refuge in their faith that a medical breakthrough will surely arrive just in time to save them from old age. Realist rhetoric, such as it is, lacks punch, energy, and daring. The Denialists proclaim their faith in a thousand-year life span. Realists offer a dutiful vision of "successful aging," that, at its best, is capable only of delaying and minimizing the worst parts of aging. Culturally speaking, this is very thin gruel. A magnified version of Realism would be most likely to offer us all the excitement of wet socks.

Historically, AARP's magazine (aka *The Magazine*) has been the best place to explore the Realists' brand of age resistance. *The Magazine*'s advocacy for social programs that benefit older people is real and powerful, and its writers and editors have shown little tolerance for Denialist fantasies. Subscribers look for and get practical strategies for better living in late adulthood. The articles mostly feature headlines like these:

"Juices or Smoothies: Which Is the Healthier Choice?"
"Unplug and Renew with a Relaxing Vacation"
"Staying in Touch Is Good for Your Health"

The Magazine and its readers also have a special fondness for lists.

"Five Shopping Tips That Will Save You Money"
"Eight Inexpensive Ways to Winterize Your Home"
"Five Great Immune-Boosting Foods"

Nearly every issue features on the cover a man or woman who is at least semifamous. As befits the purpose of *The Magazine*, starlets need not apply. Instead, we are offered models who blend youthful vigor with a gray-templed, gently wrinkled "maturity." Once a celebrity passes this delicate point, he or she disappears and is never seen or heard from again. Issue after issue, *The Magazine*'s soft-focus cover portraits capture the essence of Realism, perfectly.

Just as the Squares accepted the adulthood that was offered to them during the First Crucible, Realists endorse the commonsense notion that simple diligence offers the best hope of delaying or deflecting aging. They harbor no illusions about defeating their foe and know very well what lies ahead of them. An amplified Realism would, not surprisingly, enlarge the role that failure plays in the process of aging. Whereas the Denialists see aging as an "alien invasion" and rail against it as something that is being done *to* them, Realists internalize the blame. They say, mournfully, "I used to walk five miles a day, but after I broke my hip, well . . ." Temporary success is available but only to those who are willing to work at eating better, exercising, and plowing through books of word and number puzzles. Assuming the blame for one's inevitable and ultimate failure is a heavy burden for any individual to carry. Indeed, it is hard to imagine the postwar generation willingly shouldering such a load.

SCROLLING

There is a commonly practiced but little recognized strategy for dealing with the pessimism and guilt that lurk beneath Realism's commonsense exterior. It is called "scrolling," and it allows Realists to maintain the illusion that we can pause aging at just the right moment. A look back at Jane Fonda's career as an actress, activist, and exercise guru can illustrate how scrolling works. Born the daughter of American acting royalty in 1937, she achieved stardom when her first movie *Tall Story* premiered in 1960. At the height of the First Crucible, her opposition to the war in Vietnam led her to visit Hanoi. She went on the radio to condemn American political and military leaders as "war criminals" and was also photographed sitting on an antiaircraft battery. The visit earned her the enmity of the Squares along with the nickname "Hanoi Jane."

The political fallout led to Fonda's being "gray-listed" in Hollywood; she worked only intermittently in the 1970s. She won her second Best Actress Oscar in 1979 for the film *Coming Home*. She also starred in the hit *The China Syndrome* as reporter Kimberly Wells. Injured during filming, she had to give up her usual ballet classes and started working with future business partner Leni Cazden. Before long the Leni Cazden workout became the Jane Fonda Workout. The release of *Jane Fonda's Workout Book* hit a generational bull's-eye: it was among the top five nonfiction bestsellers for sixteen months and has since sold 17 million copies. On April 24, 1982, Fonda released her video workout, launching an empire of home-video aerobics. The forty-five-year-old Fonda was reborn as an exercise guru.

Fonda's resurgence in the 1980s included seven major motion picture roles and twenty-three workout videos, the last of which was released in 1995, just two years shy of her sixtieth birthday. She then retired from both the film and fitness industry to enjoy more time with her new husband Ted Turner.

After a fifteen-year hiatus, Fonda announced her return to the world of aerobics with a new fitness DVD in 2011. In the intervening years she had undergone one hip replacement and a knee surgery and been diagnosed with osteoarthritis.

This First Crucible celebrity's *continuing* commitment to fitness thrilled the folks at AARP, who tweeted the news: "Jane Fonda to release new workout videos for aging baby boomers. Nice!" On her blog JaneFonda.com she offers visitors this sort of advice: "Exercise those smile muscles and feel your best both mentally and physically. . . . Tune in to BeFit for more Prime Time Health Tips from Jane Fonda every

Tuesday." AARP's enthusiasm for Fonda's advice was, of course, based on common sense. It really is better to age as a person who is physically fit, and people who smile really do feel better than those who frown. It is also true that regular exercise adds "years to life and life to years."

Jane Fonda is very likely to continue exercising and might even release a new exercise program when she hits ninety in 2027. She will not, however, be treated to a cover story in *The Magazine*. Despite her status as a First Crucible celebrity, despite her nonagenarian "buns of steel," she will be scrolled into obscurity. Once Jane Fonda can no longer emulate the appearance and actions of a person living in late adulthood, she will disappear and so will her videos and exercise routines.

It is in this vanishing act that we begin to identify the contours of a magnified Realist future. Because they lack the Denialists' sunny capacity for refusing to accept aging, Realists need extra help reconciling the *reality* of aging with their *desire* to remain adults. When Realists insist on applying the test of "still" to themselves and others, they unwittingly foster the phenomenon of scrolling. Realism develops and manicures an endless series of perfectly age-dusted celebrities to replace the ones who have disappeared. The faces change but the image of a singular, abiding resistance to age endures.

If scrolling only concerned celebrities with books and movies to sell, it would be more of a curiosity than a problem. Once we become aware of it, however, it is easy to see the phenomenon in everyday life. People we worked with for years retire and disappear from our lives. We remember that nice guy with the fishing photos and the grandkids and wonder, sometimes years later, Where is he now? The older woman who lived down the block and was so nice to the kids vanishes one day and is never heard from again. An obituary catches us by surprise as we read about someone we once knew well but haven't thought of in years. Out of sight. Out of mind.

The postwar generation uses scrolling to alleviate its growing pes-

simism about the reality of aging. In its most benign form, it is responsible for the ubiquitous photos of the physically attractive, relentlessly
cheerful couple who always seem to be walking on a beach. Over the
decades, the older models have scrolled off the bottom of the screen
while their younger versions have appeared at the top. This is how
advertisers are able to ensure that the couples who are pitching their
products to "mature" audiences will always be just the right age.

Retirement communities also make heavy use of this approach
and for good reason. They have long served as Realist strongholds, and
those who enter into this world quickly encounter much more aggressive forms of scrolling. Despite their rhetoric (and that nice couple
pictured in the brochure), these "communities" often operate as rigidly
segregated societies that practice a highly evolved form of discrimination. The bias, in this case, has little to do with age and a great deal
to do with the ability to function as an independent adult. The spry
centenarian is celebrated as a respected member of the community in
a way that the sixty-year-old living with dementia can never be. Inside
these miniature worlds a byzantine set of rules and expectations gov-
erns where people can exercise, where they can eat, and where they
must live. Independent residents are entitled to take their meals in the
main dining room—until they require such assistance as a wheelchair,
at which point they are scrolled to another, less desirable dining area.
Some retirement communities have published maps of their campuses
that lavishly detail the health and wellness center and scroll the community's nursing home right off the page.

A Realist victory in the Second Crucible will intensify scrolling and
apply it on a culture-wide scale. Just as the postwar generation's manic
adulthood spared no one, the practice of scrolling will be adopted by
members of every generation. During the long decades of their adult
preeminence, the postwar generation became so accustomed to being
powerful *actors* that they forgot how easily they could be acted upon.
Here lies the essential flaw of Realism. Its proponents believe that their

diligence, good habits, vitamins, and exercise will protect *them* from irrelevance. They presume that they will always be the ones doing the scrolling and never the ones being scrolled.

Many in the postwar generation have already had the experience of being in a mixed-age business meeting or social gathering where someone makes a cultural reference or uses a catchphrase from a television program that dates back a half century or more. These bits of cultural flotsam are instantly recognized and understood by their generational peers while the younger people in the room mostly nod without understanding. The humor of "Sock it to me!" is lost on a majority of Americans living today. First Crucible slang is as alien to young people today as "twenty-three skiddoo!" was to the postwar generation during its own youth. Meanwhile phrases like "I, for one, welcome our new insect overlords" and "All your base are belong to us" stump the many millions who never missed an episode of *Rowan and Martin's Laugh-In*. The postwar generation is already being scrolled off the pop culture screen.

Placed in the hands of America's rising generations, scrolling will be used for purposes very different from what the Realists might intend, or desire. It is, after all, an instrument of social control that privileges those who look and act younger over those who look and act older. Realism's energetic fatalism actually entitles the young to set the postwar generation aside as soon as its members fail to keep pace. Scrolling is meant to comfort those who fear age by making the old disappear, but it also provides the rising generations with the means to carry out a culturally sanctioned coup against the postwar generation and its titanic adulthood. If this seems harsh or unlikely, it is worth remembering that this is simply a generational version of the fate that already awaits Jane Fonda and her exercise videos.

Those who once imagined themselves to be stardust would be fed, medicated, and sheltered while the generation they belong to fades into a silent, colorless irrelevance. Realism seems safe. It seems like common sense. It rejects the bizarre rhetoric and fantasies of the Denialists. It treasures sensible shoes, tax tips, flax seed, bran, and brain calisthenics. Beneath this bland surface, however, lies a fear of and disdain for aging that rivals that of the Denialists. A Realist victory would pave a road leading straight to the postwar generation's lonely tombstone. Those few who came to visit might read its epitaph, "Rust never sleeps."

17

IN THE BALANCE

If the vision of a Denialist or Realist outcome from the Second Crucible seems less than appetizing, there is a third possibility. The Enthusiast subculture remains at the time of this writing a small, underground movement, in large part because it embraces aging in ways that Denialists and Realists find almost impossible to believe. Might the Enthusiasts emerge from obscurity and become the dominant cultural force that shapes life beyond adulthood? Given that they exist within an ageist society, the Enthusiasts, along with their beliefs and practices, will likely be considered to be countercultural (perhaps dangerously so), if and when they do come to wider attention.

Enthusiasts gleefully violate the dominant understandings of age and aging that pervade American society, and they endorse a unique and uniquely powerful concept of "life beyond adulthood." They draw inspiration for their vision from people and cultures around the world and throughout history. Viewed from this global perspective, the Enthusiasts are, strange as this may seem, something akin to the First

Crucible's Squares. Against all odds and in the face of ageist bigotry, the Enthusiasts can sing the words "Wouldn't it be nice if we were older . . ." and mean them.

The Enthusiasts search for and work to develop a deep, historical understanding of life beyond adulthood. This is something that our society needs but cannot yet appreciate. Although the Enthusiasts' belief that growth can and should continue across the life span is rarely encountered outside this subculture, an abundance of research supports their perspective. The idea that human beings can outgrow adulthood is at once ancient and noble. The Enthusiasts take the countercultural notion that older people need to grow and radicalize it by insisting that the development of a healthy society is dependent on such growth. Enthusiasts are eager to enter into and fully inhabit an old age they have spent a lifetime constructing.

This desire to outgrow adulthood is powerful, normal, and so far at least, uncommon. It is this frustrated and unacknowledged impulse that accounts for so much of the postwar generation's foreboding sense that life is out of balance. If the Enthusiasts came to dominate the post–Second Crucible era, they would serve as a massive, magnified and amplified cultural counterweight to the hyperkinetic, productivity-driven cult of adulthood.

The conventional narrative surrounding the postwar generation concentrates on its supposed idyllic childhood and dalliance with dissent, but the First Crucible's icons (many of whom continue to play a role in public life) will have little to do with the legacy of their generation. The misplaced emphasis on youth and a hardened nostalgia have combined to create a cultural prison from which the Enthusiasts fully intend to escape. Its walls must be breached if the postwar generation is ever to find its way to the freedom it needs to once again grow, to discover, to tackle and solve our most important and pressing problems.

A RUNAWAY TRAIN

It's been 65 million years since Earth's last great extinction event. The culprit on that occasion was a six-mile-wide meteor that crashed into the sea near what is now the location of the Mexican town of Chicxulub. For centuries after the impact, Earth was rocked by volcanic eruptions, firestorms, earthquakes, and tsunamis, and nearly 75 percent of all living species perished. Hard times.

When, in 1961, a group of postwar generation Activists gathered at a tumbledown lakeside camp to craft what became known as the *Port Huron Statement*, they lamented, "A shell of moral callous [sic] separates the citizen from sensitivity of the common peril: this is the result of a lifetime saturation with horror." The reference is to living in the shadow of a nuclear cold war. The youthquake that once seemed to promise a new era of peace and justice was quickly curdled by the ongoing militarization of society and our economy.

On a cultural level, we have also spent decades living, largely without protest, under the suffocating power of the postwar generation's cult of adulthood. We have watched as the dangerous trends identified by the authors of the *Port Huron Statement* were magnified by the workings of their own generation. Although threat of immediate nuclear annihilation has receded in the years since the *Port Huron Statement*, other equally dangerous and much less fixable global threats have taken its place. In May of 2011, a group of highly respected paleontologists published an article claiming that the planet's sixth mass extinction is now under way. "The modern global mass extinction is a largely unaddressed hazard of climate change and human activities." This time around it is humanity that is playing the role of the death-dealing space rock.

Nor are these imbalances merely political or technological issues. We live in thrall to a savage doctrine of independence. From cradle to grave we are taught that there is no collective action that can or should be undertaken by any group—unless it can be shown to turn a profit. During the long reign of the postwar generation's adulthood, the American gospel of wealth cast off all residual restraints and became a domineering, soul-searing ideology. To a degree unprecedented in American history, people believe that great wealth is itself evidence of worthiness. The poor, if and when they come to the attention of the powerful, are dismissed as being undeserving of support or even simple compassion. In Ayn Rand's terms (much aped by her contemporary fans), half the country now consists of ungrateful "moochers and looters." Our plutocracy has disposed of quaint notions of reciprocal obligation and the common good and pledged itself exclusively to its own further enrichment. This venality would have horrified the students who authored the *Port Huron Statement*, if they had been able to imagine such a thing happening on American soil.

For all these reasons, it is understandably hard to believe that a generation whose manic adulthood has served so well and so long as an instrument of destruction could, in its final decades, become a force for good. It is in the end of the postwar generation's adulthood (rather than its beginning) that we can find the seeds of redemption and renewal. The end of the postwar generation's adulthood will offer one last chance to repair the damage that has been done.

The idea that adulthood and the vigor and power of adults are the only forces capable of changing our world is gradually being exposed as a dangerous and damaging error. The passage of time will assert its dominion over our society. Its iron law is and will remain more powerful even than the culture-distorting force of the postwar generation. It is time that, each and every day, moves the once immovable postwar generation one day closer to a new way of living.

Millions of people can sense the power of this transition but for most the feeling remains diffuse and undefined. All they can say is that life is somehow out of balance. Koyaanisqatsi. People find themselves living in a way that calls for a new way of living but cannot explain why this is so or what can be done to restore a sense of balance. Few outside of the Enthusiast subculture are able to connect the personal sensation of koyaanisqatsi to the massive global imbalances that are pulling life on Earth out of balance. Our families, our communities, and our planet are being seriously damaged by a malignant enlargement of adulthood.

Throughout history, societies have relied upon elders and elderhood to serve as a check on the excesses of adulthood. Unfortunately for us all we are living in a time when the world is being ruled by adults without elders' supervision. We are all on board this runaway train. We are all witness to the habitat destruction, the systematic exploitation of the young and the vulnerable, the warehousing of the old, the escalation of income inequality, and the rise of a global plutocracy. We are all being governed by manic adulthood that has distorted historic understandings of time, money, childhood, and relationships.

The most important question facing American society and culture today is, Where will we find the elders we need to pull us all back from the brink of destruction?

18

2011

January

4 Tunisian street vendor Mohamed Bouazizi dies after setting himself on fire, sparking antigovernment protests in Tunisia and later other Arab nations. These protests become known collectively as the Arab Spring. **6** For the second time in as many years, Charles Manson is found to have a cell phone in his possession. Prison spokesman Terry Thornton offers no details about where Manson got the phone or whom he might have called. **8** A gunman opens fire on a public meeting held in a supermarket parking lot in Casas Adobes, near Tucson, Arizona. US Representative Gabrielle Giffords is shot in the head but survives. Six others are killed. **9 Tom** *lies in bed, alone and heartbroken. This is his sixty-fifth birthday and, for the first time in his life, his mother forgot to make a cake for him. The doctor says that she has Lewy body dementia.* **12 Flo Marsh**'s *nephew Floyd emails her. "Hey, I'm looking to make a move to LA, Any chance I could stay with you for a while?" Alice loves the idea.* **14** The movie *Plastic Planet* is released. It examines how plastic affects our bodies and the health of future generations. **24 Tom**'s *sister, Vicky, drives* *down from Verona, where she lives and runs a beauty shop. She looks after her mother while Tom sits at the bar at the Hofbräu.* **25** *Before she leaves, she tells Tom, "I'll be down next weekend—after work."* **26 Melanie** *has been flying with Continental Airlines for twenty years. She is a shop steward for her union and likes her work. She and Kevin endured three painful miscarriages before they decided they were not meant to have children.*

February

11 Egyptian president Hosni Mubarak resigns after widespread protests calling for his departure. The military declares that it will hold power until a general election can be held. **13** Lady Gaga releases "Born This Way" as a single.

March

3 A group of biologists announce in the science journal *Nature* that the sixth great extinction event is under way. **10 Tom** *returns from the barn and finds his mom on the floor of the kitchen. He calls 911.* **11** The most powerful earthquake ever known to hit Japan generates a tsunami that reaches heights of up to 133 feet. **15 Tom's** *mother is moved to the ICU and put on a ventilator; the doctor tells him that there is nothing more they can do. The minister from the Methodist church arrives. They pray. Tom decides that his mother wouldn't want any "heroic" measures. He tells the doctor that it is okay to "unplug" the ventilator.* **28 Tom's** *mother is buried in the family plot next to her husband and little Wayne. The fraternal organization Eastern Star puts on a lunch in her honor; twelve women attend.* **29** An estimated 2 billion people watch the wedding of Prince William, Duke of Cambridge, and Catherine Middleton at Westminster Abbey in London.

April

1 The US National Highway Traffic Safety Administration reports 32,788 traffic deaths, the lowest annual number since 1949. **7** In an interview on MSNBC, Donald Trump says of President Obama, "His grandmother in Kenya said he was born in Kenya, and she was there and witnessed the birth. He doesn't have a birth certificate or he hasn't shown it." He continues, "He has what's called a certificate of live birth. That is something that's easy to get. When you want a birth certificate, it's hard to get." **8 Flo** *leans against the kitchen counter and smiles. Floyd is sitting at the kitchen table entertaining her friends with stories from his days in Alpha Phi Alpha. He is, she thinks, a good man, and seeing him so bright and happy makes her wonder what it would have been like if she had had a son of her own.* **9** Hugh Hefner, the creator of *Playboy*, turns eighty-five. **22 Tom** *goes to the mailbox expecting to find the usual assortment of bills and junk mail. He finds a check for life insurance he didn't know his mother had. The check is for $5,000.* **30** *Tom buys his first computer and has a man come out to install a satellite dish so he can get the Internet. He patches the roof on the double-wide.*

May

1 President Barack Obama announces that Osama bin Laden has been killed during an American military operation in Pakistan. **13 Tom** *discovers Facebook. He finds Marsha's page. It is marked as private. He sends a friend request and, after a couple of days, she accepts. She is a dermatologist living in LA; her husband is a neurosurgeon. They have a four-year-old son named Wayne.* **14 Melanie** *and Kevin arrive at Yellowstone for a long-delayed vacation. They take long walks and talk about their future. The work they have done for so many years no longer seems to suit them. It's time, they agree, for something new, but neither of them can say what that might be.* **18 Flo** *takes a call from a headhunter. She gets up and closes her office door. He talks to Flo at length about a position as a dean at Columbia.* **25** *She* *has hidden news of the call from Alice for the past week. An unaccustomed heaviness hangs over the house. Flo wants the position as dean but knows that Alice will be opposed.* 28 Flo *and Alice fight bitterly over the job prospect in New York. Flo's nephew slips out of the house, unnoticed.*

June

3 Melanie *attends a ceremony celebrating twenty years of service to Continental Airlines.* 8 Melanie *overhears two passengers talking about the Grassroots Festival of Music and Dance. It seems like something she and Kevin would like. She calls him and he loves the idea. Continental flies to Ithaca, New York. If they can get the time off, they decide to go.* 15 Flo *breaks the news to Alice, who sobs, "What about our house? What about our friends?" Flo begs Alice to understand that she has spent her entire life preparing for this moment. She owes it to . . . people . . . to reach for this brass ring. Alice asks, "Don't you owe me anything?"* 17 Floyd *tells* Flo *and Alice that he's found a place to live. He moves out.* 20 Tom *fiddles with his webcam and then connects with his daughter on Skype. He meets his son-in-law and grandson for the first time.* 29 An election decides that the AFA will represent all the flight attendants of the newly merged United Airlines–Continental operation.

July

8 *Atlantis*, the last of NASA's operational space shuttles, launches for the final time. 9 Tom's *daughter emails him. "Hey Dad, what would you think about coming out here and spending a little time with us?" He replies, "Can't afford it, hon." She writes back, "It's our treat."* 21 Space Shuttle *Atlantis* lands at the Kennedy Space Center, thus concluding NASA's space shuttle program. 23 Rita *fights traffic all the way to the airport. She is heading out on what both she and Bob know will be a grueling swing through Asia.* 24 New York becomes the fifth and largest state to legalize same-sex marriages.

August

9 Flo *books her flight to New York while Alice is sleeping in the next room.*
10 Tom *climbs into his rusty pickup truck and drives three and a half hours to
Newark Airport. He paces nervously at the gate until his flight is called. He
boards Continental 17 to LA. It is his first flight since he returned home from
Vietnam.* **13** Construction of the Berlin Wall began fifty years ago today.
14 Flo *comes into the kitchen and tells Alice that she is leaving for New York
for the interview. Alice does not respond. Flo loads a suitcase into the car and
drives herself to the airport.* **14 Tom**'s *daughter bids him farewell at security,
and he hugs her close as he whispers "I love you" into her ear. He feels that
his visit with her has opened a new chapter in his life.* **14** *After the flight from
Shanghai lands at LAX, Rita retreats to the Continental Club. She tries to
work but is too jet-lagged to concentrate. Instead she stares listlessly at a blar-
ing television. When her flight to Newark is called, she gathers her belongings
and walks to the gate just as first class is being boarded.* **14 Melanie** *is working as the lead flight attendant on the red-eye from LA to Newark. Kevin
will be coming in from Houston. They'll take the afternoon flight to Ithaca.*
15 Rita *is startled awake when the wheels of Continental flight 107 touch
down at Newark's Liberty International Airport, on schedule, at 5:35 a.m.
eastern daylight time. She leans forward and rubs the back of her neck. She
knows, from long experience, that nothing she can do will relieve the dull ache
in her temples. Rita trudges up the Jetway, retrieves her luggage, and drives
home. The house is empty, as she knew it would be. Bob is at work. The
twins are away at college.* **16 Flo** *spends the day in interviews and leaves the
campus feeling that she is likely to be a finalist for the position. It is perfect for
her. Before heading back to the airport, she wanders aimlessly through Central Park. The energy of the city feels good to her. She could live here.* **18 Flo**
*returns home. The house is quiet but tension remains. There is a change
coming; they can both feel it.* **18 Melanie** *and Kevin are pressed up against
the front of the infield where Donna the Buffalo is playing the festival's closing show. They are ecstatic: the music, the food, the people, the freedom, the
energy all seem to fit them so perfectly. The sun is rising when they lie down*

to sleep and they promise each other that they will come back. **21 Tom** *quits drinking.*

September

14 Flo *finds an email from the search committee in her inbox. She hesitates, then opens it. "We are pleased to inform you that you are one of three finalists for the position as dean." She gets up from her computer and walks into the kitchen, where her friends are sitting at the table laughing and talking. She knows and loves them and they love her. Alice smiles weakly and takes Flo's hand tentatively into hers. When the moment passes, Flo excuses herself and returns to her computer. Taking a deep breath, she clicks reply and types, "I am honored to be chosen as a finalist but I have decided not to pursue the selection process further." She clicks send.* **17** The Occupy Wall Street protest gets under way in Zuccotti Park, near New York's Financial District. **25** Google and the Israel Museum publish the digital Dead Sea Scrolls online. The new website gives users access to searchable, fast-loading, high-resolution images of the scrolls, explanatory videos, and background information.

October

9 Heavyweight boxing champion Leon Spinks marries his longtime girlfriend, Brenda Glur, in Las Vegas. Friend of the couple Tony Orlando serves as best man. **13** Aubrey de Grey speaks before a packed auditorium at the Johns Hopkins University in Baltimore. **13 Melanie** *and Kevin return to Ithaca, this time for a week. They have done their research in advance. They visit the Finger Lakes School of Massage together and imagine what a new career in the healing arts might feel like. It feels right.* **22 Rita** *somewhat nervously makes her first appointment with the dermatologist her friends are raving about. The woman is, she has been told, a magician. She paces in the waiting room and briefly considers leaving before her name is called. In the exam room the doctor gives practiced answers to Rita's ques-*

tions. They both know that she is going to go ahead. After being reassured that the injections feel "like having your eyebrows plucked," Rita signs the consent form. **25** **Rita**'s *husband Bob returns home from a trip and as soon as he sees her says, "Hey, you look great!"* **31** This is the symbolic date the UN selected to mark the point when the global population reaches 7 billion.

November

22 *At Thanksgiving,* **Flo** *toasts Alice and acknowledges that she had lost sight of how important her wife, her friends, and her home were to her. "For these things, and so much more, I am truly grateful."* **22** **Rita** *and Bob's twins are home for Thanksgiving. They both know immediately that their mother is getting Botoxed. They roll their eyes but do not laugh.* **30** United Airlines completes its takeover of Continental. Continental Airlines ceases to exist as a separate air carrier.

December

5 **Melanie** *and Kevin can't escape the feeling that something has been lost. The merger with United has been bumpy, to say the least. "It's not like it used to be." They had been thinking about working another ten years before retiring, but an offer comes around from the company. They can get out early, much earlier than they thought. They take it.* **15** The United States formally declares an end to the Iraq War. **29** **Melanie** *and Kevin receive an email informing them that they have both been accepted to the School of Massage Therapy. They will start in the fall of 2012. That evening they huddle close together with their laptop in bed and pore over real estate listings. They will sell their condo in Houston and buy a house, a nice little house, in Ithaca.*

PART IV

LIFE BEYOND ADULTHOOD

19

I AM . . .

I am, among other things, a father, a husband, a farmer, a writer, a musician, and a teller of stories. I am also a physician, a geriatrician—a specialist in the care of the old. The first half of my working life was spent largely in the company of very old people, and these elders helped me grasp a handful of valuable truths about life, love, and happiness. They showed me how, given sufficient time, even the smallest changes can remake us. They insisted that I continue to grow. Few things, in my experience, are more soulful and more fruitful than being a patient and faithful companion of the very old, the frail, and the infirm. My patients helped me accept who I was, who I am, and who I am becoming.

The elders I have known inspired all that I have written in the preceding chapters, but those pages also contain a note of caution. I have been careful to couch my discussion of the postwar generation's past and future in terms that carry my meaning while at the same time doing what I could to avoid arousing the reader's natural wariness about issues related to age and aging. For those who have made it this far and are willing to go farther yet, I will make a simple promise. In the chapters

that follow, I will surrender caution and introduce you without reservation to a secret world. It is a place where elders hold their heads high,
where age functions as a virtue that is capable of great and wondrous
things, where the slings and arrows of ageism fall harmlessly to the
ground.

Prejudice and bigotry of all kinds take root where people fail to
understand the experience of others as *individuals*. People who casually
dismiss the humanity of others come to rely on the most superficial and
unrevealing of signs. Skin color, accent, and gender are used in this
context and made the basis of unjust and unwarranted assumptions
about others. American society has made strides toward addressing the
morbid flaws of racism and sexism (and we have very far to go), but the
struggle against ageism is just beginning.

The previous chapters offer a context that allows us to redefine
aging from an issue that involves "them" to an issue that involves "us."
But what can we say about the elders? What do we know about the
largely unexplored realm which they inhabit? How do elders (generally) understand and use concepts like time, money, spirituality, meaning, worth, and relationships? The world of the elder and the terrain of
elderhood differ from the experience of living as an adult in much the
same way that adulthood differs from childhood. The child peers into
adulthood and gains only the most rudimentary understanding of what
it is like. We can do better.

I am the ambassador from elderhood, and this section is dedicated
to those readers with the courage and curiosity necessary to cast off (at
least for the moment) the ageist bigotry that surrounds us and to enter
(for a little while) into a time and place where age and aging stand
alongside that which is right and good and true.

20

THE FIRST
GRANDMOTHER

Our opposable thumbs, quirky two-legged gait, and excessively large heads are not the only features that distinguish our species. Human beings also possess a highly distinctive life cycle. Regardless of their life span, all nonhuman mammals make do with just two life stages. The first, juvenile phase is a time of growth and development; the second, an adult phase that commences with reproductive maturity.

Unlike all other living creatures, human beings possess a remarkable third age, a life beyond adulthood. While aging is commonly, and wrongly, thought to begin at birth, it actually gets under way as soon as full reproductive maturity has been established. The typical human begins aging very soon after his or her twenty-eighth birthday. The aging process then unfolds in a linear and highly predictable fashion for the remainder of our lives. Aging isn't the exception to the human experience, it's the rule. Our third age, which transcends and supersedes adulthood, ranks as one of humanity's least acknowledged and most important attributes. Around the world and through history, the expansion of human longevity and the ability to make fruitful use of old age has been a cornerstone of human progress.

People understand that telling an adult that he is "acting like a child" is derogatory and hurtful. At the very least, good manners require us to be truthful when we refer to others by the life phase they inhabit. A person who has yet to reach maturity is living in childhood and is rightly called a child. A person who has "come of age" and is living in adulthood should be called an adult. A person who has outgrown adulthood has become an elder living in elderhood. This evolution is related to but not defined by one's chronological age. More than anything else, our journey across the life cycle relies upon our capacity for growth and development. Elders are unique among all earth's living creatures in the genius they apply to finding and making use of the virtues that are hidden inside of aging.

We are the only species on Earth that makes fire, fashions wheels, and grows old. Unlike all other mammals, we have been molded and refined not just by parents but also, crucially, by grandparents. Although we rarely think of ourselves this way, we are the descendants of perhaps as many as two thousand generations of grandparents. As such we are the richly entitled heirs to an ancient tradition that has provided us with a universe of language, myth, faith, ritual, and ceremony. All these gifts came to us down through the ages and across an unbroken chain of elders. In ways we barely understand, and certainly do not appreciate, life beyond adulthood has become essential to our humanity.

University of Utah anthropologists Kristen Hawkes and James O'Connell and UCLA anthropologist Nicholas Blurton Jones have proposed a "grandmother hypothesis" to help explain humanity's unique approach to intergenerational interdependence. During the 1980s, Hawkes and O'Connell lived and foraged with Tanzania's Hazda hunter-gatherers. They observed older women collecting food for their grandchildren. While this behavior may seem perfectly ordinary (Spoil the grandchildren!), they speculated that it might actually represent one of the most important distinguishing characteristics that separates humans from their primate cousins. All other apes, after all, collect food only for themselves after they are weaned.

Their hypothesis works like this: When grandmothers help feed their weaned but not yet mature grandchildren, their daughters can wean their young more quickly and, therefore, produce more children at shorter intervals. The very tangible value of this assistance resulted in the development of a hugely expanded postmenopausal life span. In evolutionary terms, success breeds success. The first grandmother's daughter had more children than other women, and when those children grew up, they passed their longevity genes to their children and grandchildren. And so on and so on.

According to Professor Hawkes, "In other great apes, females, if they make it to adulthood, they usually die in their childbearing years." It is during adulthood that our primate cousins become "old, frail and gray and less able . . . all the things that we associate with old age." Human beings changed primate aging into human aging. "It happens to all of us, but it happens slower and later to us compared to the other great apes." The grandmother hypothesis helps explain how we gradually found the virtues hidden within the necessity of aging. Dr. Hawkes and her colleagues tie grandmothering and humanity's spectacular longevity together: "When there's grandmothering, that makes more grandmothers. And it makes longevity increase from an apelike range into a humanlike range."

While historians dote upon emperors, kings, and generals, it is actually our grandmothers who made us what we are today. A full appreciation of the remarkable link between grandmothering and longevity makes the contemporary fascination with youth seem as bizarre as a decision to arbitrarily abandon the use of fire, shiver in the cold, dark night, and eat our meat raw. Around the world and through history in countless different ways, human elders have been esteemed for the value they have contributed to their families, their tribes, and even their nations. That our society could so easily reduce them to objects of pity or recipients of a grudging charity says much more about the young than it does about the old.

The postwar generation's cult of adulthood has condemned us to life inside an aging society that persists in worshipping youth. There is an unnamed yearning in the place where we ought to find a vibrant and respected elderhood. As a result, members of the postwar generation are especially prone to interpreting normal aging as an egregious personal failing. The sensation that one is living in a way that "calls for another way of living" can be seen as a sign of failure, but it can also be taken as a summons to further growth and exploration. There is a life beyond adulthood waiting for us, and its potential has been with us since the dawn of our humanity. The frenetic, yearning urgency, the burning sense of possibility, and the bottomless faith in "effectiveness" might still surround us—but help is on the way.

Time pushes the postwar generation forward even as its own merciless cult of adulthood pulls it back. The Second Crucible is already breathing life into the new subcultures that will define this era. Members of the postwar generation are already beginning to embrace and endorse (mostly unconsciously) the Denialist, Realist, and Enthusiast points of view. American society's profound ignorance of elderhood will, however, complicate this passage and make the coming years more turbulent and painful than they need to be.

GETTING STARTED

The best way to begin the journey toward an understanding of and appreciation for elderhood is with a confession. Aging is real, it is inevitable, and it is good for us. Because we live in a society that lionizes youth and in which every incentive is offered to those who would deny and delay the appearance of signs related to aging, making this admission can be a painful and difficult step. Nevertheless, this is the first step on the long journey out of adulthood.

The best place to begin this exercise in truth telling is in front of a mirror. Many members of the postwar generation can empathize with what Rita Benson-Sorrentino experienced on August 15, 2011:

> *She stood in the shower and let its hot rain wash the grime of travel from her body. She was tired but knew that it would be a mistake to sleep. There was work to do. She wrapped her hair in a towel and palmed an opening in the misted mirror. Her face leapt into view and surprised her. Old. She pushed the word away and remembered the L'Oréal ad she'd seen on the plane. "Worried about wrinkles? We'll help you fight back."*

We've come to believe the especially enticing lie, that "adulthood lasts forever." Most people are so attached to this belief that they are willing to defend it even at great personal cost. They are determined to "fight" aging. This desire is the source of a great deal of the unease and unhappiness that is afoot among members of the postwar generation. During the Second Crucible, the most important cleavage line within the postwar generation will be between those who wish to stay young (Denialists and Realists) and those who want to grow old.

When I first uncovered this demarcation line, I was fascinated by how clearly it marked the boundaries of adulthood in American society. I was on the phone with one of America's leading advocates for older people, and decided to ask her, "Are you an adult?" This proud, beautiful, and wise seventy-five-year-old woman answered instantly and forcefully. "Of course!" This was a person who had thought long and hard about aging in America, but even she had been ensnared by our culture's rigid attachment to adulthood. Is it any surprise that the rest of us would be so concerned about our wrinkles, creases, and imperfections?

Although many will find this hard to believe, it is within our power to stand in front of a mirror, study what we see there, and then acknowledge, without reservation, that we are no longer young. I am not the person I was twenty years ago, and neither are you. Admitting this to ourselves is one of the most culturally transgressive and liberating things we can do with just a mirror and a bit of privacy. We can learn to read the story of our lives as it has been written around our eyes and mouth and across our foreheads and cheeks. We can begin to reinterpret the changes as signs of important signifiers of our unique journey through life.

This is where we tender our resignation from the cult of adulthood. This is where we step off the treadmill of greed, hurry sickness, and effectiveness and set ourselves free. This path to personal happiness and fulfillment has just two steps: First, stop pining for what is already gone. Second, start searching for the person you were meant to become. Take these two steps and you will be ready to begin your own, incredible journey into life beyond adulthood. This advice, as simple as it may be, is difficult to follow. In a youth-obsessed society, there is a price to be paid for the kind of honesty I am recommending. During the First Crucible, there were many people who, though they lived outwardly Square lives, inwardly admired and even embraced the unabashed daring and freedom of the Activists and Hippies. Today, reasonable people do want to "look their best" and do take commonsense steps to obscure the signs of aging. Far from condemning such actions, I am advocating for a shift in perspective. Relinquishing one's *claim* on youth is a revolutionary act that cannot, by itself, expose one to ageist bigotry.

Compared with the First Crucible's generational journey out of childhood and into adulthood, the effort to leave adulthood behind will be maddeningly difficult and confusing. Americans currently understand life beyond adulthood about as well as they know the dark side of the moon. Persistently and deliberately misinterpreted as mere decline, elderhood actually offers rich rewards to those who manage to outgrow the frenzied jangle of adulthood and enter voluntarily into its vastly more soulful way of being.

UNDERSTANDING ELDERHOOD

Elderhood, rightly understood, is an instrument of culture. It has been protected, sustained, and nurtured across millennia because it can bind families, communities, tribes, and even nations together. Although powerful voices now claim, wrongly, that this precious endowment is an unaffordable luxury, we need elders more than ever before. We need them because they are critical to the function of the magnificent tripartite intergenerational dance of reciprocity that has been swirling around humanity for thousands of years. (See figure 1.)

FIGURE 1
THE INTERGENERATIONAL TRANSMISSION
OF CULTURE AND ASSISTANCE

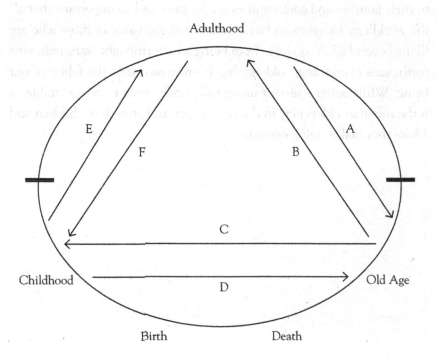

A. Support provided to elders by adults
B. Assistance elders give to adults
C. Gentling and acculturation of children by elders
D. Assistance and affection given to elders by children
E. Participation in work of adults by children
F. Food, shelter, clothing, and affection provided to children

We are both the creators of and the products of a complex multi-generational system of exchange. This is one of the most specifically human of all our traits. Over the ages this distinctive pattern of mutual dependence has shaped us, served us, blunted our worst tendencies, and magnified our best. It is elderhood that unifies and humanizes this pattern of interdependence. From their origins in the radical and unprecedented act of grandparenting, through their development of elderhood as a unique third age, elders have earned a respect that was founded on the value they create for humanity. The contributions they have made to their families and communities are so great and so important that all the world's major religions have emphasized the value of those who are living beyond adulthood. Far from being an afterthought "sans hair, sans teeth, sans everything," old age has been woven into the fabric of our being. While aging is almost universally understood to be inevitable, it is the role that elders play in the nurturance and growth of children and adults that makes aging essential.

21

SAGE-ING

I began my medical career as a family doctor, and during those years I devoted a significant part of my practice to obstetrics. Among the most soulful moments of this work came when I held a newborn, just seconds old, in my arms and looked into that child's eyes. I always felt that I was witnessing something that was exquisitely precious, a human being seeing the world for the first time. When I shifted into geriatrics, I had the honor of being present at the bedside for many peaceful, profoundly meaningful deaths. The bodies of the people I was caring for were frail, battered, and sometimes broken, but in their presence I could feel the power, and the truth, of a life that had been lived fully and completely.

Human infants, as adorable as they can be, have no story, no past, no loves gained and lost, no triumphs, and no acquaintance with grief. Those who are fortunate enough to reach elderhood, however, possess all these things in abundance. Elders spend a lifetime exchanging new-born perfection for something infinitely more valuable—a story. The ancient Greeks told of the affair between Selene (the Moon goddess) and a young shepherd named Endymion. She fell in love with him and begged Zeus to grant him immortality, which he, reluctantly, agreed to do. When she returned to her lover, Selene found him in a slumber from which he would never wake. Zeus knew that aging is the constant companion of a life worth living, and one who would not age could not truly live.

Nowadays, we have the unprecedented opportunity to think about and choose between many different narrative arcs for our own life story. For many of us, the earliest chapters of our lives fell into a comfortable rhythm as we passed through the way stations our culture had prepared for us. The passage through elementary, middle, and then high school, followed by further education or entry into the workforce or a branch of the military, is a well-worn developmental pathway. Unfortunately, as people approach midlife and beyond, the kinds of clear-cut cultural signals that stimulate growth and change become far less common. The false belief that aging equals decline, combined with the lack of cultural direction, leads millions of people to become stuck. These limbo episodes make it much more difficult to continue the story of our lives.

I recently visited an old friend from medical school who had spent two decades on the faculty of our alma mater and risen to the rank of full professor. "But," he said, "I started to realize that I had mastered my job and that the next five years would probably be just like the last five." The competence that so often accompanies the arrival of late middle age is a subtle kind of poison. It leeches the sense of possibility from the unwary and, far too often, condemns them, like Selene's human lover, to a life without growth.

One well-known approach to this problem is known in the vernacular as the "midlife crisis." My friend from medical school responded to the "need for change" by taking a new and more challenging position at another university. He and his wife will move out of the home where they raised their children as soon as their youngest enters college. They will start a new life in a new city—together. Many other people respond to the growing need for change by adopting much less sensible tactics. Men are especially well known for embracing adolescent fantasies (most famously cars and younger sexual partners) during midlife. Although this behavior is heavily stigmatized, it actually represents an earnest response to a unique developmental challenge.

A midlife crisis is the consequence of our changing relationship with memories of our younger self. These memories form the foundation of our identity, and we normally suppose them to be fixed and unalterable. In fact, they are subject to a nearly constant but unconscious process of revision. As we move past midlife (which honestly must be said to end in our forties), the memories we have of our youth become more distant, and in the press of daily responsibility, they are recalled less frequently. Dr. Judah Ronch, dean of the Erickson School at the University of Maryland, Baltimore County, describes the consequences of this process:

> The more remote an unused memory gets, or the more you retrieve
> it without strengthening it by real experience, the more [memo-
> ries of youth] change to conform to contemporary experience. . . .
> The margins of memory of self are constantly changing with our
> experience. If the major activity that our memories of self gets is
> reminiscing, rather than doing and storing new experiences, then
> memories of self become less and less about the person and more
> about the memories.

Our youth-obsessed culture places a premium on maintaining an authentically youthful self-identity. Living life as a harried adult makes it increasingly difficult to maintain such an identity. The much-maligned balding man with the too-young girlfriend is actually engaged in a reconstruction project. He is trying (some would say desperately) to maintain the authenticity of his memories, and therefore his self, by rejoining them with real-life experiences. He is attempting to recapture the enlarged zone of possibility that was available to him when he was young.

Contemporary society does endow young people with a wide range of possible lives. Indeed, the number of possibilities can become so large that it leads to a kind of developmental paralysis. Our culture helps youth manage this difficulty by providing social structures that permit and even encourage uncertainty and ambiguity. For example, during the early years of my own adolescence, I hoped to join my uncles in earning a living as a stonemason. A couple of years later, I changed my mind and decided to become a high school health teacher. Once in college, I conceived a desire to go to medical school. Throughout this process I was reassured that my indecision was normal and that I could "be anything I wanted to be." I relied on and was sustained by a cultural narrative that said, "Young people are allowed to change their minds."

During adulthood, people are expected to settle into a small number of fixed identities. We are allowed, for example, to be a mother and a firefighter. Adults who express role ambiguity and fail to "stick with" things are condemned for their immaturity and lack of seriousness. This emphasis on role persistence helps adults fulfill expectations of reliability and productivity. Years stretch into decades and we gradually become very good at our jobs and, if we are lucky, competent at parenting. As this sense of mastery grows, it naturally becomes an ever-larger part of our identity. Adults who are asked, "What do you do?" understand the question to mean, "What are your most important adult roles?" More than anything else, how we describe these roles tells other people who we really are.

A dawning and largely unspoken awareness of the iron law, combined with an incipient feeling that the end of adulthood is approaching, tempts members of the postwar generation with a dangerous question: "What comes next?" Even when the question remains unspoken, our culture offers an unambiguous answer: "There is nothing more. You are what you are."

Even as the iron law works its way with us, our society continues to insist that we remain confined to adulthood. Even as our adult powers begin to wane, we are told that adulthood lasts forever. We live in a society where the number of "possible lives" available to older adults contracts with the passage of time, and this creates an insidious developmental trap. What is most surprising about this situation is that so few men and women actually experience a midlife crisis as they struggle to escape the sensation of being trapped in a way of living that no longer suits them.

Fortunately, there is a little-known but vastly more effective approach to solving the developmental difficulties that arise in late adulthood. Instead of attempting to reanimate memories of youth, we can revisit our past with an eye toward understanding the person we might yet become. We can reject the dominant cultural narrative of loss and decline and embrace a personal narrative based on growth and change. We can design an approach to life beyond adulthood that restores to us, in its mature form, the experience of living with many "possible lives" in front of us. Best of all, there is no sports car required.

REB ZALMAN GROWS UP

The icon of the Enthusiast movement was born in Zhovkva, Poland, in 1924. Zalman Schachter-Shalomi (commonly known as "Reb Zalman") grew up in Vienna, escaping the Nazis in the late 1930s and making his way into France, where the Vichy government placed him in a detention camp. With great difficulty, his family arranged passage to the United States in 1941. Ordained as an Orthodox rabbi in 1947, Shachter-Shalomi was later directed to visit college campuses and work with Jewish college students. During the 1960s, his experimentation with the "sacramental value of lysergic acid" led him to leave the Chabad Lubavitch Hasidic community. He went on to become one of the main architects of the Jewish renewal movement and has had, by any measure, an enormously successful career as an author, teacher, and spiritual leader.

Shortly after his sixtieth birthday, Schachter-Shalomi began to feel that his life was out of balance. Koyaanisqatsi. He recalls, "I felt in the midst of being successful in what I was doing, that I was depressed and I couldn't understand the reason why." Instead of buying a Corvette, he embarked upon a forty-day retreat at the Lama Foundation in New Mexico. During his time in the desert, Reb Zalman came to understand that "my lifestyle hadn't changed from the time that I was younger, that I wasn't listening to my body. Then I began to look deeper and see that not only did I have to change the way in which I used my body, but also the way in which I started to think about the future." A man who had eluded the Nazis, helped found an important religious movement, and distinguished himself as a scholar had been transformed by the act of confronting his mortality.

Despite his long history of success and eminent qualifications as a spiritual leader, Reb Zalman had fallen prey to a virulent form of declinism. Even as he entered into his seventh decade of life, he continued to believe that success was defined by his sturdy capacity to avoid change. He believed that in order to be the person he had always been, he had to do the things he had always done. In an effort to lift the pall of depression, he began to thoughtfully and diligently reconsider his life not for the purpose of resurrecting the past (reminiscence) but to better understand his future. He summarized his difficulty: "You come to the age of sixty-three and you get into that period for which we don't have models in society." His postretreat desire to create a map of life beyond adulthood led him to write *Age-ing to Sage-ing: A Profound New Vision of Growing Older.*

The book inspired a Spiritual Eldering movement that places a thoughtful life review at the start of an extended late-life growth process. Schachter-Shalomi describes his version of being "saved": "Imagine I've been typing along on my computer and I was on a roll and it was so wonderful, the words were just flowing from me and then suddenly there's an electrical outage and I lost the file, and I didn't save it. And so I asked myself, What would it be like if I lived a life and all the files of awareness and experience and learning would get lost when I die?" An honest accounting of our memories, of the story we tell ourselves about who we are and who we have been, is the first prerequisite for becoming an elder.

Reb Zalman writes, "Our task in elderhood is to give ear to that inner voice which has been calling us to authentic life and to complete its call to the best of our ability." How does this work? Schachter-Shalomi organizes this work into the five broad categories of Life Review, Wisdom Creation, Legacy Transmission, Self-Care, and Life Completion.

What can we truthfully say about our successes and our failures? Across the span of a half century or more, we cannot avoid injuring people we love and neglecting obligations we have professed to hold dear. These transgressions, properly accounted for, can provide us with some of life's most valuable lessons. Being able to admit that one has been wrong and that these errors have harmed others opens the door to reconciliation and healing. The act of forgiveness, the surrender of grudges, and the repair of broken relationships are all essential to the process of growth in late life.

A significant part of Reb Zalman's own feeling that life was out of balance came from his continued reliance on practical knowledge and skills as the pillars of his self-esteem. Growing into elderhood requires us to change. Wisdom, properly understood, is insight into the problems of daily living. The reason that wisdom endures across millennia is that, despite advances in technology, the problems of living have changed little since ancient times.

The development of a legacy requires a lengthy and highly cooperative journey of discovery. The goal is to unearth and then seek to understand the deepest truths of the life one has lived. Tribal cultures employ a wide variety of strategies for helping their elders accomplish this work. Having an established role as a teller of stories, for example, promotes the sort of self-reflection and interaction that can spur this process. Spiritual Eldering helps people discover and then share the fundamental truths that have shaped their lives.

Enthusiasts value good health and the feeling of vitality because these things allow them to carry out their exploration of life beyond adulthood. The nature of physical, mental, and spiritual health change in elderhood but are no less important than they were in childhood and adulthood. The desire to care for oneself is often conflated with the desire to "stay young." Reb Zalman's forward-looking perspective on health honors the dictum "use it or lose it" and nurtures the sense of well-being that fosters further growth and development.

No matter how spiritual we may feel, our bodies are and will remain mortal. Those who work regularly with the dying speak of two distinct forms of loss. The deaths of children and younger adults are said to occur "out of time." The grief is compounded in these cases by the feeling that the deceased was denied the opportunity to complete life's full journey. Deaths that occur "in time" are spoken of in terms like "It was her time" or "He had a good life." The concept of "life completion" as a developmental goal helps people prepare for the end of life so that they can truly be said to have died "in time."

Early in *Age-ing to Sage-ing*, Schachter-Shalomi outlines the value of eldering: "The use of tools such as meditation, journal writing, and life review allow elders to come to terms with their mortality, harvest the wisdom of their years, and transmit a legacy to future generations. Serving as mentors, they pass on the distilled essence of their life experience to others. The joy of passing on of wisdom to younger people not only seeds the future, but crowns an elder's life with worth and nobility."

THE MIDLIFE CRISIS VERSUS SPIRITUAL ELDERING

The conventional midlife crisis and Spiritual Eldering both offer a solution to the problems of living in late adulthood. The former allows people to "reset the clock" of development by bringing memories of youth (and its possibilities) to life through lived experience. The latter looks forward to growth that has yet to occur. For Reb Zalman, "Eldering is what you participate in consciously and willingly. Spiritual means beyond sensory, beyond affect, beyond reason. . . ." The fact that "midlife crisis" is a universally understood term and "Spiritual Eldering" is (at the time this is written) known only to the Enthusiast cognoscenti is evidence of our long immersion inside a hard-charging, highly effective adulthood.

Academic studies suggest that fewer than 10 percent of adults experience what would properly be called a midlife crisis. Many millions, however, know the feeling that their lives are out of balance. The self-help bookshelf is well stocked with volumes that aim to help adults solve this riddle of dis-ease and nearly all of them locate the problem within the personal narrative of an individual life. The traditional model of success is to strive for advancement in our careers and perfection in our domestic relations. This perspective works well enough until the passage of time begins to make us aware of aging and its limitations.

Our culture proposes a false dichotomy, "Shall we age or shall we remain the same?" The Enthusiasts counter with "Shall we age or shall we sage?" Our society is in desperate need of people with wisdom born of long experience. Where shall we find such people? Reb Zalman concludes, "I hope you sense what a glorious future awaits you in old age. No longer will you dread the evening of life as a time of unremitting suffering and futility, but as an opportunity for continued growth in consciousness and service to humanity. What a vista, what a wonderful adventure, what a miraculous window of opportunity awaits us in old age!"

Elders and sages, rightly understood, are much more than aged people. They are heirs to a social status rich in honor and dignity. They are agents of change, guardians of both our past and our future. They are what we may yet become.

22

SLOW

The postwar generation's tumorous enlargement of adulthood has warped our perception of time: almost everyone is familiar with the experience of time poverty and hurry sickness. Less evident but even more significant is the elevated value our society places on time spent at work over and above less "productive" pursuits. Advanced digital technologies have simultaneously fueled economic growth and radically depleted our stock of "social capital." We are both highly adept at turning time into money and laughably inept when it comes to turning money into meaning.

Morning, noon, and night we are surrounded by laborsaving technologies that people living just a generation ago would have described as miracles. Given this, we ought to be so at ease and have so much free time that long walks along the river on a summer afternoon and evenings spent playing music with friends are seen as routine activities. But we aren't and we don't. Indeed, our culture has taken us in the opposite direction. Our brief mortal lives are increasingly given over to a desire to turn our time into money. When not at work, we search clumsily for the time we need to be with each other.

SPEED KILLS

Robert Levine, the author of *The Geography of Time*, recalls seeing the following inscription on the narrow-gauge Darjeeling Himalayan Express: " 'Slow' is spelled with four letters; So is 'life.' 'Speed' is spelled with five letters; So is 'death.' " A condensed version might have read, "Speed kills." The postwar generation's entry into elderhood offers us all an opportunity to reevaluate our need for speed. Elders don't have to "run higher and jump faster" because they've been there, done that. Instead, this phase of life calls on us to let go of *fast* and embrace *slow*. Members of the postwar generation will find it especially difficult to wean themselves from the fast life. After all, what reasonable person ever chooses slow over fast?

In American society *slow* has a range of meanings and few of them are positive. The standard dictionary definition of the word sets the tone. Slow cars and computers "move only at a low speed." Slow novels are "boring and uninteresting." Slow people are "dull and unintelligent." Except for the writings of a few (fascinating) contrarians, it is nearly impossible to find the word *slow* being used as a term of praise.

In fact, the word *slow* becomes even more dangerous and demeaning when it is used in the context of aging. This is where American society adds an extra layer of disapproval. It is a terrible thing, we are told, terrible when a fit and vigorous person "loses a step" and starts to "slow down." Older drivers are relentlessly criticized for driving too slow. Older people catch our attention when they cross the street because they move so much more slowly than the adults who surge around and ahead of them. People experience foot-tapping frustration when older relatives take "too long" to get to the point. Holiday celebrations that place multiple generations around a single table almost always find young people finishing their meal well ahead of their older relatives. The fact that older people generally work, walk, talk, drive, and eat more slowly than younger people reinforces already highly negative stereotypes about aging.

We don't need elders to speed up; we need our society to slow down. If we are fortunate and Enthusiasts' beliefs about the intrinsic value of aging dominate the Second Crucible, people of all ages will benefit when this natural, healthy embrace of slow is magnified and amplified by the postwar generation. Living life more slowly is an art that can help us break free of the time machine's insatiable demands. Slow living is essential to the creation of social capital. This distinctive form of wealth cannot be measured in dollars and cents. It exists entirely within the intangible currency of healthy, vibrant families, communities, and nations.

SLOW LIFE

America's traditional devotion to hard work and success was transformed into an unreasoning obsession with speed, performance, and "effectiveness" during the postwar generation's long sojourn through adulthood. Now millions of people are waking up to the fact that this obsession can also cause intense personal distress and dissatisfaction. People living in late adulthood are increasingly being torn between a desire to stop chasing every shiny object that comes into view and a cultural imperative that measures success entirely in terms of speed and productivity. Koyaanisqatsi. Success in resolving this tension and breaking the cycle of guilt and blame it inspires in us will depend greatly on our ability to embrace a truly slow life. While we can be certain that our culture will continue to insist that fast will always outperform slow, those who lay claim to the title of elder have access to a new kind of freedom, one that pays little heed to who is winning which race.

Sometimes beautifully and lovingly, sometimes harshly and painfully, our decades of living teach us that faster is not always better. It is impossible, for example, for even the most loving parent to accelerate the speed at which a toddler eats her breakfast. The seconds may be racing past and it may be true that "we should have left seven minutes ago," but a young child cannot and should not be made to experience urgency in the same manner as an adult. The businessman driving to an important meeting blows his horn and cuts off other motorists— and "saves" just seconds of his time. On a more intimate level, many couples who have been together for a long time feel the urgency and thrill of sex begin to wane. The "quickie" that once served as a way to spice things up can become a habit. Sex conducted in a fast and orderly fashion may be highly "effective," but it also robs a relationship of its intimacy and passion. Connecting with another person, actually being with that person, takes time. If that time is constantly compressed and distorted, the connection can be lost.

When I was in medical school, I arranged my academic schedule so that I would have time for a transcontinental bicycle ride. After flying from Boston to San Francisco, I started the long journey home with a ride down the Pacific Coast Highway. I soon came upon a narrow and, I thought, abandoned stretch of beach, where I could "baptize" my bike. As I rolled its back tire into the Pacific Ocean, I caught sight of a middle-aged man strolling along the beach. He was shirtless and his chest bore what I recognized as a fresh scar, probably from heart bypass surgery. We soon struck up an amiable conversation, and I noticed how at ease he was and how carefully he studied the sun and the sky, the gulls and the splash of salt water on rock. We parted company, but I never forgot him. Through him I had glimpsed the pleasure that can be found in a proudly and joyfully slow life.

Our culture's embrace of fast food, fast cars, fast conversations, fast families, and fast holidays is so powerful, it sometimes takes a near-death experience to make us reconsider the need for speed. There is, fortunately, another, less traumatic way to gain insight into the value of slowness. Those who can find the courage to admit that they are no longer young and will never again be young can also begin to appreciate the possibilities that a new, less frenzied, life might hold. Beginning the journey into elderhood is good for us because it leads us toward the unique sources of meaning and purpose that are available only to those who are willing to live slow.

Our society makes it hard for us to embrace slowness. Adulthood has barricaded nearly all of the exit ramps that lead away from the fast life. Members of the postwar generation increasingly find themselves driving faster and faster down life's highway even as they begin to wonder where exactly that road is taking them. While we are all supposed to aspire to a better "work-life balance," experience teaches us that work will almost always take precedence over play. We've internalized our culture's hard necessity: we have to live fast if we want to hold on to our status, our livelihood, and even our house.

In the Covey tradition, our culture has come to regard anything less than a full objective and subjective commitment to performance as a guarantee of failure. On the shelves of the secondhand store in my neighborhood, there are rows of remarkably inexpensive used computers, each one of which was at one time the fastest computer money could buy. Now they are dusty relics, one step removed from the landfill. Older people who aren't as fast as they used to be or (even more dangerously) not as fast as they need to be are evaluated in similarly negative terms. If they are lucky, they'll be called "lazy" or "complacent." If not, the young will shake their heads and say, "What do you expect? He's really slowing down."

Although we are often encouraged to think of ourselves as such, people are not machines, and a dawning interest in slow is not equivalent to obsolescence. The First Crucible pop music duo Simon & Garfunkel reflected on slow living over a half century ago; rereading lyrics from "The 59th Street Bridge Song" creates an eerie feeling given what was to come. "Slow down, you move too fast." The first line of the song now seems to echo as if it comes to us from a strange and distant land. The lyrics celebrate the intrinsic value of time and of direct sensory experience. There is so much freedom and so little pressure that the lyricist has plenty of time for nonsense syllables: "Ba da da da da da da da . . ."

The song offers a vision of life lived without the constraints and limitations that are so rigorously imposed by conventional adulthood. Revisiting these lyrics on the cusp of the Second Crucible lets us interpret its message in a new light. The singers believe that the freedom to work when one chooses to and rest when one wants to is a way of living that has intrinsic moral and aesthetic value. On reflection it seems obvious that a culture that compels us to work when we are weary places little value on personal well-being. Being able to rest when we are tired is transformative precisely because it is in doing so that we begin to see the world as it is, rather than as we wish it to be. The freedom to embrace a slow life that permits this kind of reflection is one of the most important gifts elderhood has to offer.

The good news in all of this is that the iron law never rests. It is always at work, always moving the postwar generation closer to life beyond adulthood. Our culture identifies the diminution of endurance and vigor that comes with age as an especially painful type of loss, but these changes can also honestly be seen as part of a complex process of preparation. The waning energy that accompanies the end of adulthood helps to ready us for elderhood in much the same way that puberty prepares us for the difficult task of outgrowing childhood and entering into adulthood.

The passage out of adulthood is the postwar generation's final and most challenging developmental task. This endeavor will require millions of people to develop fluency in a new and unfamiliar language of change. Adults, who have been so busy for so long, will require practice and a good deal of encouragement before they can learn to say the words "Slow is better" and mean them. The encouragement and inspiration we need are fortunately close at hand. There are a range of little known but deliciously creative slow movements here in America and around the world that can help us see how the slow life really works.

SLOW MONEY

The Slow Money movement was, strangely enough, founded by a long-time venture capitalist. His name is Woody Tasch, and unlike most investment advisers, he urges people to invest in companies and ventures they can literally see grow. The idea that such growth actually belongs in the realm of the real—rather than in, say, the domain of synthetic credit default swaps—has enough common sense in it to make it unusual. Tasch argues that the best investments are local, including things like crops in a field and cattle grazing in a pasture.

In his book *Inquiries into the Nature of Slow Money: Investing as if Food, Farms, and Fertility Mattered*, he asks, "What if you had to invest 50 percent of your assets within 50 miles of where you live?" People are increasingly demanding that they know about and understand the ingredients in their food and should, he argues, follow similar rules with regard to their investments. Tasch, a chairman emeritus of the "Investors' Circle," touts a concept he calls "nurture capital." This is slow money, because it is invested in things that need time to grow. Slow money is ideally suited to stimulating healthy local growth because it supports investments that can be seen and touched.

SLOW MEDICINE

In their article "It's Time to March," two of geriatric medicine's wisest elders, Drs. Knight Steel and T. Franklin Williams, argue that the current specialist-dominated, technology-oriented industry of "fast medicine" is failing to meet the most important needs of patients and that someone needs to step on the brakes. Multiple studies from the Institute of Medicine have found that the speed at which medicine is practiced today literally kills. Fortunately, an alternative to conventional practice is beginning to gain credibility.

First popularized by Dennis McCullough in his book *My Mother, Your Mother: Embracing "Slow Medicine," the Compassionate Approach to Caring for Your Aging Loved Ones*, this approach to care imagines health-care providers, families, friends, and neighbors and elders working together as a team. Research suggests that when this teamwork-oriented approach is combined with effective, unhurried communication, it can dramatically improve care. In particular, sometimes difficult and often-avoided conversations about issues related to comfort, honor, dignity, and the end of life can minimize inappropriate, often dangerous medical interventions. While fast medicine and its awe-inspiring technology continue to dominate in the media, slow medicine is beginning to change how medicine is practiced in the real world. Thoughtful conversations, skillful teamwork, and a reverence for the individual do take more time, but they are powerful tools for creating better lives for doctors and patients alike.

SLOW FOOD

When Carlo Petrini founded the Slow Food movement in 1986, it is unlikely that he imagined how widely his commonsense approach to food would spread. He was, initially, spurred to action by two seemingly unrelated events. The first was the opening of a McDonald's restaurant in the heart of Rome. The other was the poisoning of hundreds of people by cheap wine that had been diluted with methanol. Petrini saw the dangers that were being created by the explosive growth of fast food and mourned the loss of local food sources that were trustworthy, safe, and delicious.

He founded the global nonprofit Agricola and continues to work to preserve traditional and regional cuisine and help farmers match plants, seeds, and livestock to the characteristics of their specific ecosystems. Every local Slow Food group has a leader who is responsible for promoting local artisans, local farmers, and local flavors through regional events such as taste workshops, wine tastings, and farmers' markets. The Slow Food movement unabashedly embraces hedonism, tranquility, conviviality, and the richness we experience when we share good food in good company. It is a nearly perfect match for elders and elderhood.

SLOW CITIES

The Slow Cities movement celebrates the value of "specific-ness." Like the Slow Food movement from which it grew, Slow Cities celebrates local differences that can be "seen from the outside and felt from the inside." An international network of slow cities have signed pledges aimed at encouraging the development of slow approaches to good eating, hospitality, services, facilities, and the fabric of urban life. A group calling itself Slow London wanted to encourage Londoners to take time for lunch and issued an open invitation to a panel discussion on the "Slow Revolution." The event's participants included Carl Honoré (author of *In Praise of Slow*), Kate Fletcher (coiner of "slow fashion"), and Gervais Williams (author of *Slow Finance*).

The movement's proponents believe that our hot, fast, frenetic world can give rise to a countervailing effort to create and maintain tight connections to land, climate, weather, streets, buildings, and most of all, people. This powerful localism results in the polar opposite of the stunning blandness that afflicts so many American neighborhoods and communities and shopping centers.

SLOW SEX

Nicole Daedone is the author of *Slow Sex: The Art and Craft of the Female Orgasm*. She has spent the last decade teaching a technique for slow pleasure that she calls "orgasmic meditation." Just as the Slow Food movement leads devotees to develop an in-depth knowledge of and appreciation for local produce, Daedone encourages couples to take time to explore female genitalia and its response to contact. She writes, "The habits of receptivity, appreciation, awareness, true intimacy—are 180 degrees opposite from the habits that rule our conventional world." She encourages women to cultivate the ability to communicate during intimate moments, because doing so fosters the ability "to state their needs outside the bedroom."

Daedone is not the only one who is encouraging couples to dial back the speed of their lovemaking. Diana Richardson, author of *Slow*

Sex: The Path to Fulfilling and Sustainable Sexuality, combines her experience studying under the tantric master Osho with practical guidance for couples. Her approach is just as "slow" as Daedone's but offers a more spiritual perspective. "Slow sex," she writes, "is definitely not some kind of technique as in 'a-b-c' leads to 'x-y-z.' It's not something you do but rather something that you become. . . . Slow sex is a journey in which each and every day counts." Richardson counsels patience and reminds readers that time has the power to change us in ways that force cannot; her description of slow sex also describes much of the journey into elderhood. "It's a slow journey that can extend over many years and into old age. That is how it is turning out for me, and I can definitely say that I did not plan for it to be this way. Very gradually one thing led to another through curiosity and practice."

23

DEEP

The psychological and emotional terrain of elderhood is poorly understood by young and old alike. In place of wisdom and insight, our culture has presented us with superficial and misleading explanations for why elders behave the way they do. This lack of understanding is, for example, largely responsible for the well-known archetype of the "grumpy old man." You know the one. Many people remember him living in the house on the corner. As the end of the school day drew near, he took his position on the porch, like a sailor standing watch. He waited quietly, listening, anticipating.

As you and your friends came down the street, he leaned forward, just a little bit. You looked for him, up there on the porch, but didn't see him. You giggled—and decided to cut the corner. The moment you stepped on his iridescent green lawn, he was up and out of his chair. "Get off my lawn, you damn kids!" You ran as fast as your new sneakers would carry you and disappeared around the corner. His duty done for the day, the old man retreated to the comfort of his recliner and a remote control.

Almost everyone knows a story like this. Some people will even swear that they are related to this man. But misted childhood memories and a culture of ageism show him in a false and unflattering light. What really accounts for grumpy old men? The answer is far more complicated and interesting than is commonly supposed. On the most superficial level, most people believe that old men are grumpy *because they are old.* They believe, incorrectly, that life beyond adulthood is an unfortunate time dominated by rheumatism, bowel complaints, and a fading memory. Because our culture primes us with such beliefs, this is most often what we see when we look at older Americans.

Having an appreciation for elderhood as a distinct phase of human development allows us to reimagine the terrain of life beyond adulthood and see this man, and his behavior, in an entirely new light. We can start by acknowledging that adults find the habit of yelling at schoolchildren to be a strange and somewhat disturbing practice. The unyielding responsibilities imposed by jobs, mortgages, car payments, and college funds make most adults wary of offending other people (and other people's children) without good cause.

The elder who lives in the house on the corner is free to adopt an entirely different calculus. He lives on Social Security and a pension, his house is paid for, the kids are grown and have moved away, and the Buick in the driveway will last him for the rest of his life. The social constraints mandatory for adults no longer apply to him—and he knows it. He possesses a freedom to choose that adults have difficulty even imagining.

As we saw in the research on happiness, it is the adult-aged population that is burdened with the unhappiness that is supposed to be the domain of old age. While some people are irritable from birth onward, it is more often true that elders seem "grouchy" or "crabby" because they are free to act as they prefer. Although he did not appear to recognize this pattern in his own family, Realist guru Dr. Gary Small's description of his wife's centenarian grandmother applies here: "She never forgot a birthday, an anniversary or a single holiday. And God forbid you forgot to send her a card or call her on her birthday—you'd hear about it for ages." As an adult, an esteemed professor, and a best-selling author, he is accustomed to being shown a considerable amount of respect. She is 103 years old, lives in a third-floor walk-up, and has no reason to defer to him, flatter him, or refrain from criticizing his various breaches of etiquette. Dr. Small's written passage reveals his injured ego more clearly than he might have intended.

An Enthusiast elderhood enables people to increasingly express their true selves, often in ways that would not have been tolerated when they were younger. Elderhood, properly understood, is actually a delicious form of liberation. It grants us new forms of freedom. Even pop culture has begun to recognize the latitude that age can offer to elders. As an adult, actress Betty White played Sue Ann Nivens on *The Mary Tyler Moore Show* and, even more famously, Rose Nylund on *The Golden Girls*. In her eighties, she experienced renewed career success—this time as her true, elder self. She felt free to tell the kinds of risqué jokes that would have swiftly ended the career of her younger self. One example makes the point: "Why do people say 'grow some balls'? Balls are weak and sensitive. If you wanna be tough, grow a vagina. Those things can take a pounding." Betty White the elder is transparent, profane, funny, and most definitely not *careful*.

Near the conclusion of Simone de Beauvoir's late-life masterpiece *Coming of Age*, she observes, "Once we have understood what the state of the aged really is, we cannot satisfy ourselves with calling for a more generous 'old age' policy, higher pensions, decent housing and organized leisure. It is the whole system that is at issue and our claim cannot be otherwise than radical—change life itself." Elderhood unlocks the psychological shackles of adulthood in much the same way that adulthood releases us from the constraints imposed by childhood. Aging offers us a new frame of reference that we can use to reinterpret and redevelop the entire American cultural landscape.

Betty Friedan's last major published work was a lengthy and carefully developed reconsideration of aging. *The Fountain of Age* plumbed the unexpected depth and strength that is hidden within life's third age. In one of the book's most engaging chapters, Friedan tells of being challenged to rappel down a three-hundred-foot cliff during an Outward Bound–type expedition. She declined the invitation. Her hosts insisted. She literally held her ground. While such an experience would leave most adults with feelings of failure and shame, she experienced it as tangible evidence of her new freedom. As an elder, she understood that "I don't have to compete to prove myself—I can live with the fact that I'll never rappel and that failure doesn't really matter one way or another."

Freedom really is another word for "nothing left to lose."

GEROTRANSCENDENCE

Swedish gerontologist Lars Tornstam spent decades carefully interviewing elders, and this work led him to develop a theory he calls "gerotranscendence." He suggests, quite provocatively, that human development in late life isn't just a possibility; it isn't something that is reserved for the fortunate few: it is instead a vital necessity for all. Tornstam asserts that we need to grow in late life and that obstructions to such growth actually violate our human nature. His detailed knowledge of the emotional terrain of "life beyond adulthood" allowed him to challenge orthodoxy and explore the most misunderstood features of elderhood. Gerostranscendence is founded on the idea that the "drive" for growth can be best understood in terms of the following attributes:

1. The individual becomes less self-occupied and at the same time more selective in the choice of social and other activities.
2. There is an increased feeling of affinity with past generations and a decreased interest in superfluous social interaction.
3. The individual might also experience a decrease in interest in material things and a greater need for solitary "meditation." Positive solitude becomes more important.

4. There is also often a feeling of cosmic communion with the
   spirit of the universe, and a redefinition of time, space, life,
   and death.

Tornstam's ideas have been enormously useful to me as I have
worked with elders and their adult relatives. He helped me see elders in
a new and much more advantageous light. As a physician, I had been
instructed in a thoroughly negative and highly declinist understanding
of age and aging. I knew a great deal about stroke, osteoporosis, dementia, congestive heart failure, and emphysema and very little about the
virtues of elderhood. The medical profession continues to ignore or
demean the notion that elders have access to strengths and a richness
of experience that are largely unknown to adults. Tornstam's theory of
gerotranscendence helped me transcend my own medical education.
These are powerful insights.

   While I have always done my best to help my patients manage
their clinical conditions, I developed a new interest in helping them
fulfill their developmental potential. Where I had once insisted on the
value of social activities, I began to honor my patients' desire to engage
with others more selectively. Although we live in a society that often
belittles the elder's natural tendency to revisit and reinterpret the past,
I began to listen more carefully to the stories elders were willing to tell
me. I came to agree with Tornstam that among the most important of
all of elderhood's developmental tasks is the construction of a life story
that feels right and true to an elder.

   Younger relatives often have a difficult time understanding the
stories elders tell and retell. Whenever people tell me that an elder is
repeating the same stories, I look for evidence that this is behavior indicating the onset of dementia or a side effect of a medication. If that
is not the case, I suggest they understand such repetition as part of a so-
phisticated effort to address unresolved conflict, long-suppressed anger,
and sometimes disappointment. The point is that both the story and its

repetition have purpose, meaning, and value. Imagine an adult telling a budding musician who is playing the same song over and over to stop or to "play something else." It takes vastly more time and effort to discern the meaning of one's life than it does to learn how to play a particular song on a clarinet. In both cases, the offer of support and understanding is exceptionally helpful.

Elders are also likely to begin reevaluating and readjusting the balance between possessions and relationships. This shift can, and often does, feel oddly disorienting to younger relatives. I have often counseled younger relatives who are distressed, for example, when a grandmother opens her jewelry box, the one that has been on her dresser for half a century, and begins giving away some of her most loved pieces. In my experience, many elders reach a point where pride of ownership becomes less important than the giving of a gift they believe will be treasured long after they are gone. Elders can be some of the least materialistic people in American society.

In a similar fashion, elders can also change aspects of their behavior that had seemed integral to their personalities. A woman who once insisted on never appearing in public without being carefully coiffed shows a new and, to some younger relatives, shocking willingness to go out to dinner in a tracksuit. People who are growing are also changing. Although our culture makes it easy to forget this, elders begin to display new dimensions of their being in precisely the same sense that children take on new traits, new priorities, and new beliefs as they enter into adulthood.

What Tornstam refers to as a "cosmic" redefinition of space, time, life, and death is actually a decisive shift away from adult preoccupations and toward a much more nuanced understanding of one's place in the universe. Sometimes this drive expresses itself in a religious spirituality and regular participation in religious services. Less obviously, this trait can also manifest itself in a very private reflection on death's relentless approach.

As a geriatrician I have been with hundreds of elders as they have died. I have seen them be "tortured" by medical technology; I have seen them struggle with grief and longing. I have seen them resist in every possible way and to the last possible moment the going into "that good night." Elders are a complicated lot and it is rarely wise to describe them in sweeping terms.

In my practice I have engaged in countless end-of-life conversations with elders. As I began to mature as a physician, these talks became much easier for both doctor and patient. I found that most elders, by the time they talked to me, had already given careful consideration to what they did and did not want at the time of their passing. They are, mostly, eager to talk about these things to someone who can listen without judgment. They show remarkably little fear of death. Because they understand that they are mortal, and that knowledge helps relieve them of the egocentrism that bolstered them in their adult years. They know that, after they are gone, the world will carry on perfectly well—without them. Of course, the depth of these insights varies greatly between individuals but, taken together, I think they provide strong support for Tornstam's belief that there is a "cosmic" dimension to elderhood.

An elder's growing affection for solitude is also cause for much concern among families and professionals. Because we live in an adult-dominated culture, an elder's normal desire for solitude is very often confused with loneliness. These two states of being are actually very different from one another. Loneliness is always painful. In particular, it is the pain that comes from seeking but not finding companionship. In the words of the First Crucible song, "Lonely man cries for love and has none." Solitude is that distinctive pleasure we experience when we choose to be alone. Some adults can recall living in a house filled with young children and retreating into the bathroom, locking the door, in order to be alone, even if for just five minutes. Elders have a much more expansive understanding of solitude than adults. Many elders find that solitude offers them an open, boundaryless space that is not restricted by the expectations of others.

Solitude provides a safe haven that also helps elders budget their time in ways that optimize their changing levels of energy and interest. I remember when the concerned daughter of a patient of mine dropped by to see me because she was worried about her parents. They were approaching their sixty-fifth wedding anniversary and the family was busy planning a picnic and family reunion to celebrate the milestone. Her mother took her aside and told her, "We don't want a party." She asked why. "It's just," her mother said, "it's just too much." The daughter thought it might be the cost, but that wasn't the case. "We just don't want to do it." The daughter told me that her parents had always enjoyed gatherings with friends and families and their children. This reluctance was something new and it concerned her. She wondered if her parents might be depressed—or worse.

Her parents' health was good; this problem was actually being caused by a new and largely unacknowledged generation gap. The First Crucible's troubled generation gap had featured 80 million adolescents on one side and their Spock-reading parents on the other. The Second Crucible generation gap will feature elders on one side and their worried adult relatives on the other. In their time, members of the postwar generation will play both parts in this second intergenerational drama, just as they did in the first. In the case of the family picnic described above, the younger relatives knew that they would enjoy the party and that the adult versions of their parents would likewise have looked forward to it. What they were unable to see was their parents as the elders they had become, nor did they understand how elders think about time, energy, and relationships.

I explained to the daughter that her parents were becoming, in Tornstam's words, "more selective in the choice of social and other activities." This selectivity is evidence of wisdom, not failure. I suggested that they could begin to bridge this generation gap by going ahead with the picnic, taking plenty of pictures, and understanding why the matriarch and patriarch had elected not to attend in person. They could, as a family, also arrange for a year-long series of weekly visits that would not overwhelm or overtax the elders.

Much of the distress that enters into the relationships between elder parents and adult children has its roots in generational misunderstandings. The postwar generation can diffuse much of this angst, if they are willing to learn about, accept, and finally embrace the nature of elderhood. It behooves them to do so, and not just because it will improve their relationship with their parents. Despite the rhetoric of the Denialists and Realists, elderhood does, in fact, await those who once believed that they were stardust, that they were golden. In fact, the very best way for members of the postwar generation to teach their own children how to love, honor, and most of all respect elders is to learn how to do so themselves.

Elderhood offers a depth that far exceeds either the untested innocence of childhood or the frenzied activity of adulthood. This depth, however, comes at a cost. Age requires new, unfamiliar, and sometimes quite unpleasant sacrifices from us. The acceptance of these changes is part of the price of admission to life beyond adulthood. We can gain access to wonderful new forms of freedom here, if we are willing to explore. We've been told that old age offers us nothing that the adult does not already possess in abundance, but this is a lie. For Americans, and especially for members of the postwar generation, elderhood remains an undiscovered country. We can explore its terrain only if and only when we find the courage to go deep inside ourselves.

Those who are willing to slow down and deliberately let go of the desire for control are rewarded with a feeling of accomplishment that exists beyond adulthood's stunted declarations of success and failure. Elderhood asks if we are willing to accept the fact that we are mortal and rewards those who are willing to do so with a lightness of being known only to those who have lost their fear of death. How do I know these things? I learned them from elders. I have been beside them as they lived and died. I have done my best as a physician and, often, as a friend to ease their burdens, and they, in turn, have shared their truths with me. This is how I came to know that elderhood is deep.

24

CONNECTED

The Grimm brothers collected the tale of the Old Grandfather and His Grandson in the nineteenth century, and it was probably already hundreds of years old when they first heard it. In this version of the story a very old man, who can "scarcely hold his spoon" begins to spill his soup on the tablecloth. The grandfather is soon evicted from the family table and made to sit in the corner behind the stove. His son and daughter-in-law also took away his spoon and gave him his food in a wooden bowl. Once when they were all together the little grandson pushed some pieces of wood together on the floor. The father asked his son what he was doing, and the boy told him, "I am making a wooden trough so you may eat from it when you are old!" In the Grimms' telling, "The man and woman looked at one another and then began to cry. They immediately brought the old grandfather to the table, and always let him eat there from then on. And if he spilled a little, they did not say a thing." This intergenerational transfer of respect and resources is the oldest and most elemental form of social security.

Most (though certainly not all) societies around the world and

SECOND WIND ~ *219*

through history have taken care to ensure that older people are granted rights and considerations that are distinct from those pertaining to the young. We can see the value of such special designations when we look at, to choose one example, the peoples of the Iroquois Confederacy. The "Great Law" that governed the union of these five (later six) tribes reserved a special place in society and government for the tribe's elders. Because the clan mothers decided which men would serve as chief, they kept a special watch over children at play. Those who acted in a selfish or cruel manner were removed from consideration for future leadership positions. They would also "impeach" a leader who failed to act in the interests of the common good. Perhaps most importantly, these old women were given the power to veto declarations of war. The wisdom of their elders kept peace between the tribes for nearly seven hundred years.

The value that elders can provide to their communities is so great that anthropological research has identified remarkably few cultures where the young kill or abandon the old. Examples of gericide are largely confined to peoples living in the harshest and most unforgiving environments. The Yakut people of North-Central Siberia, for example, engaged in a culturally sanctioned "forsaking" of infirm older people. Waldemar Jochelson, writing in 1933, noted that "aged people are not in favor; they are beaten by their own children, often forced to leave their dwellings and to beg from house to house." Nearly three decades later when Tokarev and Gurvich studied the Yakut, they found that little had changed. The old were still given little to eat, were still poorly clothed, and were still being reduced to "total destitution."

Contemporary American society occupies a strange and unsettled middle ground between the extremes of pious respect and sanctioned abuse and neglect. Our rhetoric always aspires to the former while our practices too often veer dangerously close to the latter. What does set American society apart from so many others is our deliberate segregation of older people. With rare exceptions, this separation of young from old is unknown among tribal and highly traditional peoples. Giving lectures at scores of universities, I nearly always ask students in the audience who grew up with an older person (friend or relative) as a regular part of their everyday life to raise their hands. Over years, I have watched the number of raised hands dwindle. I recently gave a lecture to a group of thirty undergraduates at an elite university, and when I asked this question, not one hand went up.

For nearly all of human history, children, adults, and elders have lived with, worked with, celebrated with, and grieved with one another. No one had to think about "fostering intergenerational relationships" because such relationships were exquisitely normal. Although dense family clusters that remain tied to a single community for many generations (older people will recognize this as "the home place") retain an important place in American iconography, few of us live in this way today. When confronted with the facts regarding our society's radical and destructive practice of age segregation, most people respond with nostalgia. "It used to be," they say, "that older people were respected. You know, families took care of their own." This appeal to kinfolk and tradition might feel good but it also disregards the realities of contemporary American life.

One of the least noticed but most important consequences of the age segregation is the destruction of the historic alliance between children and elders. When we separate the old from the young, children wind up living entirely under the supervision of adults. This, it turns out, is rarely a good thing. Because I grew up surrounded by older relatives, I learned early on that I could count on them to temper my parents' natural tendency toward strictness. In particular, my maternal grandfather, a truck driver by trade, was known inside the family as "the Lawyer." Whenever I got into trouble I knew that, sooner or later, his American Motors Rambler would roll up the driveway. My grandfather would sit down at the kitchen table and plead my case for me. "Now, don't be too hard on Billy, he's a good boy." The Lawyer almost always won a reduction in sentence. Families that no longer have access to the restraining influence of elders often find it difficult to contend with the unrelenting and unhealthy pressure that adults and adulthood apply to children and childhood.

Because they occupy a station that lies outside adulthood but also possess long experience with living life as adults, elders are the social group best positioned to roll back many of the cult of adulthood's most damaging excesses. At least, they would be if our society was able to see their true worth. Our contemporary aging apartheid does damage to society at large by disconnecting elders from their families and their communities. It isolates them in old age ghettos (some of which are very finely appointed) and deprives us all of the value of their lived experience. Elders can and should be people of influence, but for the exercise of this influence to be felt they must be connected to the people around them. Elders can help undo the adultification of childhood, but only if they are involved in the daily lives of children. They can inspire and guide adults, but only if they live in a world where the wisdom of elders is held to be at least equal in value to the expertise of adults. Connecting elders to each other and to younger people is a highly practical strategy for improving the lives of people of all ages.

Problem

The growing prevalence of childhood obesity is frequently blamed on children. Its true causes, however, are complex and include, at a minimum, the rise of the fast food industry, the fall of shared family meals, the popularity of television and gaming, and the disappearance of unrestricted, unstructured, and unsupervised outdoor play. Although they are rarely willing to shoulder the blame, adults and their relentless adultification of society are actually major contributors to this "children's" epidemic. Adults are entirely responsible, for example, for the marked decrease in the number of children who walk to and from school every day. The *Wall Street Journal* profiled the "car kids" phenomenon in 2010:

"First, the 'car kids' are herded into the gym. The guards make sure all children sit still and do not move or speak during the process," reports a dad in Tennessee. Outside, "People get there 45 minutes early to get a spot. And the scary thing is, most of the kids live within biking distance," says Kim Meyer, a mom in Greensboro, N.C. When the bell finally rings, the first car races into the pick-up spot, whereupon the car-line monitor barks into a walkie-talkie: "Devin's mom is here!" Devin is grabbed from the gym, escorted to the sidewalk, and hustled into the car as if under enemy fire. His mom peels out and the next car pulls up. "Sydney's mom is here!" Kerry Buss, a curriculum developer in Fairfax County, Virginia, says her son's school does this, "and this is the same school that took out the bike racks to discourage kids from biking." It's also the school her husband attended as a child. Back then, "he and his sister walked to school like every other kid in the neighborhood. It was unheard of that there'd be a bus, much less a car line."

The practice of driving children to and from school when they could walk or bike aggravates childhood obesity, increases traffic congestion, and adds to the greenhouse gases in the atmosphere. Most people would find it unlikely that elders could have anything to contribute to such a tangled mess of interrelated problems. They would also be wrong.

Solution

In 2003, an Italian environmental group developed and implemented the concept of a *piedibus* (literally "foot-bus" in Italian). These bus routes have drivers but no vehicles. Each school day a mix of adult staff members and elder volunteers clad in fluorescent yellow vests lead lines of walking students along the town of Lecco's winding streets and through the schools' gates. Each piedibus has a regular route and assigned stops—just like a "real" bus.

At the Carducci School, 100 children, or more than half of the students, now take walking buses. Many of them were previously driven in cars. Giulio Greppi, a 9-year-old with shaggy blond hair, said he had been driven about a third of a mile each way until he started taking the piedibus. "I get to see my friends and we feel special because we know it's good for the environment," he said.

Lecco's environmental auditor estimates that the piedibuses have eliminated more than 100,000 miles of car travel and prevented thousands of tons of greenhouse gases from entering the atmosphere. This innovation has already spread to the United States, and here, as in Italy, elders make up a substantial fraction of the "piedibus" drivers. The piedibus doesn't just increase physical activity among children and elders, it also connects them to each other and expands the influence elders have in the lives of the young.

Problem

Troubled young people who are sheltered in unstable home environments are at risk for substance abuse, academic failure, and juvenile delinquency. Foster families who would like to provide a loving home for these children and teens are often discouraged by the overwhelming amount of care these young people require. At the same time, older people find it difficult to acquire affordable housing that doesn't place them into an old-age ghetto. These three generations face what seem to be completely unrelated difficulties.

Solution

When connection becomes an organizing principle, we can escape the limitations of existing family structures and bring people together based on their intentions rather than their DNA. The Generations of Hope model of community development creates mixed income intergenerational communities that are designed to support elders, foster parents, and at-risk youth all at the same time. What makes this possible is a culture of reciprocity. When they become part of a Generations of

Hope community, elders agree to volunteer at least six hours per week to the foster families who also live in the community. In return for this support, they receive a reduction in rent. This results in the development of strong, mutually beneficial relationships between foster parents, the at-risk youth they are raising, and the intentional grandparents who live "next door."

As the elders age, and their need for support increases, the foster families pull together to meet these needs. They do this because they feel connected to these elders. Experience has shown that making sure these elders remain in their lives has value. The genius of the Generations of Hope model lies in the way it endows members of each generation with opportunities to give and receive care. Research on this model shows that it increases the health and well-being of the elders, decreases emotional and behavioral difficulties among the foster children, and enhances the quality of life of the foster parents.

AGING IN PLACE

A woman in her early sixties puts her problem this way: "My friends and I talk about it all the time. We all want to sell our houses and buy a house we can live in together. We'll have a nice garden and share the cooking and housework. We'll live together the way we did when we were in college. The thing is, every time I bring it up with my husband, he gets angry. He says he doesn't want to live with 'strangers.' He says he's never selling the house. Never."

This couple is trapped inside an "aging in place" fantasy, which holds that staying in one's home is best, no matter what. Aging in place is seen by millions to be the best strategy for staying in control of one's life and safeguarding one's status as an adult. A survey conducted by AARP found that "92 percent of Americans aged 65 and older want to live out their lives in their current homes; even if they should need help caring for themselves and 82% percent would prefer not to ever move from their current homes." Given the prevalence of ageism in American society, this attitude is very understandable. It is also wrong.

New York Times columnist David Brooks summarized the folly behind our quest for independence: "Over the past 30 years, there has been a tide of research in many fields, all underlining one old truth—that we are intensely social creatures, deeply interconnected with one another and the idea of the lone individual rationally and willfully steering his own life course is often an illusion." Aging in place is actually a form of Denialism, and it works about as well as all the other age-combating strategies available today. Living alone is something human beings have, historically, had very little experience with, and it is a very hard thing to do. Over time, normal human aging relentlessly magnifies its difficulty. Although Americans heartily endorse the concept, staying alone in one's own home is a loser's game. The longer an older person "ages in place," the more likely he or she is to fail at remaining independent.

AGING IN COMMUNITY

The frustrated woman in the example above is more concerned about *how* she is going to live than about *where* she is going to live. Although she would be unlikely to identify herself (or her friends) in this way, she is actually aligned with the burgeoning "aging in community" movement. The Enthusiasts who are driving this movement believe that aging is the ultimate team sport and that we all need and can benefit from the development of new ways to grow old—together. Human beings have a long history of creating "intentional communities" that allow small numbers of like-minded people to come together to share the rhythm of daily life and pursue some noble aim. What is new is the desire to use this approach to foster a better, more connected elderhood.

One of the biggest problems the aging in community movement faces is that *The Golden Girls* made it look so easy. Creating a real com-

munity is actually very hard work. The show's main characters lived together, laughed together, and loved each other, but we never got to see
the details of how they made their shared household work. Living together requires people to solve and re-solve a myriad of legal, economic,
cultural, and psychological questions. As of today, most people find the
prospect of just "staying put" to be far easier than bringing a "shared
household" to life. The good news is that, led by some truly remarkable
Enthusiasts, a growing number of people are succeeding in the effort to
remake their own communities. Here are some of the most notable of
these pioneering efforts.

VILLAGE TO VILLAGE NETWORK

The Village model began in 2001 in the Boston neighborhood of Beacon Hill, in the form of a self-governing, grassroots, community-based
organization focused on the sole purpose of enabling people to remain
living in their homes and communities as they age. In 2010 the Beacon
Hill Village partnered with the community development organization
NCB Capital Impact to help replicate the Village model nationwide
through the Village to Village Network. Made up of local, member-
driven, nonprofit organizations, each Village evaluates, organizes, and
coordinates supportive community programs that build social connections and civic engagement. As of 2013 there are already ninety-five
other Villages and many more in the planning stages.

SENIOR CO-HOUSING

Co-housing is currently the fastest growing model of "intentional
community." The idea was imported from Denmark by architect
Charles Durrett in the 1990s and has grown tenfold in the last decade.
Co-housers join together to design, plan, and oversee the construction
of their community. The built environment typically takes the form
of a cluster of small houses and a larger central "common house" that
is shared by all. This process takes years to complete, and the intense

cooperation required gives life to a robust feeling of community and mutuality among all involved. A group of nuns who left their order over philosophical differences with the Church hierarchy brought one of the first senior co-housing projects to life. Another project, Elderspirit, has twenty-nine households located along the scenic Virginia Creeper Trail within easy walking distance of downtown Abington, Virginia. This community is dedicated to "personal growth, mutual support and an embrace of spirituality."

THE GREEN HOUSE PROJECT

I am a committed nursing home abolitionist. For more than two decades my wife Jude and I have traveled the world teaching elders and their care partners the principles of the Eden Alternative as part of our commitment to creating a world where elders are no longer institutionalized for the "crime" of frailty. At the turn of the century we both realized that the buildings that were being used as nursing homes were aging faster than the people living inside them. The Green House model makes nursing homes obsolete by providing people who would otherwise be living in a nursing home with community-based alternatives that provide an abundance of privacy, better health, and a greater sense of well-being. With the help of a multiyear grant from the Robert Wood Johnson Foundation, the model has already been replicated in more than two dozen states.

EVERMORE

Founded in 2012 by the irrepressible Sarah McKee, this approach to community offers people access to shared housing with private living areas and easy access to communal spaces. Her approach relies on a clever method of converting financial capital into social capital. Part of the equity invested by elders into the building's apartments is used to create a revenue stream that supports the community life of the people who live there. Instead of living in sixty different houses on sixty different streets, elders are able to organize into six neighborhoods of ten apartments each. Every neighborhood has, at its center, a well-furnished kitchen and living area. As the need for support increases, elders can join a "care cooperative" that oversees the support these elders need to remain a part of their community.

It is just as novelist William Gibson has said: "The future is already here—it's just not very evenly distributed."

25

UNCOMMON SENSE

Denialism is a harsh mistress. Her demands are unrelenting and the rewards she is willing to bestow upon her followers are meager. Denialists are so eager to embrace the *idea* of a future anti-aging miracle that they are nearly always willing to overlook the flawed reality of anti-aging technology. In the years ahead, the desire to be spared from aging will continue to run well ahead of the reality, and the result will be anti-aging rhetoric that goes even farther beyond the bounds of believability. In the aftermath of the Second Crucible, the inevitable and highly visible aging of the postwar generation will greatly diminish the number of people who are willing to believe in the prospect of a thousand-year life span spent entirely within the bloom of youth.

The Realists, bolstered by their devotion to common sense, pose a different type of cultural challenge. They have no need of miracles and their perspective on aging is routinely validated by observations made in the course of daily life. When Realists proclaim that aging is an unpleasant reality that can and should be resisted, people believe them. The alignment between their rhetoric and reality makes them much more credible than the Denialists. When Realists insist, "Use it or lose it!" people nod their heads. They remember, all too well, what happened to Dad after he broke his ankle on that fishing trip.

This reliance on what we see to inform what we know deceives us much more often than we suppose. Almost all our ancestors, for example, believed that the sun rose in the east, rode high into the sky, and at the end of the day, sank into the west. This is clearly what appears to happen, and in medieval Europe, this commonsense cosmology was reinforced by the theology of the Roman Catholic Church. Nicolaus Copernicus challenged this belief in his masterwork *De revolutionibus orbium coelestium*. In its pages, he daringly separated truth from appearance and then supported his conclusions with surprisingly accurate mathematical calculations. The Church responded by banning the book for three centuries. The idea that the earth moves while the sun remains fixed is a near-perfect example of uncommon sense.

Enthusiasm's greatest value lies in its ability to expose and then explore dimensions of experience that common sense and ageism have hidden from our sight. For example, everyone *knows* that mental agility declines with age. Indeed, multiple well-designed scientific studies have verified the waning power of the mind in late life. Such studies matter little to the Denialists. They place their faith in a yet-to-be-discovered technology that will rescue them from such a fate. Realists, in contrast, use this information as a spur to ever greater diligence. They hope that (still unproven) brain exercises and antioxidant-rich diets will delay the decline they know must come. Meanwhile, the Enthusiasts ask, "Is there something more to be discovered here? Are we missing something important?" They know well that, sometimes, common sense is a little too common.

THE SPEED TRAP

People of all ages are familiar with the experience of knowing a name, having that name right on the tip of the tongue—and still not being able to produce the name. The man who created the first English dictionary, Samuel Johnson, was familiar with this circumstance and the meaning that society attached to it. In 1783 he wrote:

> There is a wicked inclination in most people to suppose an old man decayed in his intellects. If a young or middle-aged man, when leaving a company, does not remember where he laid his hat, it is nothing; but if the same inattention is discovered in an old man, people will shrug up their shoulders, and say, "His memory is going."

As is so often the case with elderhood, the problem is derived mainly from our ageist culture. What Dr. Johnson didn't know is that someday neuroscientists would provide a surprisingly commonsense explanation for age-related changes in memory. It turns out that younger brains are good at quickly recalling bits of information (like a name or where you put your hat) because they have a relatively straightforward filing system. Older people, by dint of long experience, store memories within a more diffuse network of brain systems. The author of a 2011 study published in the journal *Brain Research* described the effect: "We're all accessing the same brain networks to remember things, but we have to call in the troops to do the work when we get older, while we only have to call in a few soldiers when you're younger." This simple insight can help explain a few of the normal but puzzling mental phenomena associated with aging.

First, there is abundant evidence that mental agility declines with age. If that sentence makes you feel uneasy, recall that there is also abundant evidence that our maximum foot speed also declines with age. While both of these things are true, only the former is stigmatized. Almost no one becomes anxious when they think about not being able to run the hundred-meter dash in under thirteen seconds. Nearly twenty years ago, Betty Friedan, in her book *The Fountain of Age*, did us all a favor when she drew attention to research that asked, "Are there virtues more precious than mere agility?" Ohio State psychologist Roger Ratcliff and his colleagues have been exploring this terrain for more than a decade, and their studies have taken our understanding of mental agility to a new level. While their peers defined agility solely in terms of speed, Ratcliff's team chose to explore the relationship between speed and accuracy.

One of their most important studies evaluated three hundred subjects of varying ages as they watched as a group of asterisks flash on a computer screen. The number of on-screen asterisks was classified as either "small" (31 to 50) or "large" (51 to 70). After viewing each image, participants were asked to assign it to one of these two groups. While increasing age was clearly associated with decreased speed, the accuracy of the older subjects matched that of younger people. When Ratcliff's team then actively encouraged the older participants to focus more on speed and not worry about accuracy, their reaction time matched that of the college students in the study.

The results of these kinds of studies can be understood as an amalgam of biology and culture. Age does "change our minds," but the meaning we assign to these changes is heavily influenced by the society in which we live. In this case, the elders in the study understood that defects in accuracy are more stigmatizing than slower reaction times. Given this bias, a rational older man has every reason to avoid having people say of him, as they did of the man who forgot his hat, "His memory is going." Ratcliff explains, "Older people don't want to make errors, so what they do is adopt a more conservative decision criteria and that slows them down." Other studies have shown that, while younger people are better at finding patterns in strings of numbers, the reluctance of older people to jump to conclusions help them outperform younger people when it comes to identifying strings that have no pattern. This ability to not be drawn into the error of seeing patterns that aren't there, this ability to reserve judgment, is the basis for some impressive new elder-oriented mental abilities.

Day-to-day interactions with elders and research studies both indicate that age can increase our ability to extract the essential meaning of a story, event, or social situation. Older people are better than young people when it comes to capturing the gist of things. How do they do this? Having seen similar situations in the past is helpful, but having more experience is just part of the answer. As we age, our brains distribute memories across a wider range of brain structures compared to when we were young. Retrieving and using these memories therefore requires the simultaneous engagement of multiple cognitive systems. This more global activation helps older people see a "big picture" that younger people often miss.

But that's not all.

The changing, age-related distribution of memory and cognition also makes it more likely that our memories will sporadically "misfire." Neuroscientists have done considerable work on this tip-of-the-tongue phenomenon. They define it as a failed attempt to retrieve a word, number, or name from memory (partial recall sometimes produces a letter or syllable) combined with the feeling that recall is immanent. Our ageist culture leads nonneurologists to call this a "senior moment."

People do become anxious whenever an age-related word retrieval hiccup occurs. Tellingly, the resulting flustered confession of failure emphasizes speed rather than accuracy. Also common are (sometimes joking) rehearsals of ageist stereotypes. The function of these protestations is to shift the emphasis from a failure of accuracy (Lost your hat, did you?) to a speed problem. This is why they are referred to as "moments." These events can, and should, be used to help people better understand the distinctive contours of the elder mind.

An Enthusiast's approach to age-related word-finding glitches runs something like this. First, remain calm and carry on. There is no reason to panic and no cause for anxiety. This is normal. Second, don't struggle to find the word you need; consciously slow down. This is an opportunity for you to widen the activation of your mind; who knows what new ideas and interpretations might emerge out of this process? Third, if you are in the company of others, use this opportunity to dispel ageist stereotypes. Something like this will do: "People used to call them 'senior moments,' but it's really more like mind expansion. As we age, we use more of our brains, which helps us see general patterns more clearly, but it can also make retrieving a particular word more difficult. Anyway, as I was saying . . ." The loss of mental agility can also give us valuable new abilities, if we know where to look for them.

HARDENING OF THE LIFESTYLE

The Realist perspective is largely responsible for the idea that the ideal state for people living beyond adulthood is stasis. This is the tyranny of *still*. As long as we can *still* do the things we used to do, others can't really say that we are getting old. Or so the Realists believe. The problem with this perspective is that it undercuts the ethic of growth and development that is such an important part of the lives of younger people. Our society disapproves of stasis during youth and, rightly, labels it as a form of failure. The difficult transition from childhood to adulthood is smoothed by the belief that growth is normal and expected. People who are "growing up" can expect society to facilitate the transition from childhood by normalizing curiosity and discovery. Even more helpfully, the road out of childhood is well provisioned with rest stops and has good signage all along the way.

Unfortunately, the same cannot be said about the journey into life beyond adulthood. Far more people get stuck in adulthood than get stuck in childhood. In fact, the inability to outgrow adulthood is the most pervasive and least recognized of all developmental disabilities. The earliest sign of this developmental delay is the ache that comes from living in a way that calls for another way of living. Koyaanisqatsi. The question, which neither the Denialists nor the Realists have an answer for, is, "How do we get unstuck?" The postwar generation's ability to find and make use of the tools it needs to outgrow adulthood will do much to determine whether we will have the elders we need to restore balance to society as a whole.

Being imaginative, curious, open to change, and willing to explore new ways is the best possible preparation for overthrowing the tyranny of *still*. The goal here is to help people (of all ages) understand how it is possible to grow, change, and adapt over time while remaining true to themselves. The concept that best explains this capacity for change with continuity comes from developmental psychology and is known as "trait transformation." Although our core personality traits (the big five are extroversion, agreeableness, conscientiousness, neuroticism, and openness to experience) remain remarkably stable across the life span, how these traits are displayed changes as we age.

An example drawn from early childhood development can help illustrate how trait transformation works. When researchers test the ability of very young infants to track moving pictures of human faces with their eyes, they find that some babies score much higher than others. When they retest the same infants several months later, however, the infants who tested high on the tracking test score much lower. Why? It turns out that the trait being tested is sociability, and for very young infants, following a picture with their gaze is being sociable. As their social skill set grows, they are no longer interested in moving pictures: they want to connect with real people. A talent for following pictures becomes, with time, a talent for making and keeping friends. The process of trait transformation is active throughout our lives and has helped to make AARP's Experience Corps a major success. People with long and successful careers flock to this nationwide volunteer program because they are eager to use their skills in new and different ways.

THE CLOAK OF INVISIBILITY

A friend of mine—a woman in her midfifties—decided to let her Enthusiast freak flag fly and stopped dyeing her hair. In place of the jet-black mane I had always known her to have, she began sporting a very crisp shade of silver. The problem, as she later told me, was that after she "went gray" people stopped seeing her: she became invisible. On airplanes, in stores, at meetings, and on the street people stopped seeing her the way they had before. When she started coloring her hair again, it was as if the cloak of invisibility had been lifted. She was once again seen as a person of worth, a person worth noticing.

Although the historic roots of racism are very different from those of ageism, it is worth noting one point of similarity. For nearly a century, the Pullman Company hired African-American men to serve as porters on its thousands of sleeping cars. It was customary throughout that period for Pullman's customers (all of whom were white) to refer to every porter as "George," no matter what his actual first name might be. The practice was rooted in the antebellum South, where slaves were commonly named after their masters. The porters were, in these terms, George Pullman's boys. Oral histories taken from these porters frequently emphasize how demeaning it felt to not be known as an individual.

Just as racists are likely to say, "They all look alike to me," those who (often subconsciously) endorse ageist stereotypes often fail to see older people as individuals. For my part, I was fortunate enough to be mentored by the late T. Franklin Williams, a giant in the field of geriatrics who also had the gift for making complicated things seem simple. He would often tell young physicians, "When you've seen one eighty-year-old, you've seen *one* eighty-year-old." It was his way of reminding us of the central role that polymorphism plays in defining the contours of life beyond adulthood.

When I was just out of residency, one of the least satisfying duties I was called on to fulfill involved conducting physical exams on the hundred or so kindergartners who started school each fall at our rural school district. They were, I am certain, all unique individuals to their parents. They were also all four or five years old, about forty pounds and about forty inches tall. After the first three hours, I must say, they all started to look alike to me.

My complaint about the monotony of the work was, in this case, well founded. It turns out that human beings are endowed with an important but little-appreciated trait that unfolds across the life span. When we are young, we are very much like other people our age. As we enter into midlife this begins to change. As Bennett Cerf once observed, "Middle age is when your classmates are so gray and wrinkled and bald they don't recognize you." By late adulthood it becomes apparent to even the least observant person that people who are your age are much less like each other than they used to be.

This tendency toward growing differences within an age group helps explain some interesting and seemingly unrelated phenomena. For example, the lower polymorphism of childhood let Drs. Spock and Watson write highly practical and very detailed books whose precepts could be applied to nearly all children. I know that some readers may be disappointed by this book's failure to make specific recommendations for and about those in search of life beyond adulthood. The general guidance offered in "Slow," "Deep," and "Connected" is actually matched to the more general needs of people living in late adulthood. Imagine a book about elderhood that aped childcare experts by claiming to know what people who are fifty-seven need and how they are so very different from people who are fifty-six or fifty-eight. This false certainty would be quickly revealed as nonsense. Tragically, the people among us who are the most diverse, have the most distinctive personal histories, and the richest stories to tell, are routinely dismissed as being so similar to each other as to become invisible.

My own awakening to this issue occurred when an elder removed her cloak of invisibility and made me listen to her. I was just thirty-one years old, fresh out of residency and working part-time as a physician in a nursing home. On that day I was called to see this woman about a rash on her arm. I entered her room with all my customary bravado. I examined the rash and informed her, in a too-loud voice, of my diagnosis. As I prepared to leave, she took hold of my arm and pulled me over to the bed so that I was looking into her eyes. As I did so, I saw *her* for the first time. She was very old, with pale, almost translucent skin and limpid blue eyes.

She said, "I'm so lonely."

I don't recall what I said in response, but I know that I excused myself and returned to the nurses' station. There I wrote a note in this woman's chart and ordered a medication for her rash. I left the nursing home and went on with my busy day. Later that night her image returned to me. I had *seen* . . . not the way a doctor sees a patient but rather as one human being sees another. She was a person with a vital and unmet need. When I woke the next morning, I knew that I had to do something about the problem of loneliness. I began to visit the nursing home when I was not on duty. I would sit quietly in a corner with a speckled composition book in my lap and practice seeing the people who lived there. As a result of this experience, my wife, Jude Meyers Thomas, and I founded the reform movement known as the Eden Alternative and dedicated ourselves to combating the plagues of loneliness, helplessness, and boredom.

One of the most important ways for older people to become elders is for them to *insist* that others "look them in the eye." Although this may seem egocentric, there is nothing selfish about such a demand. Elderhood possesses a depth and diversity of experience that is valuable only to the degree that it is shared. The cloak of invisibility doesn't just conceal the elders in our midst, it also removes a rich palette of possibility from our sight. When I was young, an elder helped me overcome my inability to see elders as people and, in doing so, led me to discover my life's work. Without speaking the words, she said, "Look at me!" and I did.

Challenging the dehumanizing power of ageism is difficult work and, as Enthusiasts who've gone gray and then resumed coloring their hair will tell you, it can also inspire fear and self-doubt. Fortunately, we can rely upon and be inspired by the example of people like Frank Rollins. Mr. Rollins, a retired Pullman porter, recalls the importance of insisting on being seen as an individual. "I would walk into the car, and I would say, 'May I have your attention please. My name is Frank Rollins. If you can't remember that, that's okay. You can call me porter—it's right here on the cap, you should be able to remember that.' "

We would all do well to follow his example.

26

CRONING

In an essay first published in 1946, George Orwell lamented, "To see what is in front of one's nose needs constant struggle." While it is easy, from the distance of a century or more, to mock magazine articles that warned against young women "sitting in a place that is too narrow; read not out of the same book; let not your eagerness to see anything induce you to place your head close to another person's," it is much more difficult to see and name the damage that our culture's youth-centric definition of womanhood is doing to us all. Indeed, seeing it requires "constant effort." In contemporary American English the conjunction of the words *old* and *woman* bring forth a murderer's row of negative images and attitudes. Fortunately, there are among the Enthusiasts a growing number of women who are willing and eager to challenge this unthinking and unyielding bias.

They're striking back against sexist ageism by taking hold of and redefining words that are currently being used to demean older women. The word *crone*, for example, is familiar to most people but is rarely said aloud because it expresses a caustic level of bigotry. The act of calling a woman a name that means "withered old hag" requires a level of cruelty beyond what we encounter in our daily lives. If the word sounds antique, that's because it has roots that go much further back than most people know. *Crone* has a lustrously beautiful heritage that reaches back into ancient times.

The modern English word *crone* descends from the ancient Greek word for time—*kronos*. For thousands of years this word was used to refer to a "woman wise with time." The image of an old woman who was wise, kind, and gentle was well known to the German peasants who first told the Grimm brothers the story of the grandfather, father, and son. The folklore gathered by the brothers also contained the story of "Mother Holle." In the most common telling she was an old woman, a weaver of fate, who lived at the bottom of a well and gave each person exactly the reward he or she deserved. We can still catch glimpses of Mother Holle in the popular but sanitized image of the "fairy godmother."

George Orwell made a career out of closely observing the uses and misuses of language. His counsel is useful here: "At any given moment there is an orthodoxy, a body of ideas of which it is assumed that all right-thinking people will accept without question." Where once the worth of a woman was judged according to her purity, piety, and submissiveness, we now live under an orthodoxy that ties a woman's worth to the youthfulness of her appearance. In an inversion of thousands of years of appreciation for the value of older women, we now assume that youth is necessarily superior to age. If that seems to be an overstatement, a quick trip to the local magazine rack will make the point. The faces, words, insights, and wisdom of older women are missing from all the most popular publications. Orwell concludes, "Anyone who challenges the prevailing orthodoxy finds himself silenced with surprising effectiveness."

Given the Orwellian circumstances that prevail around questions related to women and age, it is difficult to imagine how small bands of Enthusiasts could ever overturn the prevailing orthodoxy. Their solution is, as we will see, both ancient and wise. These women gather together and bestow upon each other the venerable title of "Crone." They refer to this practice as "Croning," and these ceremonies are endowed with tremendous power. Croning transmutes the power of the word crone. What was an instrument of harm becomes an honored title. Mother Holle would be proud.

The countercultural elements of croning have kept the movement underground; few people have ever heard of the practice. The lack of visibility should not, however, be confused with a lack of influence. I travel widely and I find crones nearly everywhere I go. I see them because I know where to look; I get to talk to them because I know what to say. Though they remain out of sight, their gatherings give women a glimpse of what an Enthusiast future might look like. Such a future would be especially beneficial to women because society penalizes aging women much more severely than aging men.

I know that readers who are not (yet) crones may be wondering what a Croning ceremony looks and feels like. There are many variations on the theme of Croning, but all such ceremonies have a few commonalities. First, there is a strong communal feeling to these events. Women who have already accepted the title of Crone gather together, sometimes adding younger women to the company when they bestow the title. Second, there is an explicit recognition that the whole of a woman's life cycle is endowed with worth and dignity, with love and loss, with triumph and suffering. These ceremonies combine a celebration of this wealth with a summons to continued growth and development. Third, Croning is an entirely voluntary and informal affair. There is no Crone licensing board, there are no tests or qualifications, there is no accrediting body. It is a primal expression of women helping women.

I'll illustrate the experience of Croning with an excerpt taken from my novel Tribes of Eden. I've read this passage to a number of Crone gatherings, where it has been received with enthusiasm. Near the end of the novel one of the main characters, a woman named Emma, has reached an age that allows her to become a crone. I use the age fifty-seven for reasons that are explained below, but any age over fifty will do. The chapter starts with a spirited day-long party held in anticipation of the evening's ceremony. As twilight descends on the land, Emma and the women who will participate in the ceremony take their places around a labyrinth with a kind of circular walking path used for meditation. The old crones who lead the ceremony are named Haleigh and Hannah. Emma is their niece.

Haleigh and Hannah stood together in the center of the labyrinth. At moonrise, Haleigh's frayed voice asked, "Who among us is ready to become a crone?"

Emma answered, "I am."

"Come forward."

Emma walked into the center and took her place beside them. She looked up into the darkening sky and found the pale yellow light of Saturn high overhead. The planet stood in the very spot it had occupied on the day she was born. Once every 19 years, three times in all, it had returned there. This was her fifty-seventh birthday. She lowered her gaze. Around her, ordered according to their ages, stood a circle of women and girls. Each held an unlit candle. When the Strawberry Moon climbed high enough to cast a shadow, Haleigh faced Emma and asked. "Who are you?"

"I am Emma of the Shire, the daughter of Val, the granddaughter of Jude and Kianna. I am a healer, a post rider, a lover, a midwife, an artist, and a teller of stories. I am both the daughter of and the mother of the Tribes of Eden. I am the one people call the Peace Maker."

Hannah lit the candle of the youngest among them. The girl, just four years old, solemnly turned and lit the candle held by the girl to her left. Soon, a dozen tender faces glowed with reflected light. Emma thought of her childhood. She remembered growing up, wild and free, racing barefoot across meadows heavy with morning dew.

When the light came to the young women, she remembered the world as it was when she was their age.

The flame passed to the mothers, women in the thickest part of life. It was the time of making, the time of love and sacrifice. She thought of the men she had known and loved. They'd married other women, started families of their own. Motherhood was a joy she would never taste.

Then came the young crones, these were the women she'd known since childhood. She looked into their faces and saw her own. The wrinkles, etched by time, the lines of worry and laughter, those were hers as well. The knowledge that their lives were already more than halfway lived, they shared that too. Lit from above by the light of the moon and from below by a candle; they were beautiful, and so was she.

Finally, the flame passed to the Old Crones. She admired them. Admired their poise, the graceful way they draped the mantle of age across their shoulders. They were what she might still become. When the candle held by the oldest crone was alight, the circle was complete.

It was Hannah's turn to speak. "A crone understands that she must give before she can receive the gifts of age. Are you prepared for this exchange?"

"I am."

Hannah escorted her niece to the east most point of the circle. "Your limbs once did your bidding without hesitation. Your face was smooth and unblemished and you knew little of life's worries or cares. Are you willing to set your youth aside?"

"I am."

"I offer you Elderhood in return. Know that your mind and body are just as they should be. You are as you should be. The crone finds new beauty in age. It is a loveliness that the maiden cannot know. Honor this beauty and it will honor you."

Hannah walked slowly to the south of the circle. "Once you held within you the potential for bringing forth new life. Now your wise blood flows no more. Are you willing to surrender the dream of making new life?"

Emma laid her hand upon her womb, ready, at last, to leave its aching emptiness behind. She said, "I am."

"Then age shall bring you the gift of understanding. Your wisdom, your patience and your counsel will allow you to guide the young of many mothers."

Hannah found the circle's northern edge. "For too long, you've taken the promise of good health for granted. Are you ready to accept weakness and frailty when they come into your life?

"I am."

"In time, and if fortune favors you, you will enrich the lives of others by allowing them to care for you. I offer you the blessing of knowing how to receive that care gracefully."

Hannah brought Emma to the west most point of the circle. "During your youth you clung to the belief that you were immortal. Are you ready now to surrender that illusion?"

"I am."

"Accepting that death will come gives depth to life. As a Crone you will have so much less to fear. I give you the freedom to speak and write and do as you think best."

They returned to the center of the circle and Haleigh said, "In the company of these women in this place on this night, you begin a new journey. You are, my dear sweet Emma, a Crone of the Tribes of Eden."

Their candles raised high, the women came forward to congratulate the Shire's youngest crone.

• • •

In the story that develops between the covers of the *Tribes of Eden*, the Croning ceremony is cultural. The women of the Shire experience it as a customary event that would be understood as a normal part of every woman's life. Contemporary culture, in contrast, regards an event like this as being alarmingly countercultural. Instead of initiating a woman into "life beyond adulthood," our society erects razor wire fences around elderhood—and then electrifies them. In fact, the prejudice against embracing one's own aging is so powerful that many of the people reading about this ceremony for the first time may well find some part of themselves recoiling from its premise. We have been taught that we must fight a war against aging and peace talks are simply out of the question.

When the flame reaches the oldest crones, we encounter another tug on our preconceived notions. Emma's response to them is admiration. She values "their poise, the graceful way they draped the mantle of age across their shoulders. They were what she might still become." She sees their beauty and wants it for her own.

I do understand that people living in an intensely ageist society often find reading about and thinking about crones to be difficult. The good news here is that you don't have to do anything. If the description of a croning ceremony offered above helps some people think a little differently about the nexus of age and gender, that counts as progress. Those who felt inspired by the "women of the Shire" should remember that there is no reason you can't emulate them. You are free to borrow the words and actions set forth above for your own use. Even better, you and your friends can create your own Croning ceremony. Gather together and let the oldest woman in your circle bestow the title of crone upon the younger.

Men can, and should, join the struggle against sexist ageism. This bigotry has a profoundly negative impact on the lives of our mothers, wives, daughters, and friends. No one is immune from it, no matter how rich and famous she might be. Workplace discrimination based on sex and age belongs near the top of any list of ills that should be eradicated, but there is more, much more, that needs to be done. As Orwell said, it needs a constant struggle to see what is right in front of our noses; this is particularly true when it comes to America's bias against older women. One seemingly trivial example helps reveal how far we have to go.

Every year at Halloween millions of girls and women dress up as "witches." Anyone who has ever tended the candy bowl on Halloween has seen these costumes. They seem ordinary, customary, and sometimes even cute. The crone's point of view, however, quickly reveals the ugliness behind this practice. Witch imagery (I am talking here about the traditional forms, not the antiseptic television offshoot) dates back hundreds of years. These stereotypes, which seem so innocent on October 31, are actually powerful instruments of cultural warfare. Europe endured a three-hundred-year-long witch hunt (1450–1750) that led to the execution of 50,000 to 100,000 people and the torture of at least as many more. The witch imagery that dates from that time is designed to degrade and diminish the value, the worth, and the importance of women "wise with time."

Because we live in a time when a woman's face is thought to define her worth (Young, good. Old, bad.), encouraging young people to don a witch's "face" is an especially useful strategy for demeaning older women. The witch's prominent nose and ears are exaggerated expressions of the facial changes that accompany age for men and women alike. Bone growth stops before we enter into adulthood, but the cartilage in our ears and nose keeps growing for the rest of our lives. The mocking exaggeration of normal facial characteristics is unfortunately familiar to African Americans. Those who traffic in such things are rightly called racists.

A "witch's wart" is also commonly used to mar the young trick-or-treater's face. Normal aging results in an enlargement of the sebaceous glands that are responsible for secreting the oily substance that helps keep our skin healthy. Because these glands are often associated with hair follicles, these enlarged glands can seem to have a hair growing out of them. This is normal and has nothing to do with warts. Likewise, aging results in the redistribution of subcutaneous fat in the human face. The fat pads surrounding the eyes and chin of older people become less prominent, making those features appear relatively larger. The witch's coarse hair and reedy voice are also exaggerations of normal phenomena. The "evil" in evidence here is entirely on the side of those who take pleasure in mocking, shaming, and dismissing older women.

Enthusiast women who dare to gather together in circles of mutual support and dare to assert the truth of their age and the existence of their wisdom will, inevitably, be accused of "witchy" behavior and beliefs. People will dismiss them as ugly and old and claim that their ceremonies are pitiful exercises in self-consolation. In fact, the crones among us are laying the foundation of a better way of living, one that will benefit people of all ages. A Croning ceremony may be in your future, or in the future of a woman you care about, but even if it is not, you can point out and condemn the prejudice against older women wherever it appears.

We would not allow daughters or granddaughters to go trick-or-treating in blackface, nor would we tolerate their appearing in public costumed as a "greedy" Jew. We should not tolerate their dressing up as "witches." Because they are growing up in an ageist society, few girls and young women appreciate the damage that sexist ageism does to older women. Those of us who do understand its impact have an obligation to help others see the message that these costumes send about "women wise with age."

27

ELDERTOPIA

When I was in medical school, I was taught that menopause was an example of "primary ovarian failure." It wasn't until I had worked with elders for many years that I began to challenge that view. Gradually, I began to see the complex mental and physical changes that accompany menopause as a means of transformation. As is the case with all real and lasting change, there are parts of the process that are decidedly unpleasant. No one welcomes hot flashes or vaginal dryness, nor should they. In our youth, we struggled with the emotional upheavals, hormonal storms, and acne outbreaks that accompany puberty, but we all knew where it was taking us: we were in the process of becoming adults. Very few of the many millions who are now poised to leave adulthood understand that aging is what changes an adult into an elder.

A lifetime spent living in and coping with our youth-centric society makes it hard to identify or appreciate the distinctive virtues that define elders and elderhood. Several years ago, I wrote a book called *What Are Old People For?* When it was released, I hurried down to the local bookstore so that I could admire it on the shelf for the first time.

I searched the store—no book. Finally, I asked an earnest young clerk for help. He looked it up on the computer and then announced, quite cheerfully, that the store had three copies. He added, without missing a beat, "They're in the death and dying section." Without meaning to, this young man gave me the most concise definition of what America thinks of "life beyond adulthood" that I have ever encountered.

We live in an ageist society and we are inundated by propaganda that insists aging, like smallpox, will be eliminated in our lifetimes. We are told the nation is going to be bankrupted by the selfish demands of countless frail old people. In particular, the media reliably emphasize the cost of Social Security and Medicare while at the same time discounting the dignity and stability these programs offer to millions of people. Decades of growth in productivity have expanded our access to financial capital while at the same time depleting our stock of "social capital."

We need the love and acceptance that come from healthy families, neighborhoods, and communities much more than we need a new high for the Dow Jones Industrials. We need elders, more than ever, because of their unique ability to connect us. They are the human equivalent of superglue.

In order to develop fully, elders need access to a slow, deep, connected way of living. The "fast" life that suits adults so well interferes with the normal development of elders because it leads them to keep running a race that they can never win. I was recently on a plane and overheard an older man comment on his much younger seatmate's New York City Marathon T-shirt. "You know," he said, "I ran a two-eighteen in 1982." When every race goes to the swift, all elders have to offer the rest of us are their memories of how fast they used to run.

The mania for adultish independence and achievement also lies behind the American consensus on "aging in place." Everyone wants to "stay at home," even if the only advantage conferred is the illusion of independence. Far too often the price that must be paid comes in the form of an excruciating self-exile from membership in a supportive community. In contemporary American society people rarely encounter or maintain relationships with elders who are not also close relatives. As a result, millions are denied access to the emotional honesty and foresight of people who are able to imagine and accept the idea of their own death.

Although the specifics of their role have varied widely around the world and through history, elders have used their capacity for wisdom and peacemaking to influence their families and communities. Wisdom plays little part in the workings of an elder-poor society like ours. Few can even say, rightly, what "wisdom" is. In my work with elders I have found the following to be a useful definition of wisdom. "Wisdom consists of insight into the problems of everyday life gained through an abundance of experience." While not every old person is wise (and there is no fool like an old fool), a room full of eighty-somethings inevitably contains more wisdom than a room full of twenty-somethings. It is the accumulation of life experience, and an awareness of their own mortality, that has long enabled elders to become skillful peacemakers.

A thousand years ago the "Great Law of Peace" endowed clan mothers of the newly formed Iroquois Confederacy with the power to select men for leadership positions, impeach them if they failed in their duty, and veto declarations of war. Since then it has been the duty of old women to ensure that "the Chief Statesmen shall be mentors of the people for all time. . . . With endless patience they shall carry out their duty, and their firmness shall be tempered with a tenderness for their people. Neither anger nor fury shall find lodgment in their minds, and all their words and actions shall be marked by calm deliberation."

In 2004, three women—Jyoti, Ann Rosencranz, and Lynn Schawecker—sent a letter of invitation to fourteen grandmothers all descended from tribal peoples:

> We are approaching our indigenous Grandmothers to ask for help and guidance in these times, so that we may make relations between peoples and nations, reinforce the prayer of unity and listen to our elders who

hold earth based ways of life and prayer. The dream of the vision is that our indigenous Grandmothers who hold traditional lines of medicine and healing come together in council, not to mix, but to share their teachings and prophecies. We need the voice of our Grandmothers in this time so we can bring sustainability to our communities, to our peoples and to our planet.

Thirteen Grandmothers agreed to meet in Upstate New York, on land that had once been governed by the Iroquois Confederacy and its "Great Law of Peace." They issued this statement of purpose:

WE ARE THIRTEEN INDIGENOUS GRANDMOTHERS who gathered from the four directions in the land of the people of the Iroquois Confederacy. We come here from the Amazon rainforest, the Alaskan Tundra of North America, the great forest of the American northwest, the vast plains of North America, the highlands of central America, the Black Hills of South Dakota, the mountains of Oaxaca, the desert of the American southwest, the mountains of Tibet and from the rainforest of Central Africa.

We have united as one. Ours is an alliance of prayer, education and healing for our Mother Earth, all Her inhabitants, all the children and for the next seven generations to come.

We are deeply concerned with the unprecedented destruction of our Mother Earth, the contamination of our air, waters and soil, the atrocities of war, the global scourge of poverty, the threat of nuclear weapons and waste, the prevailing culture of materialism, the epidemics which threaten the health of the Earth's peoples, the exploitation of indigenous medicines, and with the destruction of indigenous ways of life.

We, the International Council of Thirteen Indigenous Grandmothers, come together to nurture, educate and train our children. We come together to uphold the practice of our ceremonies and affirm the right to use our plant medicines free of legal restriction. We come together to protect the lands where our peoples live and upon which our cultures depend, to safeguard the collective heritage of traditional medicines, and to defend the earth Herself. We believe that the teachings of our ancestors will light our way through an uncertain future.

These ideals stand worlds apart from the Squares' declaration of "conservative principles" in the *Sharon Statement* and the Activists' assessment of American society's ills in the *Port Huron Statement*. These are older women speaking purposefully and authoritatively about the state of the world and what must be done to repair the damage being done to it by humanity. Some readers will find it difficult to take the grandmothers' intentions seriously. Their belief that "the teachings of our ancestors will light our way through an uncertain future" seems naive to people long accustomed to living under the sway of unrestricted adult power.

The Thirteen Grandmothers and their youthful allies have since organized Elders Councils all over the world. These gatherings typically last a week and are structured around the needs and capacities of the grandmothers. The diary of one gathering of the grandmothers goes like this:

- Monday: Children's Day—The elementary school students had questions, then gifts; a beautiful luncheon, prepared by older students, concluded the visit. Grandmother Margaret Behan said, "This school and what they are doing here gives me hope." Grandfather Stalking Wolf, the Lipan Apache elder who instructed Tom Brown Jr., taught the children wilderness skills.
- Tuesday: Women's Day Gathering—A brilliant blue sky and sun shone on the four hundred plus women gathered for a pic-

nic. The grandmothers spoke after lunch, followed by a question and answer period. Each grandmother received poignant queries.

- Wednesday: Men's Gathering—In the evening, the grandmothers went to the local community college for the Men's Gathering. Nearly two hundred men attended. The evening ran two hours overtime as the men shared personal and spirited exchanges with the grandmothers.
- Thursday: A Day for Healing and Community—The grandmothers were given private appointments with volunteer health practitioners in the morning. In the evening, all the grandmothers and eighty invited guests came together at the Community Center to discuss healing of the racial divides within the community.
- Friday: Closing Ceremony—Grandmothers held the closing ceremony, with the extinguishing of the Sacred Fire, and the dismantling of the Buffalo Skull altar. Before lunch, the grandmothers received Dorothy Cotton for tea. A grandmother and a guide for many people, Ms. Cotton was one of Martin Luther King's close associates and dear friends.

How many adults can say that they have ever done so worthy a week of work?

Can you?

AN EARTH ELDER

The exercise of a profoundly spiritual, highly influential elderhood is not limited to indigenous peoples. It is possible to outgrow adulthood and find, at last, a legacy that William Tyndale described as the "reason wherefore one was sent into this world." Nearly five centuries after Tyndale wrote those words, a terminally ill man named Fred Lanphear explained why he founded the Earth Elder movement.

Although recently diagnosed with ALS, I do not fear my impending mortality, but I do fear for the fate of our home, Planet Earth, and for future generations whose lives will be impacted by the consequences of climate change, species destruction, and the general decline of the health of the planet. Our generation has been a major contributor to the actions that are compromising the health of the planet and we must be accountable and do all that we can to correct the disastrous trajectory we are on.

A person diagnosed with a terminal disease has the freedom (not always exercised) to state the truth as he or she sees it:

As an elder, I have a unique perspective to share with my peers and more importantly, with the generations that will follow me. I have decided to take on the mantle of Earth Elder, one who speaks and cares for Earth and future generations.

Who would or could stop him from doing this?

Many of my long-held assumptions have been challenged and radically changed. In the past, I arrogantly believed that science and technology would ultimately provide solutions to all our human needs. The focus on human needs without consideration for other species and our common habitats is the contradiction that we are finally recognizing. We are integrally connected and can no longer isolate or elevate ourselves apart from other life forms.

If we allow it to work its way with us, the process of aging can lift the scales from our eyes. This new vision allows elders to see things that adults are blind to, just as adults understand things that children cannot grasp.

As an agricultural scientist I once contributed to the development and promotion of pesticides. Since discovering the consequences of continual use of pesticides, I have now dedicated my agricultural practices to being totally organic. Many of the practices that I once considered to be sacrosanct I can now see are of questionable value. It is particularly challenging to be faced with your past errors of judgment, but also freeing to be able to accept what has happened and take action to correct and/or change those practices.

All human growth depends on a willingness to face "past errors of judgment." After the First Crucible, American society encouraged, validated, and actively mythologized the postwar generation's reconsideration of its youthful distemper. Even as late as 2000, presidential candidate George W. Bush was able to blunt the impact of reports of an arrest for driving while intoxicated and possible cocaine use simply by asserting, "When I was young and irresponsible, I was young and irresponsible." The Second Crucible will be more conflicted than the first in large part because American society often confines the confession of adult errors to the deathbed. Among the gifts of elderhood is the freedom to admit and begin to correct one's adult mistakes right now—today.

The time is ripe for elders to reclaim their rightful role of speaking for Earth and future generations. Those of us who are willing to accept the challenge need to come together in local groups, connect via the Internet, and periodically gather in council to share our experiences, learnings, and emerging vision of our role.

As I face my mortality, I feel a sense of urgency in taking steps to help build the movement of Earth Elders now. This is not something we can put off to another time, as many of us are in or approaching the final time of our lives. It is urgent because of impending planetary shifts that may be irreversible, such as global warming and the accelerated extinction of species.

Instead of spending his final years raging against his body's lethal betrayal, Fred Lanphear opened his mind and his heart. Elderhood enabled him to turn his attention toward matters much larger than himself. Elderhood inspired him to carefully consider questions that would not be answered until long after he was gone. Elderhood transformed an old man living with a degenerative neurological disease into an exceptional human being.

THE ELDERS

With the help of Graça Machel and Desmond Tutu, Nelson Mandela set about bringing together a small, dedicated group of elders who, he believed, could contribute to resolving global problems and easing human suffering. The members of this guild have all, in Mandela's words, "earned international trust, demonstrated integrity, and built a reputation for inclusive, progressive leadership." When he announced the formation of the Elders in July 2007, on the occasion of his eighty-ninth birthday, Mandela described the organization's mission:

The Elders can speak freely and boldly, working both publicly and behind the scenes. They will reach out to those who most need their help. They will support courage where there is fear, foster agreement where there is conflict, and inspire hope where there is despair.

Elderhood needs to operate in the political realm. Although old age changes the body and mind and the force of time erodes the capacities of youth, the inalienable rights of the elder, however, remain undiminished. Barry Barkan, founder of the Elders' Guild, has long observed that happiness, joy, and pleasure can be made available to us all no matter what age we might be. In his "Live Oak Definition of an Elder" Barkan reminds us that

Moreover, an elder is a person
Who deserves respect
And honor
And whose work it is
To synthesize wisdom from long life experience and
Formulate this into a legacy
For future generations

Nelson Mandela's Elders have honored the ancient alliance between young and old by placing a special emphasis on the effort to protect children from exploitation by adults. Child marriage affects millions of girls worldwide because, in Graça Machel's words, "Girls have no status, no protection, and no prospects in many families and communities—and this is simply the way things are. Inequality is so entrenched that it isn't even questioned." Their age and status allow Elders to advocate for girls in ways that adults cannot. Elders exist to "amplify the voices of those who work hard to be heard, challenge injustice, stimulate dialogue and debate, and help others to work for positive change in their societies."

Because they are to be seen as above and outside adulthood's conventional struggle for power and control, Mandela's Elders do not hold public office and do not seek political or legislative power. This freedom from ambition enables the Elders to "speak boldly and with whomever they choose on any issue, and to take any action that they believe is right." When undertaking initiatives, the Elders are committed to listening to the views of all groups and individuals—and especially women and young people. The Elders work both publicly and behind the scenes and at all levels—local, national, and international—lending support and advice when invited, and sometimes when it is not. Adults seek and wield power. Elders accumulate and use influence.

American society, so long and obsessively concerned with the lionization of youth and its attendant virtues, is now faced with an urgent need to change aging. The number of centenarians living in the United States doubled during the past twenty years and will likely double again by 2020. We live in a society which, paradoxically, enables millions of people to reach old age and then afflicts them with pernicious, outdated and easily disprovable stereotypes, prejudices, and beliefs about aging. America's young and old are subject to a corrosive ageism that has saturated our culture so completely that no single thought, idea, book, or campaign will be enough to free us from this bigotry.

The question the postwar generation's Second Crucible will pose and then answer is, What forms, structures, and intentions will define life beyond adulthood? Will members of this generation cling to their faith in youth and devote their final decades to chasing after ever more meager affirmations of their waning vitality, energy, and productivity? Will they mount an intergenerational war against their own children and grandchildren? Or will they consent to change and follow another, more rewarding path? The iron law of aging knows nothing of mercy and it never tires. It will continue to push the postwar generation away from the sources of adult power. Will it also lead the postwar generation to embrace the role of elder? Could those millions of babies born into the aftermath of war actually become the elders who will save the world?

No matter which faction prevails during the Second Crucible, the experience of aging in America will be remade. It must be remade. If fortune favors us and the Enthusiasts do emerge as the leading cultural voice in the rise of a new old age, we will likely see a major revision of the psychology and physiology that define old age today. This new science will be placed in the service of an engaged, influential elderhood. Traditional understandings of elderhood will be reimagined in a new post–Second Crucible society. Enthusiasm will give us access to a better understanding of longevity, one that places elders (and their needs) at the heart of our collective pursuit of happiness and well-being.

Contemporary American English lacks a word that can describe the value and vitality of ongoing intergenerational interdependence. Because I think such a word would be useful, I have coined the term *eldertopia.*

eldertopia / ell-der-TOE-pee-uh / noun: a community that improves the quality of life for people of all ages by strengthening and improving the means by which (1) the community protects, sustains, and nurtures its elders, and (2) the elders contribute to the well-being and foresight of the community. An eldertopia that is blessed with a large number of older people is acknowledged to be "elder rich" and uses this wealth to advance the good of all.

The concept of eldertopia can connect us to a life beyond adulthood that contains a rich array of human virtues and experiences. The richest, deepest, and most valuable of these experiences are largely unavailable to younger people. Age endows elders with unique perspectives on time, money, faith, childhood, and relationships that cannot be gained by any other means. We need to be in contact with the elders' point of view because it contains an antidote to the toxic adultification of American society.

Elders have a unique perspective on the tyranny of speed. They can see and understand the value of "slow," even as the world around them seems to move faster than ever. Elders have access to a reservoir of feelings and access to a level of emotional control and insight that far exceeds that available to adults. They also possess a depth that younger people would do well to emulate. Finally, elders are able to pivot away from the extrinsic outcome-oriented measures of value and toward a moment-to-moment appreciation for being with others. Although we are currently burdened by a caricature of an old age that is practically synonymous with loneliness, elders thrive when they are connected to others.

American society suffers from a malignant enlargement of adulthood, and the task of returning adulthood to its proper boundaries will, by necessity, fall to the rising generation of elders. These heroic figures will not resemble, in any way, the protean "heroes" of either the First Crucible or the cult of adulthood. They will be much more like Beatrice Long Visitor Holy Dance, a member of the Thirteen Grandmothers, and much less like Jane Fonda. They will be less like Stephen Covey and more like Fred Lanphear.

Although we do not yet know the names of the leaders who will shape the post–Second Crucible era, we do know that they will represent the postwar generation's last chance to right the wrongs that its unyielding devotion to adulthood have inflicted on our society and culture. If a misshapen life cycle was our only real problem, we could dismiss this impending shift as nothing more than the latest example of the generational self-absorption that critics of the postwar generation have long derided. Unfortunately, we are deep within a global crisis that could easily threaten our continued existence as a species. At this moment in history for both cultural and planetary reasons we need elders more than ever before. We will need them in the scores of millions if we are going to save ourselves from ourselves.

There is a new old age out there, waiting to be born. The acts of cultural creativity necessary to bring it into being will rival the daring that animated the Hippies' radical First Crucible critique of adulthood. In order for such a project to succeed, it will be necessary to possess a vastly more nuanced understanding of life beyond adulthood than our culture currently makes available to us. History and our humanity are calling to us. If we listen closely we can hear the voices of those who have gone before us. We are being summoned, as they were, to a new life as the elders of our time.

28

2021

January

9 Tom's *birthday passes without notice or celebration. He rises at four in the morning and drives to the company-owned dairy farm where he works the early shift in the milking parlor.* **12** Flo *and Alice return from shopping at their local health food grocery store. As they put things away, Flo grouses about how "healthy" everything is and how much she misses macaroni and cheese. Since a heart attack landed Flo in the ICU for a month in 2017, Alice has kept a close watch over her wife's diet.* **17** Rita *is up showered and applying makeup before six a.m. She inspects her face closely in the mirror and frets about what she sees there. It might be, she thinks, time to have some work done.* **23** Jack Nash, *an old friend of Rita's from the Arthur Andersen days, calls her out of the blue. "I need you, Rita, you're the only one that can untangle this goddamned mess." Her heart skips a beat when she hears him growl the words, "I need you, Rita . . ." She had promised Bob that she would cut down on the travel, but this was different.*

February

6 Flo and Alice load the car for the long drive to Sacramento, where they will join a protest against a proposal to turn the state's prison system over to a for-profit company. **9** When **Melanie** and Kevin return home from seeing Railroad Earth at the State Theater, they find a panicked message from her mother. *"Dad's in the emergency room. Call me. Call me!"* By the time they call, Melanie's father is already gone. Kevin makes hurried arrangements for them to fly to Nashville. **12 Melanie** and Kevin "clean out" her father's workshop. The tools are sold to a respected luthier who was once her father's apprentice. She keeps the mandolin her father played on the day she was born. **13** After a fight with Bob, **Rita** packs her bags. She is going to Hong Kong, just for a couple of weeks, that's all. They need her there. This might be her last chance to make a difference. **17 Melanie** and Kevin return home to Ithaca.

March

2 Flo and Alice begin work on a book about the work they are doing to build literacy skills among women in prison. **9 Rita** arrives early for her appointment with her plastic surgeon and thumbs patiently through the brochures that sales reps had deposited in what used to be a magazine rack. During the appointment she checks her schedule and picks the date for her surgery. **22 Melanie** rides her bike from work to their house on Auburn Street. It is just past noon and the air is cold but the sun is growing stronger by the day. She checks her email and lets the cat out. When she finishes her lunch, she grabs her bike and rides back to work. The Bikram yoga class she is teaching starts at two; she wants to be ready.

April

10 Rita has her lower eyelids done. They were just so baggy, they made her look old. It was a little thing, no one would really notice, she would just *look . . . younger.* **21 Melanie** *can't shake the strange feeling that her father's mandolin is calling to her. She picks the instrument up and cradles it in her arms, then, tentatively, plucks its strings. It is out of tune and she puts it down. The memories, however, come upon her in a rush. She sits alone in her living room and cries.* **27** On this date in 1521, Ferdinand Magellan attacks Lapu-Lapu's troops on the island of Mactan. During the battle he is injured by a bamboo spear, then surrounded and killed by his adversaries.

May

3 *Jack Nash calls* **Rita** *again; his project is moving forward. "When can you get over here? This thing is taking off like a rocket!"* **6 Melanie** *starts playing the mandolin for the first time since she was a child.* **23 Melanie** *and Kevin become foster grandparents to a young boy named Joshua.*

June

5 Rita *breaks the news to her daughters and granddaughters that their long-scheduled "family vacation" is going to have to be rescheduled. She tells them, "There's nothing I can do about it, I have to be in Hong Kong!" Her daughters are furious with her. Bob does his best to soothe their anger. "This might be your mom's last chance, she has to take it."* **6 Melanie** *takes her mandolin to a luthier to have it "gone over." The luthier is stunned when she tells him who her father is and that he made the instrument. It needs only minor repair and the luthier does not charge her. In the guitar shop downstairs she shops for a guitar—for Kevin's birthday. He'll turn sixty-two in July.* **16 Tom** *makes his annual pilgrimage to LA, this time to attend his grandson's high school graduation.* **21 Tom's** *ex-wife also makes the trip along with her husband. Time and age have washed Tom's anger away.* **22 Melanie** *relearns "Over the Waterfall" on the mandolin. It was one of her parents' favorite tunes. Kevin is exceptionally generous with his praise and encouragement. He does not know that she has bought him a guitar for his birthday.* **23 Melanie**

and Kevin are at the county courthouse watching the adoption ceremony for Joshua, the one-year-old boy to whom they have been foster grandparents. Afterward, they take him and his new adoptive parents to the Moosewood Restaurant for lunch. **23 Flo** is walking across campus when her earpiece buzzes. She taps the connect. She is told to hold for Teresa Heinz Kerry. Teresa tells her that she has won the Heinz Award for the Human Condition. Flo stops walking, sits down on a bench, and listens.

July

5 Melanie turns fifty-nine and is happier than she has ever been in her life. She loves her work and her husband. Their snug little house feels like a home in a way that only two people who have traveled constantly for decades can appreciate. She and Kevin sit on their front porch and share a bottle of wine as the glow of twilight filters through the trees. **17 Melanie** has Kevin's birthday guitar sitting on his chair at the kitchen table when he comes down in the morning. She plucks out a version of "Happy Birthday" for him on her mandolin and he cradles the guitar in his arms. He says, "I don't know how to play." She laughs. "You'll be great, I promise!"

August

17 Rita boards the flight from Hong Kong feeling very pleased with herself; everything has gone her way. Not even the layover at LAX could dampen her mood. **18** Just as they have every summer for the past ten years, **Melanie** and Kevin enter the gates of the Grassroots Festival of Music and Dance, now in its thirty-first year. These are their people, this is their tribe. They camp out for all four days, as always. Donna the Buffalo closes the show on Sunday night.

September

2 Tom, with extreme reluctance, admits to his daughter and son-in-law that he is behind on the taxes for the trailer and will lose his home property if they aren't paid soon. **16 Melanie** and Kevin play in public for the first time at a neighborhood music festival called Porchfest. **18 Tom** goes into town to pick up his mail. He sees a letter from the county clerk and his heart pounds in his chest. He tears it open and is amazed to find that the back taxes have been paid. Although the clerk's letter doesn't say so, he is certain that Marsha has paid them. He feels both ashamed and enormously loved.

October

4 Tom misses work for the first time in many years. He has a bad case of the flu and lies in bed weak and drenched in sweat. He does not see a doctor. **8 Flo** and Alice arrive in Pittsburgh for the Heinz Award Ceremony. Alice makes the final edits on Flo's acceptance speech.

November

21 Flo and Alice host Thanksgiving at their house. As the meal unfolds, Flo closes her eyes and listens to the laughter and conversation of good friends, old friends. She sips a glass of wine and it tastes good. She smiles as she thinks about how Alice would emphasize the importance of the resveratrol in the wine. After dinner, she sits down at the piano and plays music for her friends.

December

2 Tom An old friend finds Tom's body in the tool shed behind his trailer. **4 Tom's** daughter, son-in-law, grandson, and ex-wife file into the plain Methodist church where his funeral is being held. He is laid to rest next to his parents. Marsha takes Wayne for a long walk across the old family farm's pastures and woodlot. This is the first and last time that he will ever walk this *land.* **14** Rita's *daughters pointedly decline an invitation to join their parents in Mexico for Christmas.* **17** Melanie *and Kevin walk from their house to the farmers' market for the annual "end of the season" event known as the Rutabaga Curl. Potatoes, cabbages, and even frozen chickens are "hurled and curled" down the long wooden walkway. There are no set rules; the only things that really matter are style, distance, and laughter, kind of like life.* **25** Rita *and Bob video chat with their daughters and granddaughters, and when they are done, they go for a long walk on the beach. The air is warm and soft. They hold hands and look up, the sky is a piercing, cloudless blue, and she feels so . . . young.*

A BRIEF HISTORY OF
THE FIRST CRUCIBLE

The conventional history of the postwar generation's first coming of age tells of a largely monolithic "baby boom" that dabbled in youthful rebellion before finally growing up and settling down to a productive and contented adulthood. This version of events vastly understates the intragenerational conflict that pitted three highly distinctive generational subcultures against one another. These conflicts, fueled by the already overflowing supply of adolescent volatility, ignited the postwar generation's First Crucible—and nearly set America on fire.

During the late 1960s, an astonishing 40 percent of America's 200 million people were between the ages of ten and twenty-four. The immense size and demographic density of the postwar generation, and the absence of formal initiation ceremonies or rituals, combined to raise the First Crucible to an incandescent heat. Conflicts flared within and between the generations. It is worth pausing briefly to recall the most intense years of the First Crucible era because doing so will help us better understand the nature and scope of the postwar generation's Second Crucible.

WOULDN'T IT BE NICE

The word *square* echoes eerily as if coming to us from some distant and long-abandoned canyon—almost but not completely forgotten. The term now resides in a cultural twilight zone along with *transistor radio*, *sanitary napkin*, and *dual carburetors*. These things were once important to people's everyday lives, but that was a long time ago. The roots of *square* as a slang (nongeometric) term go back to the early twentieth century. At the turn of that century *square* was used to denote "upright." People used the phrase "fair and square" to praise an agreement that was deemed to be honest. Paying off a debt was often referred to as "squaring up." In 1904, President Theodore Roosevelt presented his "Square Deal" to the nation. It was in the spirit of fairness that he promoted the conservation of natural resources, the control of trusts, and the creation of consumer protection agencies.

By the mid-1970s, the word had drifted out of common use, not reappearing until 1986, when Huey Lewis and the News scored a hit with "Hip to Be Square." Lewis's pop confection brought the meaning of *square* full circle, so to speak. He enthusiastically proclaimed that he was playing it straight and that he had even cut his hair.

Time and revisionism have left us with a faded, one-dimensional memory that, if recalled at all, defines Squares as polite, diligent, well-meaning people without a scrap of imagination or daring. They were, we remember, a little too earnest and clumsy when they encountered the most exciting trends in art, music, fashion, and politics. In cultural terms it was as if they had two left feet. At the center of Square culture was an abiding faith in the traditional structures of life and human development. Their motto, if they had bothered with such a thing, might well have been Ecclesiastes 3:1: "For everything there is a season, and a time for every matter under heaven." Squares understood adolescence as a time of preparation that should lead directly into life as an adult.

This perspective helps us make sense of Square fashion's exceptionally limited repertoire. When men began experimenting with flashy neckties up to six inches wide, brightly colored suits, and longer hair-styles of the early 1960s, Squares continued to favor their fathers' gray flannel suits, plain shirt and tie, buzz haircuts, and horn-rimmed glasses. Young Square women followed the conservative dress, accessories, and hairstyles of Jackie Kennedy rather than teen mod fashion trends invading from London. These items mimicked adult styles and provided a kind of "dress rehearsal" for the clothes one would wear as a grownup.

Square music was, largely, in harmony with the styles favored by adults, some allowances being made for the surging of emotion that comes with the passage into adulthood. Squares gravitated toward pop artists like the Everly Brothers, the Dave Clark Five, and a long string of one-hit wonders. These artists rarely strayed from the traditional and wholesome sounds of popular adult artists such as Pat Boone and Johnny Mathis. Square politics, such as they were, resembled the adult version: these young people largely accepted the politics of their parents. In the first election most were old enough to participate in, Squares helped reelect Richard Nixon.

The Beach Boys provided what might well have been the Square anthem in their 1966 album *Pet Sounds*. The opening track begins with a stark question:

Wouldn't it be nice if we were older?

This desire runs counter to the youth-obsessed and age-critical sensibility that dominated the era. Compare it, for instance, with the Who's line from "My Generation":

Hope I die before I get old.

The second line from the Beach Boys expresses the singer's eagerness to "grow up."

Then we wouldn't have to wait so long.

What is being longed for here is not just physical intimacy (which is alluded to in the next verse) but rather the comforting station of adulthood itself. The best and most desirable things in life are, after all, reserved for adults. Bob Dylan, naturally, saw things differently.

I was so much older then, I'm younger than than now.

The Wilson brothers continue:

And wouldn't it be nice to live together
In the kind of world where we belong?

The Squares' intense connection to family, community, and tradition gave them a powerful, if understated, core of conviction. It also made them prone to dividing the world into *us* and *them*.

Their most enduring and influential contribution to American culture developed from the Squares' role as the nidus of a new conservative movement. These were temperamentally, if not always politically conservative people, and most Squares held closely to their parents' politics, whatever those might be. The Square daughter of civil rights activists could be counted on to endorse her parents' belief about social justice. The Square son of a Texas Republican would most likely endorse his parents' conservative political views. Indeed, an organization calling itself Young Americans for Freedom was founded on September 11, 1960, at a meeting held at the home of Mr. William F. Buckley in Sharon, Connecticut. The purpose of the YAF, as it became known, was to advocate for policies consistent with the *Sharon Statement*, which set forth a series of principles embodying the Buckley vision of conservatism. Among them:

THAT liberty is indivisible, and that political freedom cannot long exist without economic freedom;
THAT the purpose of government is to protect those freedoms

through the preservation of internal order, the provision of national defense, and the administration of justice;

THAT when government ventures beyond these rightful functions, it accumulates power, which tends to diminish order and liberty;

THAT the genius of the Constitution—the division of powers—is summed up in the clause that reserves primacy to the several states, or to the people in those spheres not specifically delegated to the Federal government;

THAT when government interferes with the work of the market economy, it tends to reduce the moral and physical strength of the nation, that when it takes from one to bestow on another, it diminishes the incentive of the first, the integrity of the second, and the moral autonomy of both;

THAT we will be free only so long as the national sovereignty of the United States is secure; that history shows periods of freedom are rare, and can exist only when free citizens concertedly defend their rights against all enemies . . .

THAT the forces of international Communism are, at present, the greatest single threat to these liberties;

THAT the United States should stress victory over, rather than coexistence with this menace . . .

Us and them. From this acorn, a mighty oak would someday grow.

Few people think of Squares these days, but if they do, the images that come to mind tend toward cat eye glasses, argyle sweaters, slide rules, and maybe Osmond Brothers concert tickets. Beneath such ephemera, however, lay an iron commitment to tradition and an unflinching acceptance of adulthood as it was presented to them. They could feel, in their bones, that there was a proper order to things, and this simple faith endowed them with an extraordinary and unexpected resilience.

They were also, it must be admitted, deeply suspicious of change

274 ~ DR. BILL THOMAS

and prone to react aggressively when new ideas or behaviors intruded upon their most cherished beliefs. The fact that others in their generation—Activists and Hippies—could not or would not fall into line was not just evidence of immaturity or foolishness, it was seen by Squares as dangerous and unpatriotic selfishness. Like many traditional and tribal cultures, Squares retained a significant level of distrust toward strangers and could easily be aroused to rejecting, mocking, and even attacking people who were not like them. Civil rights marchers, gay men, "liberated" women, antiwar protestors, Hippies, and draft dodgers would all, at one time or another, feel the wrath of the most aggressive and violent members of the Square subculture.

Squares came to be defined not by what they did but rather by what they believed and the ideas that they accepted without question.

POWER TO THE PEOPLE

The 1960s were an especially fertile period for social change movements. Many of the people we recognize as the architects of reform began their activism then. In 1962, Rachel Carson published her exposé of the impact that the pesticide DDT was having on wildlife and humans. *Silent Spring* brought a new environmentalism to life. In the spring of 1963, Martin Luther King Jr. responded to critics who were urging him to "slow down" in his "Letter from a Birmingham Jail": "Injustice anywhere is a threat to justice everywhere. We are caught in an inescapable network of mutuality, tied in a single garment of destiny. Whatever affects one directly, affects all indirectly." In 1966, Muhammad Ali—formerly known as Cassius Clay—declared himself a conscientious objector and refused to go to war. For this he was stripped of his heavyweight title, banned from boxing for three years, and initially sentenced to five years in prison. When Gloria Steinem gave her "Address to the Women of America," she observed, "Sex and race because they are easy and visible differences have been the primary ways of organizing human beings into superior and inferior groups and into the cheap labor on which this system still depends."

Members of the Activist subculture within the postwar generation fueled these emerging trends with their enormous energy, idealism, and numbers. At the core of the movement lay the so-called *Port Huron Statement*. Drafted by a self-selected and self-proclaimed group of youth activists from across the country, this 27,500-word manifesto was intended to summarize the Activist critique of society and their recommendations for reform. It begins with the words "We are people of this generation" but quickly expands its focus to people of all ages and the problems of the world as a whole. The statement offers a curious blend of the soulful ("Loneliness, estrangement, isolation describe the vast distance between man and man today") with the analytical ("These dominant tendencies cannot be overcome by better personnel management, nor by improved gadgets") and the idealistic ("but only when a love of man overcomes the idolatrous worship of things by man").

The first section, titled "Agenda for a Generation," lays out the case for change:

> With nuclear energy whole cities could easily be powered, but instead we seem likely to unleash destruction greater than that incurred in all wars in human history;
>
> With rockets we are emancipating man from terrestrial limitations, but from Mississippi jails still comes the prayer for emancipation of man on earth;
>
> As man's own technology destroys old and creates new forms of social organization, man still tolerates meaningless work, idleness instead of creative leisure, and educational systems that do not prepare him for life amidst change;
>
> While expanding networks of communication, transportation, integrating economic systems, and the birth of intercontinental missiles make national boundaries utterly permeable and antiquated, men still fight and hate in provincial loyalty to nationalism;

While two-thirds of mankind suffers increasing undernourish-
ment, our upper classes are changing from competition for scarce
goods to reveling amidst abundance;

With world population expected to double in forty years, men
still permit anarchy as the rule of international conduct and uncontrolled exploitation to govern the sapping of the earth's physical resources;

Mankind desperately needs visionary and revolutionary leadership to respond to its enormous and deeply-entrenched problems, but America rests in national stalemate, her goals ambiguous
and tradition-bound when they should be new and far-reaching,
her democracy apathetic and manipulated when it should be dynamic and participative.

The indictment the authors of the Port Huron Statement lodged
against their elders remains compelling, even a half century later. The
authors saw and provided a detailed description of a world beset by
greed, militarism, and violent social injustice. Nor did the statement's
authors flinch from criticizing their own generation, decrying in particular their peers' failure to exercise leadership that was equal to the
demands of the age. We belong, they wrote, to "the first generation
to know it might be the last in the long experiment at living." The
authors of the Port Huron Statement, with the help of millions of other
young people, went on to create a dynamic and resourceful Activist
subculture.

Even though Activists were openly critical of the "timidity" of
adults and the scale of the problems set into motion by their elders,
they also understood that the real power in their society belonged to
adults and adulthood. It was perfectly clear to the Activists that the
world needed changing, and this reality made growing up an urgent necessity for the era's young Activists. If coming of age was found to be a
necessary precondition to gaining power—and it was—then they would
do so directly, and largely without dramatics.

The forces safeguarding the social order have always found it convenient to diminish and stereotype those pressing for change. In 1968, a group of young feminists picketed the Miss America Pageant. Using something they called a "zap" action, they drew press attention to their cause by crowning a sheep and tossing "girdles, cosmetics, high-heeled shoes, and bras into a so-called 'freedom trash can.'" The event was reported as a "bra burning" demonstration led by angry feminists. But that wasn't true. Author Susan Brownmiller later explained the source of this persistent myth:

"It was the time of draft-card burning, and some smart headline writer decided to call it a 'bra burning' because it sounded insulting to the then-new women's movement. We only threw a bra symbolically in a trash can."

The feminists' affection for a natural look sans makeup and comfortable clothing and shoes became, in the popular imagination, coarse, masculine, and ugly. The African-American community's rejection of white fashion and hairstyles was ridiculed by conservative elements, black and white. A 1969 Newsweek poll asked African Americans around the nation for their opinions on the "natural" afro hairstyle and found that, while it was popular in the North, a majority of blacks living in the South disapproved.

Activists did, however, develop and communicate a radical critique of mid-twentieth-century society. They wrote, they spoke, they marched, they organized, and they demonstrated. They were passionate about the causes they supported. They were also, it must be said, a querulous lot. Although they imagined themselves to be highly practical, in truth they wasted oceans of time (and ink) arguing and rearguing basic principles. At every point in the evolution of this subculture their enthusiasm outran their competence easily and often. Activists' primary political organization, Students for a Democratic Society, reached its zenith in the lead up to the 1968 Democratic National Convention but rapidly collapsed after splintering into competing factions. Often obsessed with details that did not have practical consequences and better at talking than doing, Activists frequently made up with numbers what they lacked in organizational sophistication and planning.

They were also prone to pointing out the mote in another's eye while ignoring the plank in their own. Recollections of the era are replete with examples of unthinking prejudice. Margery Tabankin, an antiwar activist student at the University of Wisconsin, recalled that "most guys didn't take women seriously, however. They were things to fuck. . . . You went through this intense experience [at demonstrations], and you went back and had sex. . . . [Sex] was much more on men's terms." Because the Activist subculture developed out of America's culture, it contained the same deep (though in this case informal) racial segregation within it. Looking back at the iconic photo of the authors of the *Port Huron Statement* celebrating the completion of their work, it is plain to see—all the faces are white.

At the time, few Americans liked or even appreciated the role that the Activist subculture was beginning to play in society. Their parents, and nearly all the so-called Establishment, felt the sting of a vocal, unforgiving minority who were willing to use a precious freedom won with blood and treasure to explicitly criticize the failings of those who had given so much during their years in the Dark Valley. Members of the Activist subculture had a tendency to personalize issues and inject emotion into their work. They could be insufferably condescending. This superior attitude frequently alienated them from other postwar generation subcultures with whom they might otherwise have found common cause.

During the First Crucible years, Squares were highly critical of the Activists' relentless efforts to disturb and overturn the status quo. Members of the Hippie subculture were quick to observe, often with good reason, the disturbing tendency of Activists to "sell out" whenever something better came their way. The millions of members of the postwar generation who affiliated with the Activists did, despite all their failings, change American society in important ways. Perhaps their greatest contribution to their era lay in their willingness to inject the adolescent's oppositional defiance into what would otherwise be a staid and responsible adulthood.

A LIFE FOUNDED ON
PEACE AND BEAUTY

The Squares brought forth the *Sharon Statement* (with the help of William F. Buckley Jr.) while the Activists retreated to a union-run summer camp to produce their *Port Huron Statement*. But the Hippie subculture never produced a self-justifying tract of its own. They didn't see the point. *Time* magazine struck close to the truth when it noted that Hippies were "expatriates living on our shores but beyond our society." What set them apart from other Americans was not their fashion sense but rather a deeply held belief that it was possible to live a life devoted to peace, beauty, and understanding.

While Squares embraced a bumptious but direct passage through adolescence and into a well-worn adulthood, and Activists eagerly sought the perquisites of adult power, Hippies rejected the adulthood that was being presented to them. Their precise intentions are difficult to discern because they had little interest in establishing and maintaining logical consistency. As we will see, Hippies were also subjected to an unrelenting campaign of distortion, ridicule, and even violence.

A Catholic priest working in the Haight-Ashbury district of San Francisco was quoted in *Life* magazine giving this assessment of the new sense of community that was growing up around the Hippie movement:

They have some very fine ideas, they believe in sharing and they're against hypocrisy. They're for love and peace. They are honest and open. . . . They may have washed their hands of the Establishment, but in many ways that is quite understandable. Our example has been far from good.

In the summer of 1967, John Phillips captured this spirit with the lyrics he wrote for "San Francisco (Be Sure to Wear Flowers in Your

Hair)." The version sung by Scott McKenzie reached the number four spot on the *Billboard* Hot 100 and held it for a month. The image of "gentle people with flowers in their hair" peacefully embracing a summertime love-in was something new—and strange.

It was, after all, a collaboration between a Hippie (Steve Jobs) and an electronics nerd (Steve Wozniak) that led to the creation of Apple Computer. A recent book on marketing explored the business innovations pioneered by the Grateful Dead. The publisher notes, "The band encouraged their fans to record shows and trade tapes; they built a mailing list and sold concert tickets directly to fans; and they built their business model on live concerts, not album sales. . . . The Dead pioneered many social media and inbound marketing concepts successfully used by businesses across all industries today."

The word *hippie* came into use in the Bay area in the midsixties. Originally intended as a diminutive form of *hipster*, it labeled Hippies as a younger, less mature version of the Beatniks. The people within the subculture itself were much more likely to refer to themselves as "freaks" or "heads." It was common practice for people to modify these terms in ways that signified what part of the subculture they were most interested in. Thus, "Jesus freaks" were attracted to transcendental Christian spirituality and communal living arrangements that they felt echoed those of the early church. "Acid freaks" were mainly interested in going "further"—further into their own unexplored consciousness, further away from the unthinking compulsions that they felt defined life in postwar America.

Like the Activists, many Hippies favored revolutionary change in society. They differed, radically, in the means they were willing to employ to bring that change about. Hippies had little interest in attending interminable meetings or doing the work of planning, coordination, advocacy, and organization that Activists believed were essential to the enterprise of social change. Hippies preferred, and placed great emphasis on, what they considered to be the authentic ground of subjective experience. Personal growth and the subtle, indirect art of "being" meant much more to them than the structured machinations of "doing." A Hippie underground paper might carry a headline like "Alternative Society Now!" but when Activists read the article, they would find no direct, practical strategy for accomplishing this goal. The Hippies' willingness to disconnect intention from action was one of the defining elements of their subculture.

While the Hippie subculture's comparative apathy appalled and disappointed Activists, it was their apparent inability to grow up that outraged Squares. There is a critical distinction between those who cannot and those who will not take the next step down a developmental pathway. Hippies mostly fell into the latter category. Their immaturity was, for the most part, consciously chosen and deliberately (if haphazardly) combined with an ecstatic embrace of casual sex, mind-expanding drugs, and Eastern religious precepts. The Hippies' casual violation of social norms led others to suppress, mock, demean, and sometimes attack members of this subculture. David Crosby's song "Almost Cut My Hair" is a reflection on the growing tension between freaks and mainstream society. The lyricist recalls being tempted "just the other day" to surrender to social expectations. He decides to let his "freak flag fly" because—and this is the crux of the lyric—"I feel like I owe it to someone."

Crosby's sense of an ineffable but deeply shared identity and destiny also colors the pages of what many people called the "Hippie Bible." Published in 1971, Be Here Now took readers on the journey of discovery that transformed Timothy Leary's fellow Harvard University professor Richard Alpert into the guru known as Baba Ram Dass. He included this expression of solidarity in the book's opening section:

Now, though I am a beginner on the path, I have returned to the West for a time to work out karma or unfulfilled commitment. Part of this commitment is to share what I have learned with those of you who are on a similar journey. One can share a message through telling "our-story" as I have just done, or through the teaching methods of yoga, or singing, or making love. Each of us finds his unique vehicle for sharing with others his bit of wisdom. For me, this story is but a vehicle for sharing with you the true message . . . the living faith in what is possible.

There is a good reason why it is hard to write accurately about the Hippie subculture and also be taken seriously. The popular understandings of this important subculture and contemporary attitudes toward its members have been, almost entirely, based on a caricature developed and promulgated by Squares and Activists. This universally familiar stereotype features drug use, promiscuity, laziness, and a profound lack of seriousness. One of the premier Hippie-bashers of the era, segregationist and presidential candidate George Wallace, made a point to denigrate "Hippies" who showed up to protest his 1968 campaign:

> You come up when I get through and I'll autograph your sandals for you. That is, if you got any on. . . . You need a good haircut. That's all that's wrong with you. . . . There are two four-letter words I bet you folks don't know: "work" and "soap."

Wallace's critique of this subculture deliberately exaggerates its least attractive elements. Indeed, the current image of Hippies is largely the creation of the First Crucible's victors, and that history conceals the Hippies' most important accomplishment.

SQUARE UPRISING

The delirium that greeted the Beatles' arrival in the United States in February of 1964 took on a markedly different tone just two years later when John Lennon was quoted saying, "Christianity will go. It will vanish and shrink. I needn't argue about that; I'm right and I'll be proved right. We're more popular than Jesus now; I don't know which will go first—rock 'n' roll or Christianity. Jesus was all right but his disciples were thick and ordinary. It's them twisting it that ruins it for

me." This casual heresy set off a national storm of protest. The Ku Klux
Klan nailed a Beatles album to a wooden cross and vowed to take "ven-
geance" against them. The Vatican issued a statement condemning the
Beatles' dissolute and uninhibited lives. Conservative groups across the
South staged mass burnings of Beatles records and paraphernalia.

In 1967, the *National Review* published the sixty-seven-year-old
Will Herberg's dyspeptic take on Hippie culture:

> The deepest truth about the hippie style of life seems to be that
> the hippies are compulsive "enjoyers." They totally reject, in word
> and in fact, the idea of work, production, achievement; for them,
> the right kind of life is the life of enjoyment, bliss, even ecstasy.
> They wallow in life, so to speak: wallow in nature, wallow in
> "love," wallow in wallowing. Their ideal, quite literally, is a pure
> and unadulterated self-indulgence, a self-indulgence on a strange
> primitivistic level.

The hedonism and unashamed permissiveness that so disgusted
Herberg was also declared to be a dire threat to established standards of
female comportment by author Mark Harris:

> Young ladies were experimenting in drugs, in sexual license, living
> in communal quarters furnished with mattresses. . . . Girls who
> might have been in fashion were panhandling. . . . Hippie girls
> gave flowers to strangers, and they encouraged their dirty young
> men to avoid the war in Vietnam.

Even worse, from an establishmentarian point of view, was the
growing commitment to racial and economic justice. Harris continues:

> This was the thing most maddening, that these were not Negroes
> disaffected by color or immigrants by strangeness but boys and girls
> from the right side of the economy in all-American cities and towns.

Media coverage of the Hippie subculture shifted its focus to the trial of career criminal and cult leader Charles Manson. Branded a Hippie by the press primarily because of his long hair and obvious strangeness, Manson was born in 1934, had spent half his life in various detention centers, and shared none of the Hippie movement's most cherished ideals. After the release of the Beatles' *White Album*, Manson came to believe that the lyrics of the song "Helter Skelter" were actually a coded warning that foretold a coming race war between blacks and whites. The murders committed by members of Manson's cult (the so-called Family) were intended to precipitate that war and establish Manson as the white ruler over a subservient black population in its aftermath.

Time magazine, and the rest of the media, wasted no time connecting Manson's actions to the Hippie subculture as a whole. The magazine's December 1969 issue asked,

How could children who had dropped out for the sake of kindness and sharing, love and beauty, be enjoined to kill?

Dr. Lewis Yablonsky thinks that the answer may lie in the fact that so many hippies are actually "lonely, alienated people." He says: "They have had so few love models that even when they act as if they love, they can be totally devoid of true compassion. That is the reason why they can kill so matter-of-factly."

Yablonsky believes that there has been far more violence among the hippies than most people realize. "There has always been a potential for murder," he says. "Many hippies are socially almost dead inside. Some require massive emotions to feel anything at all. They need bizarre, intensive acts to feel alive—sexual acts, acts of violence, nudity, every kind of Dionysian thrill."

Society's most powerful and established voices and institutions found a growing reason to fear the First Crucible Activist agenda. Members of the Establishment began to imagine what might happen if these young people really did succeed in taking hold of the reins of power and leading America toward the future *they* envisioned. Nor was this fear unfounded: in the post–First Crucible years, many elements of the Activist agenda were enacted. Mass actions of the youth movement did, eventually, help end the war in Vietnam. They contributed to momentous gains in civil rights that helped roll back Jim Crow segregation in the South, and the women's movement transformed attitudes and eventually won, to take one example, abortion rights.

Hovering over all this turmoil was a growing concern about the violent nature of the protests. A participant in the 1967 antiwar rally and March on the Pentagon recalls that as the protesters' all-night vigil wore on,

> Someone in authority decided that the Pentagon steps had to be cleared. Rifle butts came down on peoples' heads with dull ugly wet sounding thumps. Blood splashed onto the steps. There were shouts of "Link arms! Link arms!," mixed with screams of pain and curses. People were dragged off and arrested. The brutality was appalling and the people standing on the steps began throwing debris at the soldiers. I saw a garbage can sail over my head. I feared people might be trampled in panic as they tried to escape from the clubs and rifle butts.

The adults and their allies among the postwar generation's Squares were quickly losing patience with the disorder and disrespect that seemed to define the Activist and Hippie subcultures. Opinion polling done in the fall of 1969 showed that two-thirds of Americans supported the war in Vietnam. The evening news, however, detailed an increasing number of protests against the war. As the gap between the public image of the postwar generation and the (small c)conservative beliefs of a majority of Americans widened, specific concerns were quickly generalized into moral indignation. The most important thing, it seemed, was to restore order.

BLOODY THURSDAY

A former movie actor and corporate spokesperson named Ronald Reagan rode this moral panic all the way to the California governor's mansion in 1966. Campaigning on the need to put an end to Activists' increasing use of marches and demonstrations, he won easily. Reagan promised to crack down on college students and then delivered on his promise. He singled out those in Berkeley for special criticism, calling the university there "a haven for protesters and sex deviants." In May of 1969, political conflict over what had been a land use issue regarding the fate of an abandoned lot off Telegraph Avenue boiled over.

The Berkeley administration planned to develop the lot into a student parking lot and a playing field. Student activists wanted it to become "a free speech area that wasn't really controlled like Sproul Plaza." This dispute over the "People's Park" was where Governor Reagan decided to "draw the line." On Thursday, May 15, at 4:30 a.m., he ordered hundreds of California Highway Patrol and Berkeley police officers onto the abandoned lot. By noon, roughly three thousand people, mostly Berkeley students, gathered in Sproul Plaza to discuss the government's occupation of the lot. The protesters chose to march to the site and were met there with force by the police. A riot ensued.

The governor's chief of staff, Edwin Meese III (he would later serve as President Reagan's attorney general), called in hundreds more police officers and gave them permission to use all available means to disperse the crowd, which by that time had swelled to more than six thousand. Sheriff's deputies fired shotguns loaded with 00 buckshot at people sitting on the roof of the nearby Telegraph Repertory Cinema. One of the bullets struck and fatally wounded student James Rector. According to a report published by *Time*, Rector was a bystander, not a protester. The riot at the park and the killing of James Rector would later be recalled as "Bloody Thursday."

In defense of his department's use of firearms during the protest, Alameda County Sheriff Frank Madigan said, "The choice was essentially this: to use shotguns—because we didn't have the available manpower—or retreat and abandon the City of Berkeley to the mob." In the aftermath of the riot, Governor Reagan declared a state of emergency and sent an additional 2,700 National Guard troops into the city. For two weeks, National Guardsmen patrolled the streets of Berkeley and broke up even the smallest demonstrations with tear gas.

THE ERUPTION

September 26, 1969

Responding to a question about the Mobilization to End the War, President Richard Nixon said, "Now, I understand that there has been, and continues to be, opposition to the war in Vietnam on the campuses and also in the nation. As far as this kind of activity is concerned, we expect it, however under no circumstances will I be affected whatever by it." Nixon's chairman of the Joint Chiefs of Staff, General Earle Wheeler, was much more blunt. He called the protesters "interminably vocal youngsters, strangers alike to soap and reason."

November 3, 1969

President Nixon appeared on national television to deliver what later became known as his "Silent Majority" speech. Near its end, Nixon aligned himself with "the great silent majority of my fellow Americans." After the speech, Nixon's approval ratings, which had been hovering around 50 percent, shot up to 81 percent in the nation and 86 percent in the South.

January 1970

Time magazine, which three years earlier had featured "Hippies" on its cover, proclaimed "Middle America" as the most important influence on the public stage. Reflecting on the previous year, publisher Roy E. Larsen concluded that the events of 1969 were bigger than any single individual. "In a time of dissent and 'confrontation,' the most striking new factor was the emergence of the so-called 'Silent Majority' as a powerfully assertive force in U.S. society."

April 7, 1970
In an address to the California Council of Growers almost a year after Bloody Thursday, Governor Reagan defended his decision to use the California National Guard to quell Berkeley protests: "If it takes a bloodbath, let's get it over with. No more appeasement."

April 30, 1970
President Richard Nixon: "My fellow Americans, we live in an age of anarchy, both abroad and at home. We see mindless attacks on all the great institutions which have been created by free civilizations in the last five hundred years. Even here in the United States, great universities are being systematically destroyed."

May 4, 1970
Members of the Ohio National Guard opened fire on protestors at Kent State University, killing four students and seriously wounding nine.

July 15, 1970
The motion picture Joe opened. It is a drama about an ad executive who strikes up a friendship with a blue-collar worker over their shared hatred of hippies. In the climax of the film, the duo exterminate the residents of a Hippie commune, inadvertently killing the ad executive's daughter, played by Susan Sarandon in her debut role. The film was the thirteenth most popular of 1970.

October 27, 1970
Congress passed the Comprehensive Drug Abuse Prevention and Control Act. Although President Richard Nixon would not coin the phrase "War on Drugs" until the following year, this law created the govern-

ment's legal foundation for its fight against controlled and banned substances.

December 18, 1970

Arville Garland of Detroit—dubbed the "real-life Joe" after the movie *Joe* was released—was sentenced to one count of manslaughter and three counts of second-degree murder for the murder of his daughter and three friends in their "student-hippie" residence on May 8, 1970. *Time* magazine reported, "Garland has received hundreds of letters of support. Said one California father of a teenage girl: 'There must surely be many among us who have done in our hearts what you have done with your hands. To have those to whom we have opened our hearts and treasures say "Your truth is not truth, your values are without value" can be beyond bearing.'" Other messages were simply congratulatory. One came with a twenty-dollar bill. None contained any criticism of the killings.

THE END OF THE BEGINNING

On November 7, 1972, Richard Nixon was reelected in a landslide victory. Nixon beat Democratic candidate George McGovern by 18 million votes, the widest margin of any presidential election. With the passage of the Twenty-Sixth Amendment to the US Constitution on July 1, 1971, the 1972 election was the first in which the "youth vote" would be a factor in choosing a president. Many observers felt certain that the 25 million people between the ages of eighteen and twenty-five would vote overwhelmingly for George McGovern and his plan to end the war in Vietnam. "Gonzo" journalist Hunter S. Thompson voiced this hope in the pages of *Rolling Stone*: "In a close election, even 10 percent of that bloc would mean 2.5 million votes—a very serious figure when you stack it up against Nixon's thin margin over [Hubert] Humphrey in 1968." He continued, "Think of it: Only 10 percent! Enough, even according to Nixon's own wizards—to swing almost any election."

As the election drew near, Thompson reluctantly admitted to the facts of the matter. "The polls . . . indicate that Nixon will get a comfortable majority of the youth vote, this may be the year when we finally come face to face with ourselves; finally just lay back and say it—that we are really just a nation of 220 million used-car salesmen with all the money we need to buy guns, and no qualms at all about killing anybody else in the world who tries to make us uncomfortable."

During the early 1970s, the postwar generation's philosophical center of gravity shifted decisively in the direction of adulthood, and the Squares' willingness to tolerate the Hippies' heretical perspective on adulthood curdled into a sometimes violent disgust. The resulting scorched-earth campaign of cultural warfare was meant to and did ensure that when it came to Hippie culture, not one stone would be left standing on another. The First Crucible had been extinguished, and a new and much more perilous chapter in the story of America's postwar generation was about to begin.

Acknowledgments

Every book is a collective effort, and I am grateful to all those who have helped me develop, enrich, and express the ideas presented here. In particular, Dr. Judah Ronch, and Galena Madjaroff of UMBC's Erickson School have helped me clarify my thinking about the relationship between biography and society. Rick Bowers, Emilio Pardo, Edward Newburn, and the irrepressible Beth Domingo have enriched my understanding of late adulthood as a period of growth and development. The Blogstream community at ChangingAging.org has been a sounding board for every concept in this book as well as an inspiration, chief among them elderblogger Ronni Bennett, Martin Bayne, Richard Taylor, Howard Gleckman, Marti Weston, Madeleine Kolb, Angie McAllister, Holly Whiteside, Brent Green, Richard Ambrosius, Ilene Cummings, Joy Laverde, and Catherine Yanda. Sue Penoza and Rick O'Connell heard my arguments about the centrality of health and well-being and provided valuable feedback on how they could be improved. Robert Jenkens, Susan Frazier, Anna Otigara, Terry Simonette, and the entire Green House team have and will continue to advocate for the practical relationship between elderhood and intentional community. My discussions with Mark Parkinson, Ruta Kadonoff, Dr. David Gifford, and Larry Minnix have bolstered my hope that a culture-changing reconsideration of aging is already under way. A speech delivered by Dr. Robyn Stone gave me an opportunity to test my hypothesis against one of the field of aging's sharpest minds. The Eden Alternative movement has informed this work, and I owe all of its many proponents a hearty expression of thanks. I should also emphasize the value of my ongoing conversations with Eden's Nancy Fox, Sandy Ransom, Chris Perna, Carol Ende, Mark Golden, Laura Beck, Sarah Rowan, Suzette Molina, Dr. Al Power, Denise Hyde, Steve Lemoine, and especially Rick Gamache. My web design and publicity team led by Kavan Peterson at ChangingMedia Group.com deserve special thanks—Jay Wesler, Jonas LaRance, Melissa Brumer, Hasdai Westbrook, Virgil Thomas, and Joseph Popiolkowski. It has also been my good fortune to spend time with some of corporate America's most iconoclastic thinkers, James Taylor, Willie Cho, Bryan Semkuley, Bruce Williamson, and Clarice Theisen. Christof Baer and Paul Salyards and Jack Elliot are on the forefront of integrating a new old age into American business. Deb Bryan, Dr. Carl Patow, Candace Barrett Birk, the Guthrie Theater, and the cast of *Play What's Not There* gave me the opportunity to dramatize many of these ideas in front of a live audience. I have also enjoyed and benefited from thoughtful conversations with Dr. Atul Gawande, Emi Kiyota, Jane Lowe, Joseph Angelelli, Dr. Raj Dave', Dr. Mary Jane Koren, and Wendy Lustbader. I will close with a word of thanks to what my wife, Jude, and I refer to as "the Village." These are the people who are a wonderfully warm part of my social circle when I am at home. Most of these people listened to me stumble through my early, fumbling attempts to express the ideas that make up this book: Jim Meyers, Patti Meyers, Rick Emberly, Sierra Meyers, Mike Pliss, Margo Polikoff, Mariah Prentiss, Michelle Hochstetter, A. Jay Zahn, Marci Solomon, Lynn Reitenbach, Linda Aigen, David Wiener, Patty Heaton, Dirk Davies, Ty Hall, Rob Hutchins, Jim Lombardy, Lynn and Kurt Hoyt, Camilla Faraday, Linda Folley, Don Timmons, Lisa and Brian Witchey, Patty Foster, Elijah Cardona, and Melissa Murphy.

In all endeavors, it is good to have friends.

Notes

01: Watson versus Spock

13 "Stock prices have": Irving Fisher, October 17, 1929.

14 "In the bright sunshine of prosperity": Henry Steele Commager, "After the Decline and Fall, the Promise of a New Day," The New York Times, March 3, 1957.

15 "Take the 3,548,000 babies": Sylvia [pen name], "How do you define Baby Boomers?", http://www.baby-boomers-life.com/define-baby-boomers.html, n.d.

17 Watson began his work: John B. Watson and Rosalie Rayner, "Conditioned Emotional Reactions," Journal of Experimental Psychology 3 (1920): 1–14.

18 "It is a serious question": John B. Watson with Rosalie Rayner Watson, Psychological Care of Infant and Child (New York: W. W. Norton, 1928), 5–6.

20 "every baby needs": Benjamin Spock and Robert Needlman, Dr. Spock's Baby and Child Care, 9th ed. (New York: Pocket Books, 2011), 46.

20 "I never looked at my records": Benjamin Spock, The Common Sense Book of Baby and Child Care; Bart Barnes, "Pediatrician Benjamin Spock Dies," The Washington Post, March 17, 1998, A1.

21 "Republicans created all": Benjamin Spock and Mary Morgan, Spock on Spock: A Memoir of Growing Up with the Century (New York: Pantheon, 1989), 96.

21 "illegally conspiring to aid": Bart Barnes, "Pediatrician Benjamin Spock Dies," The Washington Post, March 17, 1998, A1.

21 "totally illegal, immoral": ibid.

21 "Spock-marked generation": Spiro Agnew, quoted in James M. Naughton, "Epithets Greet Agnew in Salt Lake City," The New York Times, October 1, 1970, 22.

21 "People have said": David Beard, "Dr. Spock Still Active, Writing New Baby Book," Associated Press, June 7, 1992.

22 "My prime concern": Spock quoted by Ann Hulbert, Raising America: Experts, Parents, and a Century of Advice about Children (New York: Alfred A. Knopf, 2003), 271.

22 "a scary person": Thomas Maier, Dr. Spock: An American Life (New York: Basic Books, 2003), 241.

22 "Trust yourself": Spock, The Common Sense Book of Baby and Child Care, 1.

03: Youthquake

35 coined the term youthquake: Vogue, January 1, 1965, 112.

36 "The bikini is the most": Diana Vreeland, quoted in Grace Mirabella, with Judith Warner, In and Out of Vogue (New York: Doubleday, 1995), 135.

39 The negative and dismissive use: Turn Back the Clock: 80 years of Cub Scouting, Grand Council 2010 Pow Wow, http://phxscouting.com/PowWow/books/GCC%20PWB%202010.pdf, 2010, 74.

40 Merle Haggard was singing: Merle Haggard, "Okie from Muskogee," by Merle Haggard and Roy Edward Burris, Okie from Muskogee, Capitol Records, 1969.

40 "The duty of a revolutionary": Abbie Hoffman, Steal This Book (New York: Thunder's Mouth Press, 2002), xxiii.

41 "anonymous institutional employee": Martin Torgoff, Can't Find My Way Home: America in the Great Stoned Age, 1945–2000 (New York: Simon & Schuster, 2004), 72.

42 "the most dangerous man": Richard Nixon, quoted by Laura Mansnerus, "Timothy Leary, Pied Piper of Psychedelic 60's, Dies at 75," The New York Times, June 1, 1996, A1, http://www.nytimes.com/1996/06/01/us/timothy-leary-pied-piper-of-psychedelic-60s-dies-at-75.html.

42 "Hippy is an establishment label": Timothy Leary, The Politics of Ecstasy, 4th ed. (Berkeley: Ronin Publishing, 1998), 165.

04: 1971

46 "All right then": "Canada Holds Draftee Who Hijacked 96 on Jet," UPI, San Mateo Times, February 26, .

06: Efficiency Porn

59 "enforced standardization of": Frederick Winslow Taylor, The Principles of Scientific Management (New York: Harper & Brothers, 1911), 36.

60 An independent account: For the stories about Schmidt Montgomery, refer to Charles D. Wrege and Amedeo G. Perroni, "Taylor's Pig-Tale: A Historical

Analysis of Frederick W. Taylor's Pig-Iron Experiments," *Academy of Management Journal* 17 (March 1974): 6–27.

62 Acumen *magazine reported: Acumen,* December 1994.
65 *"What lies behind us":* Stephen R. Covey, *The Seven Habits of Highly Effective People* (New York: Free Press, 2004), 96.
66 *"It is the brain":* Garson O'Toole, "What Lies Behind Us and What Lies Before Us Are Tiny Matters Compared to What Lies Within Us," www.QuoteInvestigator.com, January 11, 2011, http://quoteinvestigator /2011/01/11/what-lies-within/.
71 *"By obedience to":* Stephen R. Covey, *Spiritual Roots of Human Relations,* 2nd sub ed. (Salt Lake City, UT: Deseret Book, 1993), 1.
72 *"I have found in":* Stephen R. Covey, *The Divine Center* (Salt Lake City, UT: Deseret Book, 2011), 240.
72 *"Renewal is the principle":* Covey, *Seven Habits,* 304.
72 *"eternal progression":* Covey, *Divine Center,* 180, 207, 213.
72 *"constantly expanding":* ibid., 207.
72 *"releases his divine":* ibid., 246.
72 *"since we truly are":* ibid., 166.

07: Greed and God

74 *"bouncy little books":* The Alger canon is described by Carl Bode of the University of Maryland, http://en.wikipedia.org/wiki/Ragged_Dick.
75 *"from the movie Wall Street":* Directed by Oliver Stone (1987; 20th Century Fox).
81 *"It's not yours":* Rachel Von Dongen, "Grassley Request Provokes Preacher," *Roll Call,* Jan. 28, 2008, http://www.rollcall.com/issues/53_84/-21777-1 .html.

08: The Time Machine

86 *"the same space of time":* William James, *Psychology: The Briefer Course* (repr., Mineola, NY: Dover Publications, 2001), 151.
86 *the first researchers to:* Marc Wittmann and Sandra Lehnhoff, "Age Effects in Perception of Time," *Psychological Reports* 97 (2005): 921–35.
88 *"Stressed Out on Four":* Daniel S. Hamermesh and Jungmin Lee, "Stressed Out on Four Continents: Time Crunch or Yuppie Kvetch?" National Bureau of Economic Research, NBER Working Paper No. 10186, December 2003, www.nber.org/papers/w10186.

09: 1991

99 *"Sooner or later, most":* Ellen Goodman, "Countering the Culture," *Gettysburg Times,* August 17, 1991, 4A.

100 California Highway Patrol: "Swaggart Plans to Step Down," The New York Times, October 15, 1991, http://www.nytimes.com/1991/10/15/us/swaggart-plans-to-step-down.html.

11: Denialism
117 psychologist Dan Kiley: Dr. Dan Kiley, The Peter Pan Syndrome: Men Who Have Never Grown Up (New York: Avon Books, 1995).
118 "we are not victims": Deepak Chopra, Ageless Body, Timeless Mind: The Quantum Alternative to Growing Old (New York: Three Rivers Press, 1994), 7.
120 Somers went on the Oprah: Jocelyn Noveck, "Suzanne Somers' New Target: Chemotherapy," http://www.huffingtonpost.com/2009/10/20/suzanne-somers-new-target_n_328063.html.
121 S. Jay Olshansky: Jeremy Manier, "Professor Sued over Anti-aging Comments: Academic Freedom at Issue in Lawsuit," Chicago Tribune, June 19, 2005, http://articles.chicagotribune.com/2005-06-19/news/0506190345_1_anti-aging-medicine-ronald-klatz-anti-aging-conference.
121 a report from CNN: Caleb Hellerman, " 'Age Management' " Is a Controversial New Medical Focus," CNN.com, May 9, 2007, http://www.cnn.com/2007/HEALTH/04/06/chasing.antiaging.med/.
122 Becca Levy, PhD: Becca R. Levy, Martin D. Slade, Suzanne R. Kunkel, and Stanislav V. Kasl, "Longevity Increased by Positive Self-perceptions of Aging," Journal of Personality and Social Psychology 83 (August 2002): 261–70.

12: Realism
124 She went without: Ann Oldenberg, "Jamie Lee Curtis Bares the Truth," USA Today, http://usatoday30.usatoday.com/life/2002-08-19-jamie-lee_x.htm.
125 Under the headline: Steve Hall, "Jamie Lee Curtis Can't Take a Dump, Hypes Dannon's Bifidus Regularis," Adrants, March 3, 2008, http://www.adrants.com/2008/03/jamie-lee-curtis-cant-take-a-dump.php.
125 based on unsubstaniated claims: Jim Edwards, "Why Dannon Let Jamie Lee Curtis Tell Lies About Activia," CBS Money Watch, December 20, 2010, http://www.cbsnews.com/8301-505123_162-42746966/why-dannon-let-jamie-lee-curtis-tell-lies-about-activia/.
125 "It's a conspiracy": "Hollywood's Plastic Surgery Industrial Complex," The Sydney Morning Herald, September 24, 2010, http://www.smh.com.au/lifestyle/beauty/hollywoods-plastic-surgery-industrial-complex-20100924-15q3e.html#ixzz2A4cAqHie.
127 "[She] lived in a": Gary W. Small, M.D., "Keep Walking to Stay Mentally

Sharp," *Huffington Post*, January 3, 2012, http://www.huffingtonpost.com/ gary-w-small-md/alzheimers_b_1170364.html.

128 *"We wish we"*: Maggie Fox, "Prevent Alzheimer's? No Evidence You Can: Panel," Reuters, April 28, 2010, http://www.reuters.com/article/2010/04/28/ us-alzheimers-prevention-idUSTRE63R5TI20100428.

128 *"I do crossword puzzles"*: Judy Lin, "10 Questions: Alzheimer's Expert Dr. Gary Small," *UCLA Today*, January 31, 2012, http://today.ucla.edu/portal /ut/10-questions-alzheimer-s-expert-228191.aspx.

13: Enthusiasm

133 *"The Poetics of Aging"*: Laura Paull, "For Baby Boomers, Aging Is the Next Frontier," *Huffington Post*, November 25, 2011, http://www.huffingtonpost .com/2011/11/25/baby-boomers-aging_n_1106529.html.

133 *"increase in the life span"*: Public Papers of the Presidents of the United States: John F. Kennedy, February 21, 1963, 189.

134 *"Life is a story"*: Norm Amundson, Poetics of Aging, November 2011, http://poeticsofaging.org/anything_slides/norm-amundson.

134 *"older people manage"*: Laura L. Carstensen, *A Long Bright Future: An Action Plan for a Lifetime of Happiness, Health, and Financial Security* (New York: Broadway Books, 2009), 16.

135 *"A Snapshot"*: "The U-Bend of Life: Why, Beyond Middle Age, People Get Happier as They Get Older," *The Economist*, December 16, 2010, http:// www.economist.com/node/17722567.

135 *unhappiest age:* David G. Blanchflower and Andrew J. Oswald, "International Happiness," National Bureau of Economic Research, NBER Working Paper 16668, January 2011, http://www.andrewoswald.com/docs/blanchosw 16668nberhappinessinternational.pdf.

140 *"How pleasant is"*: William James, *The Principles of Psychology* (1890), http:// www.wisdomquotes.com/quote/william-james-11.html.

15: Age War

147 *"self-conscious" animals:* Ernest Becker, *The Denial of Death* (New York: Free Press, 1997), 87.

149 *"To solve the problem"*: Huber Warner, Julie Anderson, Steven Austad, Ettore Bergamini, et al., "Science Fact and the SENS Agenda," *EMBO Reports* 6 (November 2005): 1006–8.

150 *"I encounter knee-jerk"*: "Big Think Interview with Aubrey de Grey," October 2, 2009, video and transcript at http://bigthink.com/ideas/16742.

154 *"There's an iceberg"*: Peter G. Peterson, inside flap, *Gray Dawn: How the Coming Age Wave Will Transform America—and the World* (New York: Three Rivers Press, 2000).

18: 2011

171 *In an interview:* Seamus McGraw, "Trump: I Have 'Real Doubts' Obama Was Born in U.S.," *Today News,* April 7, 2011, http://today.msnbc.msn.com/id/42469703/ns/today-today_news/t/trump-i-have-real-doubts-obama-was-born-us/#.UInKeoW279o.

22: Slow

199 *" 'Slow' is spelled":* Robert Levine, *A Geography of Time: The Temporal Misadventures of a Social Psychologist, or How Every Culture Keeps Time Just a Little Bit Differently* (New York: Basic Books, 1997), 6.

204 *"It's Time to March":* Knight Steel and T. Franklin Williams, "It's Time to March," *Journal of the American Geriatrics Society* 54 (July 2006): 1142–43.

23: Deep

211 *theory he calls "gerotranscendence":* Peter Öberg and Lars Tornstam, "Body Images Among Men and Women of Different Ages," *Ageing and Society* 19 (September 1999): 629–44.

26: Croning

240 *"To see what is in front":* The Collected Essays, Journalism, and Letters of George Orwell, vol. 4, *In Front of Your Nose, 1945–1950,* Sonia Orwell and Ian Angus, eds. (New York: Harvest Books, 1968), 125.

240 *"sitting in a place":* Eliza Ware Rotch Farrar, *The Young Lady's Friend* (Boston, 1837), 293.

27: Eldertopia

252 *"Thirteen Grandmothers":* The U.S. Constitution and the Great Law of Peace. Foreword by Chief Jake Swamp. Comparison by Gregory Schaaf (Santa Fe, NM: Center for Indigenous Arts & Cultures, 2004), 22–23.

255 *"Although recently diagnosed":* "Earth Elders: An Invitation," *Itineraries* newsletter, Spring 2008, http://www.secondjourney.org/newsltr/Archives/Lanphear3_08Spr.htm.

A Brief History of the First Crucible

270 *"Hip to Be Square":* "Hip to Be Square," by Huey Lewis, Bill Gibson, and Sean Hopper, Huey Lewis and the News, *Fore!,* Chrysalis Records, 1986.

271 *"Wouldn't it be nice":* "Wouldn't It Be Nice," music by Brian Wilson, lyrics by Tony Asher, Beach Boys, *Pet Sounds,* Capitol Records, 1966.

271 *"Hope I die before":* "My Generation," by Pete Townshend, The Who, *My Generation,* Brunswick Records, 1965.

272 "I was so much older": "My Back Pages," Bob Dylan, *Another Side of Bob Dylan*, Columbia Records, 1964.

272 "THAT *liberty is indivisible*": Young Americans for Freedom, "The Sharon Statement," adopted by the Young Americans for Freedom Conference at Sharon, Conn., September 11, 1960.

274 "*Injustice anywhere*": Martin Luther King Jr., "Letter From a Birmingham Jail," "*Unwise and Untimely*"?, April 16, 1963, http://www.thekingcenter.org/archive/document/unwise-and-untimely.

274 "*Sex and race because*": Gloria Steinem, address delivered at the founding of the National Women's Political Caucus, July 10, 1971, http://en.wikipedia.org/wiki/Address_to_the_Women_of_America.

275 "*With nuclear energy*": Students for a Democratic Society, "Port Huron Statement," published and distributed by Students for a Democratic Society, 1962, http://www.sds-1960s.org/PortHuronStatement-draft.htm.

277 "*It was the time of*": "Red Hot Mamas," Snopes.com, 2007, http://www.snopes.com/history/american/burnbra.asp.

278 "*most guys didn't take*": Myra MacPherson, *Long Time Passing: Vietnam and the Haunted Generation* (Bloomington: Indiana University Press, 2002), 493.

279 "*expatriates living on*": Robert Jones, "The Hippies: Philosophy of a Subculture," *Time*, July 17, 1967.

279 "*They have some very fine*": Loudon Wainwright, "The Strange New Love Land of the Hippies," *Life*, March 31, 1967, 104.

279 *John Phillips captured*: "San Francisco (Be Sure to Wear Flowers in Your Hair)," written by John Phillips, *The Voice of Scott McKenzie*, Columbia Records, 1967.

280 "*The band encouraged*": back cover copy from David Meerman Scott and Brian Halligan, *Marketing Lessons from the Grateful Dead: What Every Business Can Learn from the Most Iconic Band in History* (Hoboken, NJ: John Wiley), 2010.

281 *David Crosby's song*: "Almost Cut My Hair," by David Crosby, Stephen Stills, Graham Nash, Neil Young; Crosby, Stills, Nash & Young, *Déjà Vu*, Atlantic Records, 1970.

281 "*Now, though I am a beginner*": Ram Dass, *Be Here Now* (San Cristobal, NM: Lama Foundation, 1971), Part 1, last page.

282 "*You come up when I*": quoted in James Michael Hogan, "George Wallace's Political Revivalism: A Case Study in the Political Application of Religious Rhetorical Strategies" (master's thesis, University of Wisconsin, 1977), 11.

283 "*The deepest truth*": Will Herberg, "Who Are the Hippies?," *National Review*, August 8, 1967, 844–46.

283 "Young ladies were": Mark Harris, "The Flowering of the Hippies," The Atlantic, September 1967, http://www.theatlantic.com/magazine/archive/1967/09/the-flowering-of-the-hippies/306619/.

284 "How could children": "Nation: Hippies and Violence," Time, December 12, 1969.

285 "Someone in authority decided": Bob Simpson, "Remembering the Pentagon March," (1967), http://www.jofreeman.com/photos/Pentaremember3.html.

286 "a haven for protesters": Seth Rosenfeld, "The Governor's Race," San Francisco Chronicle, June 9, 2002, http://www.sfgate.com/news/article/The-governor-s-race-3311801.php.

286 Rector was a bystander: "Occupied Berkeley," Time, May 30, 1969.

287 "Now, I understand": The President's News Conference, September 26, 1969, http://www.presidency.ucsb.edu/ws/?pid=2246.

287 "interminably vocal youngsters": General Earle Wheeler (speech to the Association of the US Army, October 15, 1969).

287 "Middle America" as the most: Roy Larsen, "A Letter from the Publisher," Time, January 5, 1970.

288 "If it takes a bloodbath": Lou Cannon, Governor Reagan: His Rise to Power (Cambridge, MA: Public Affairs, 2003), 295.

288 "My fellow Americans, we": Richard Nixon (speech on Cambodia, Washington, D.C., April 30, 1970), http://isc.temple.edu/hist249/course/Documents/Nixon%27s_speech-on_cambodia.htm.

289 "In a close election": Hunter S. Thompson, Fear & Loathing: On the Campaign Trail '72, 1973 (repr. Simon & Schuster, 2012), 34.

Suggested Reading

GROWTH

Abrahams, Ruby. *At The End of the Day*. Eloquent Books, 2008.

This warm, often insightful book leads readers into a reconsideration of the latter decades of life. It is not an empirical work and the author does rely heavily on a mix of anecdotes and inspirational thoughts drawn from a range of Eastern and Western ideologies to support her point of view. Those who value this perspective will find much that is useful in its pages.

Bateson, Catherine. *Composing a Further Life: The Age of Active Wisdom*. Vintage, 2011.

This book offers readers a series of conversations with people who have found unusual ways of living what Bateson calls "Adulthood II." The vision she offers of a healthy human life cycle is different from the one I have developed. I do share her passion for story and storytelling as well as her commitment to ensuring that individual voices continue to be heard.

Cohen, Gene D. *The Mature Mind: The Positive Power of the Aging Brain*. Basic Books, 2006.

The late Gene Cohen was a physician, philosopher, and board game designer. His insights into "Reinventing Retirement" have helped people reframe what society has defined as a descent into obscurity and dependency.

Fry, Prem S., and Corey L. M. Keyes. *New Frontiers in Resilient Aging: Life-Strengths and Well-Being in Late Life*. Cambridge University Press, 2010.

This book adopts a "strengths-based" approach to understanding the lives and well-being of older people. The authors argue, effectively in my view, that the current "deficit-based" framework for aging is itself a source of significant disability. Most older people do capitalize on existing resources, skills, and cognitive processes and do learn and continue to grow on a daily basis. The authors show how this is possible by exploring "uncommon" insights into concepts such as social connectedness, personal engagement and commitment, openness to new experiences, social support, and sustained cognitive activity.

Grossman, I. Michael. *Coming to Terms with Aging.* RDR Books Muskegon, MI/ Berkeley, CA, 2007.

This book explicitly positions itself as an alternative to denial. The author introduces and then makes use of "Life Awareness" as a method of overcoming the fear of age and aging. This book is actually quite well suited to the needs of Denialists who are Enthusiast-curious.

Hill, Robert D. *Seven Strategies for Positive Aging.* W. W. Norton & Company, 2008.

Realists with a bit of curiosity about the Enthusiast perspective will find this book to be quite useful. The author offers practical strategies for embracing the psychology that surrounds a healthy elderhood. The chapters discussing service to one's community, forgiveness, and gratitude are especially helpful.

Jacoby, Susan. *Never Say Die: The Myth and Marketing of the New Old Age.* Pantheon, 2011.

Jacoby delivers a carefully reasoned, if sometimes snide corrective to the national religion of "can-do" positive thinking, especially as it is applied to the question of how we age. Her position can probably be best summarized as anti-pro-aging. The author takes her younger self refreshingly to task for writing bubbly articles about the merits of aging that rarely quoted anyone over sixty.

Klein, Daniel. *Travels with Epicurus: A Journey to a Greek Island in Search of a Fulfilled Life.* Penguin Books, 2012.

This lovely little book blends ancient Greek philosophy with reflections on life as it is lived on a Greek island. At its core lies a powerful refutation of the "forever young" syndrome that pervades contemporary American society. Time spent being with the old men of Hydra and reading some of the ancient world's most insightful thinkers led Klein to develop an "evolving philosophy of a good and authentic old age."

Lustbader, Wendy. *Life Gets Better: The Unexpected Pleasures of Growing Older.* Tarcher/Penguin, 2011.

Wendy Lustbader, MSW, is a wise woman with deep insights into the experience of aging in America. This book challenges settled "declinist" assumptions about the journey into elderhood and argues, persuasively, that the gains, properly understood, outweigh the losses. While I loved her last book, *What's Worth Knowing*, I find this book to be deeper, with an astonishing string of fully developed insights into life and the lives we find ourselves leading as we edge ever closer to the Second Crucible. When I first got my copy, Jude eagerly read aloud from the book before going to sleep. Wendy's clear, incisive writing reliably led us into a thoughtful conversation about our lives and our feelings about our marriage, our family, our work, and our future.

Matzkin, Alice, and Richard Matzkin. *The Art of Aging: Celebrating the Authentic Aging Self*. Sentient Publications, 2009.

Alice and Richard Matzkin are artists, and in this book they approach the experience of aging through a well-developed aesthetic sense. Both authors have entered into life beyond adulthood and, as the title suggests, have found this new terrain to be both liberating and enlightening. Notably, the pair explore how ageism corrupts our understanding of and appreciation for the older nude body. As one might expect, the book is beautifully illustrated.

Morganroth Gullette, Margaret. *Agewise: Fighting the New Ageism in America*. University of Chicago Press, 2011.

"Good stuff happens not because we are still young, but because we are not." This well-informed and especially clear-eyed contrarianism serves the author and her readers exceptionally well throughout this book. "Agewise" is a combat manual for those seeking to challenge and overcome the bigotry of ageism. Readers are shown how to reframe aging-related issues, language, and situations and shift to a more positive perspective. Before reading this book, a person with long experience might say, "I've worked in this field for more decades than I care to admit." After reading this book, a reader is much more likely to begin an introduction with a proud recitation of track record and experience.

Mortimer, John. *The Summer of a Dormouse*. London: Viking/Penguin 2000.

A collection of insightful essays on later life endowed with classic British humor.

Pillemer, Karl. *30 Lessons for Living: Tried and True Advice from the Wisest Americans*. New York: Viking/Penguin, 2011.

Karl Pillemer is a professor of gerontology at Cornell who, wisely, decided to spend five years interviewing a diverse cross-section of over one thousand elders to elicit their life advice. He refers to members of this group as "the experts." By living into their eighties, nineties, and beyond, they have been able to gain important insights into the art of living. He positions hindsight as a powerful virtue. The book is organized around six general themes (such as marriage, careers, and happiness). Each chapter ends with a "refrigerator list" of thematically organized advice. This is bite-sized wisdom that, taken together, offers a satisfying meal.

Plotkin, Bill. *Nature and the Human Soul: Cultivating Wholeness and Community in a Fragmented World.* New World Library, 2007.

This book presents itself as a guide for honoring developmental stages (e.g., the Artisan and the Master). The goal here is to support growth and development in the second half of life.

Reid, Eve. *Fearless Aging: A Journey of Self Discovery, Soul Work and Empowerment.* BookSurge Publishing, 2007.

The author makes heavy use of stories that highlight the achievement of new insights. She also offers readers well-designed exercises that facilitate introspection. The workbook-style approach is meant to offer a practical guide to the pursuit of growth in the second half of life.

Sarton, May. *Encore: A Journal of the Eightieth Year.* W. W. Norton & Company, 1995.

Poet May Sarton's journal of her eightieth year, following, as it does, on her previous journal, *Endgame: A Journal of the Seventy-Ninth Year*, elaborates on her growing identification with old age and the liberation it makes available to her. She revels in the "freedom to be absurd, the freedom to forget things . . . the freedom to be eccentric." Sarton opens a window into her octogenarian satisfactions and invites readers to look inside. Although the tone here is positive, Sarton knows better than to descend into naiveté. There are bouts of pain and ill health, wearying domestic discord, a war against fatigue, and most of all, an awareness of the "perilousness of life on all sides."

Trafford, Abigail. *My Time.* Basic Books, 2004.

This book explores how to make the most of one's so-called bonus years. A longtime columnist for the *Washington Post*, Abby Trafford has a light touch that puts readers instantly at ease. Realists will find the perspective offered here to be especially useful. From cover to cover, the emphasis is on taking control of one's time—and destiny.

THEORY

Butler, Robert N. *The Longevity Revolution: The Benefits and Challenges of Living a Long Life.* PublicAffairs, 2008.

Butler is founder of the National Institute on Aging and author of the Pulitzer Prize–winning *Why Survive? Being Old in America*. Longevity, he argues, is of little value in the absence of quality of life. This densely written, supremely credible, and painstakingly researched work was published shortly before the author's death. Butler balances the conflicting demands of a long life with those arising from the pursuit of a good life.

Butler, Robert N. *Why Survive? Being Old in America*. The Johns Hopkins University Press, 1975.
This is the original masterwork in the field of aging. Published in 1975 and awarded a Pulitzer Prize, it offers a foundational investigation of the complexities of aging. Contemporary readers will, of course, find many of the specifics offered here to be dated, but this book remains required reading for any serious student of gerontology, aging services, and public policy related to aging.

Cohen, Gene D. *The Creative Age: Awakening Human Potential in the Second Half of Life*. Harper Collins, 2000.
This book explores the role that creativity can and should play in enriching life beyond adulthood. Cohen marshals evidence that shows how creative endeavors improve mental and physical health. The creative pursuit of one's legacy can also, Cohen argues, strengthen interpersonal relationships and our sense of community. He writes, "Increasing numbers of preliminary findings from psychoneuroimmunological studies—research that examines the interaction of our emotions, our brain function, and our immune system—suggest that a positive outlook and a sense of well-being have a beneficial effect on the functioning of our immune system and our overall health. These findings are particularly strong among older persons." This is a summons to growth.

de Beauvoir, Simone. *The Coming of Age*. W. W. Norton & Company, 1996.
In *The Coming of Age*, Simone de Beauvoir applies to the problem of old age many of the insights that made her a leading feminist philosopher. At the core of this book we find a powerful insight into the social construction of old age as a social role. Much as men have constructed the female gender role, the young have largely defined the role of older people. The sections on the anthropology of age and aging are especially interesting and useful. She calls the perversion of old age "society's secret shame" and calls for a reunification of the human life cycle.

Freedman, Marc. *The Big Shift: Navigating the New Stage beyond Midlife*. PublicAffairs, 2012.
Marc Freedman has dedicated his career to helping people find meaningful

and sustaining work later in life. In this book he reframes midlife as a season of opportunity. The courage to ask, "What comes next?" can and does lead to unexpected growth and development. He takes care to link growth in late adulthood to the process of growth that accompanied the shift from adolescence to adulthood. He has a trove of stories that show how the "Big Shift" can be managed effectively.

Friedan, Betty. *The Fountain of Age*. Simon & Schuster, 1993.
    This book rocked my world when it first came out. It was thoughtful and carefully crafted, and I drank it in like the sweet intellectual nectar it is. I was especially taken by the skill with which Friedan connected the roots of sexism and ageism in our culture. It is hard to overstate how effectively Friedan identifies and undermines ageist dogma.

Green, Brent. *Generation Reinvention*. Amazon Digital Services, 2010.
    Brent Green examines how the postwar generation is changing business, marketing, aging, and the future. He deftly explores the intersection of business, culture, and sociology as it relates to our perceptions and media portrayals of aging.

Heilbrun, Carolyn G. *The Last Gift of Time: Life beyond Sixty*. Ballantine Books, 1998.
    Carolyn Heilbrun's youthful intention to commit suicide when she turned seventy is woven through these fifteen fine essays. She reflects on the unexpected pleasures of choosing "each day, for now, to live."

Moody, Harry R., PhD. *Aging: Concepts and Controversies*. Pine Forge Press, 2009.
    This book is, simply put, the standard textbook in courses on the leading edge of gerontology. While there is plenty of material that the lay reader can draw from its pages, it is most useful for those undertaking a serious inquiry into the aging process or the work of caring for elders living with illness or frailty. The book's sterling reputation is due to the ease with which its author addresses a range of difficult aging-related issues and blends personal, academic, professional, and policy perspectives into a persuasive whole.

Morgan, Leslie, PhD, and Suzanne R. Kunkel, PhD. *Aging, Society, and the Life Course*. Springer Publishing Company, 2006.
    I have taught with Leslie Morgan at the Erickson School at the University of Maryland, Baltimore County, and consider her a standout academic and human being. Her focus on integrating well-being into a larger conversation

about society is especially useful. The book works best in an academic setting, but more adventurous readers will find much here that is worth their effort.

Morganroth Gullette, Margaret. *Aged by Culture*. University of Chicago Press, 2004.

Gullete Morganroth hits the bull's-eye with this book. The idea that "we are aged more by culture than by chromosomes" is a cornerstone of my argument and serves as an especially useful antidote to our culture's casual embrace of ageist stereotypes. I am especially taken by her skillful handling of the cultural mechanisms that allow youth to define age.

Nelson, Todd D. *Ageism: Stereotyping and Prejudice against Older Persons*. A Bradford Book, 2004.

Comprehensive and scholarly in its approach, this book offers a balanced view of research on ageism. It also reveals how ageism shapes the world we live in from medical practices to portrayals in the media. Although it has been out for a while, the book remains effective, interesting, and current.

Powell, Jason, and Tony Gilbert. *Aging Identity: A Dialogue with Postmodernism*. Nova Publishers, 2009.

If the postmodern perspective is useful to you, this careful reconsideration of age and aging should serve you well.

Sperry, Len, and Harry Prosen. *Aging in the Twenty-First Century: A Developmental Perspective*. Routledge, 1996.

Members of the Enthusiast subculture who are challenging the use of aging-related slurs such as "elderly" and "geezer" will find that this book bolsters that effort by changing our focus to a new, evidence-based, developmental psychology of aging. The psychologists and psychiatrists who contributed to this book offer a new perspective: "The unity of a human life is the unity of a narrative quest. Quests sometimes fail, are frustrated, abandoned, or dissipated into distractions; and human lives may in all these ways also fail. But the only criteria for success or failure in a human life as a whole are the criteria of success or failure in a narrated or to-be-narrated quest." Reread that quote. Now reflect on your own life: what success or failures have you achieved relative to your own life quest?

Thane, Pat. *The Long History of Old Age*. Thames & Hudson, 2005.

They say that history is written by the victors. In the case of aging, elderhood (such as it is) has been largely defined by and through the writing and thinking of adults. Many people insist, for example, that old age is a new phenomenon. In fact, elderhood is likely nearly as old as humanity itself. This book serves as a healthy corrective to the bias that is introduced when adults write all the books.

Thomas, William H., MD. *Life Worth Living.* VanderWyk & Burnham, 1996.
   This was my first book, and as such, it will always have special meaning to me. I have reconsidered a number of the specifics included between the covers, but the book's main thrust—that elders suffer unnecessarily from loneliness, helplessness, and boredom—remains vitally important to me.

Thomas, William H., MD. *What Are Old People For?* VanderWyk & Burnham, 2004.
   This book reflects my thinking on age and aging during the years I was developing and preparing to implement the Green House model of noninstitutional living for frail elders. I reread it as I was working on this book and, for the most part, it holds up well. It is especially useful for those seeking to understand the functions of aging on the planes of person, community, and society.

Vaillant, George E. *Aging Well: Surprising Guideposts to a Happier Life from the Landmark Harvard Study of Adult Development.* Little, Brown, 2003.
   This textbook offers a solid introduction to the science of aging populations. The authors follow 824 people from birth through to old age. Their dedication to careful analysis allows them to make highly credible suggestions relating to health and well-being in later life. While genetics are given their due, the emphasis is on what people can do for themselves. Realists will love this book and Enthusiasts will find it to be useful if somewhat antiseptic.

SPIRITUALITY

Chittister, Joan. *The Gift of Years: Growing Older Gracefully.* Blue Bridge, 2010.
   This book has proven its worth as a guide to living for people of all ages. The writer is a Benedictine sister, who at age seventy wonders if she might actually be too young and inexperienced to publish a book about the lessons of age. Just to be sure, she "reserves the right to revise this edition when she is ninety." She reframes the final decades of life as a time of joyful connectedness, worth, and purpose. She sees elders as a force for good and insists, "Age does not forgive us our responsibility to give the world back to God a bit better than it was because we were here." *The Gift of Years* offers readers the opportunity to reflect on what it means to grow older and embraces the Enthusiast's clear-eyed optimism about the future.

Dass, Ram. *Still Here: Embracing Aging, Changing, and Dying*. Riverhead Book/ The Berkley Publishing Group, 2001.

The First Crucible icon and author of *Be Here Now* wrote this book after experiencing a stroke that limited his mobility and altered his formerly fluid pattern of speech. It consists mainly of thoughtful and well-turned anecdotes that emphasize the spiritual aspects of life beyond adulthood. Notably, Ram Dass gives meaning to his stroke by ascribing it to the "fierce grace" of his guru, who once told him, "That's the way it works. Suffering does bring you closer to God."

Fischer, Kathleen. *Winter Grace: Spirituality and Aging*. Upper Room, 1998.

This book is the best of a surprisingly small number of Christian-oriented books written from a "pro-aging" perspective. It uses the paradox of death and resurrection to show how the losses that inevitably accompany aging can actually lead to new forms of freedom. The book relies on both biblical and theological references and the life stories and reflections of older people.

Moody, Rick, PhD, and David Carroll. *The Five Stages of the Soul: Charting the Spiritual Passages That Shape Our Lives*. Anchor, 1998.

Rick Moody is one of the icons of the Positive Aging movement, and this book is one of the reasons he is regarded as a leader in the field. *The Five Stages of the Soul* draws inspiration from a wide range of spiritual traditions, including Islam, Hinduism, Buddhism, Christianity, and Judaism. Moody and Carroll weave spiritual insights into a new and refreshing reexamination of human development through the process of aging. Its depth and honesty make it a book that is often read and reread as new experiences give new perspectives on its valuable spiritual insights.

Moon, Susan. *This Is Getting Old: Zen Thoughts on Aging with Humor and Dignity*. Shambhala, 2010.

Susan Moon sees parallels between her First Crucible consciousness-raising group and her current crones group. The first was devoted to identifying and opposing sexism and the second helps her understand herself and ask, "How should I understand and embrace what comes next?" It quite properly annoys her when people say, "Even if you're old, you can still be young at heart!" She prefers the idea of dedicating herself to the work of becoming "old at heart." So do I.

Richmond, Lewis. *Aging as a Spiritual Practice: A Contemplative Guide to Growing Older and Wiser*. Gotham, 2012.

This book employs a panspiritual vocabulary (with an emphasis on Buddhism) to validate aging itself as a deeply intentional form of spiritual practice.

He backstops this perspective with well-chosen scientific studies that support his main thesis. Near the end of the book he uses his distinctive perspective to create a sample schedule for a daylong retreat.

Rohr, Richard. *Falling Upward: A Spirituality for the Two Halves of Life.* Jossey-Bass, 2011.

Rohr's critique of contemporary culture is in harmony with the First Crucible/Second Crucible construct developed in this book. He argues persuasively for a better balance between the "two halves" of life. He observes, as I have, that our obsession with the first half of life is impeding our development in the second half. There is suffering to be had throughout life, but we assign suffering in the second half of life to something Rohr calls the "shadowlands." Our fixation on age-related changes impedes our ability to create a life centered on an authentic sense of self. This book is especially useful for those who find difficulty in letting go of embarrassments and failures that now lie decades in the past.

Sarton, May. *Journal of a Solitude.* W. W. Norton & Company, 1992.

Loneliness is the pain we feel when we desire but cannot have companionship. Solitude is the pleasure we feel when we want to be by ourselves and find the opportunity to do so. In a review of Sarton's book, the *Cleveland Plain Dealer's* Eugenia Thornton wrote, "This journal is not only rich in the love of nature and the love of solitude. It is an honorable confession of the writer's faults, fears, sadness, and disappointments. . . . On the surface, *Journal of a Solitude* is a quiet book, but if you will read it carefully, you will be aware of violent needs and a valiant warrior who has battled every inch of the way to a share of serenity. This is a beautiful book, wise and warm within its solitude." That is an excellent summary of what this work has to offer the attentive reader.

Schachter-Shalomi, Zalman, and Ronald S. Miller. *From Age-ing to Sage-ing: A Profound New Vision of Growing Older.* Grand Central Publishing, 1997.

I have had the honor of attending several of Rabbi Schachter-Shalomi's lectures and I have studied this book carefully. This is where I first encountered the concept of "eldering." In the book's first section Schachter-Shalomi argues persuasively for the use of meditation, exercise, and spiritual healing as tools that can foster growth, especially for those entering into the later decades of life. In the second section Schachter-Shalomi addresses our culture's limited and limiting understanding of death.

Williamson, Marianne. *The Age of Miracles: Embracing the New Midlife.* Hay House, 2009.

Williamson asserts, "Midlife is not a crisis; it's a time of rebirth. It's not a time to accept your death; it's a time to accept your life—and to finally, truly live it, as you and you alone know deep in your heart it was meant to be lived." She also asserts, "Midlife today is a second puberty of sorts." I think that view is wrong and plainly ageist. I've included this book because the author is well known for placing an emphasis on growth and development in difficult situations, and this book does add value to the conversation about life beyond adulthood.

WOMEN

Graydon, Shari. *I Feel Great About My Hands: And Other Unexpected Joys of Aging.* Douglas & McIntyre, 2011.

This book is deliberately positioned as a response to Nora Ephron's collection of essays *I Feel Bad about My Neck.* Shari Graydon sets out to counter ageist and sexist stereotypes with the help of forty-one remarkable women over fifty, and she succeeds. Royalties from the book are being donated to Media Action, an organization dedicated to challenging the underrepresentation and sexualization of women in the media.

Hurd Clarke, Laura. *Facing Age: Women Growing Older in Anti-Aging Culture.* Rowman & Littlefield, 2010.

Facing Age is the first book in a new series on diversity and aging. In it, Laura Hurd Clarke examines the sometimes incendiary interactions that occur between a viciously ageist culture and women as they age. The author makes skillful use of in-depth interviews conducted over the course of a decade. Feminist theories about aging, beauty, work, femininity, and the body provide the foundation for this book, and the author skillfully connects them to the real-life experiences her interviewees have had with medical providers and anti-aging gurus.

Palmer Thomason, Sally. *The Living Spirit of the Crone: Turning Aging Inside Out.* Augsburg Fortress, 2006.

Thomason argues that aging encourages women to write a new script for their lives. Using extended interviews, she shows how many older women have already done this and how doing so has changed their lives. She writes, "Extemporaneous stories from other women give profound testimony to the reality that personal meaning is situated in place, time, and culture. . . . We all have a story within. If we listen carefully, we find clues of what we value and who we are becoming."

Rich, Cynthia, and Barbara MacDonald. *Look Me in the Eye: Old Women, Aging and Ageism*. Expanded edition. Spinsters Ink Books, 2001.

The late Barbara MacDonald was unsparing in her critique of the position held by older women in contemporary society. They are, in her estimation, "invisible, silenced by economic conditions, ignored by the women's movement, and, too often, not considered contributing members of society." This book helped inform my development of the concept of the "the cloak of invisibility." One reader notes, "Whenever I get tired of being old, [this book] always sets me right again."

Weintraub, Arlene. *Selling the Fountain of Youth: How the Anti-Aging Industry Made a Disease Out of Getting Old—And Made Billions*. Basic Books, 2010.

I included this excellent book in this section because, to date, the power of the anti-aging industry has been directed mainly at women. Weintraub shows how artfully ageist social constructs can be turned into fear and fear into money. The author makes excellent use of her skills as an investigative journalist to take readers inside this profitable but highly secretive new industry. Prepare to be amazed.

FICTION

Kleiner, Gregg. *Where River Turns to Sky*. Perennial, 2002.

The novel alternates between the stories of George Castor and Clara Paulson, both elders. George maintains the can-do spirit of a man who farmed for decades, and Clara is living in a nursing home after a stroke confined her to a wheelchair. A story of escape and discovery, it is my favorite novel about the realities and opportunities offered by age and aging.

Sarton, May. *As We Are Now*. W. W. Norton & Company, 1992.

Here, Sarton skillfully exposes our youth-obsessed society's toxicity, its alienation of elders, and the resulting hole in the heart of our shared culture. The difficulties experienced by her main character (Caro) are balanced, at least in part, by the virtues of quiet strength and dignity. By the end of the novel, the cloak of invisibility has been lifted and the reader is able to see Caro as a fully formed human being.

Thomas, William H. *In The Arms of Elders*. VanderWyk & Burnham 2006.

This is my first novel, written in the form of a fictionalized memoir. I write, "The truth is all wrapped up in rules, regulations, dollar signs, and self-pity," and observe that the "obsession with finding and proclaiming the difference between what is real and what is imagined conceals as much as it reveals." My goal here was to wrap truth inside a story, and I think that, for the most part, I have succeeded. The book tells of a shipwreck that leaves me and my wife marooned on a strange, unknown island called Kallimos. In this world elders have an influential voice and there is no need for "aging experts." It is here that I learn about the three plagues: loneliness, helplessness, and boredom. After coming to understand the true nature of elderhood, we are returned to this world and begin our work with the Eden Alternative philosophy of care.

This is the sequel to *Tribes of Eden*; its action begins about a dozen years after the end of that book. It is also written so that readers do not need to read the prequel. I'll let Meredith Rutter do this review for me:

Set in the near future, too near for comfort, the United States of America has crumbled. People who had become dependent on the digital/electrical grid that held everything together were set adrift. The price of gasoline skyrocketed, the stock market crashed, and "instead of providing calm reassurance, the government lurched and wobbled. . . . There was a great unraveling." Riots broke out in the streets of the major cities, and one family in particular was separated as they escaped Chicago.

As this family comes back together, with collective stories to tell, they find sanctuary and a new life in an idyllic community in upstate New York living off the "GRID," which is the name for the sinister new regime that has taken over society. This can't last forever, of course, and the new regime eventually begins zeroing in on destroying all those who would resist assimilation into the GRID.

Classic themes of good versus evil, family tensions, and the bonds shared by young and old come together in this unique book that tells a fast-paced yarn where the strength of an unusual alliance is tested and found true.

About the Author

WILLIAM H. THOMAS, M.D., is a visionary and internationally recognized expert on aging. He is an Ashoka Fellow and winner of the Heinz Award for the Human Condition. He co-created the Eden Alternative, an international nonprofit, and the Green House Project, both models to revolutionize nursing home care. In addition to teaching, speaking, and consulting internationally, he is a Senior Fellow with AARP's Life Reimagined Institute. A graduate of the State University of New York and Harvard Medical School, he lives in Ithaca, New York.